HISTORY OF ECONOMIC DOCTRINES

TO

ALVIN JOHNSON,

A GREAT AND GOOD MAN,
IN FRIENDSHIP

HISTORY OF
ECONOMIC DOCTRINES

AN INTRODUCTION TO ECONOMIC THEORY

EDUARD HEIMANN

OXFORD UNIVERSITY PRESS
LONDON   OXFORD   NEW YORK

OXFORD UNIVERSITY PRESS
Oxford   London   New York
Glasgow   Toronto   Melbourne   Wellington
Cape Town   Salisbury   Ibadan   Nairobi   Lusaka   Addis Ababa
Bombay   Calcutta   Madras   Karachi   Lahore   Dacca
Kuala Lumpur   Hong Kong   Tokyo

Preface

In writing this book the author has concentrated rigorously on the one point that appears essential to him: to show the inward logic, revealed in retrospect, of the development of modern economic thinking and thereby to place the study of economic theory in its proper setting. His aim has been to contribute to systematic thinking on the historical problem. He is thereby led to a critical survey of, and introduction to, the entire field of economic theory. Although no special knowledge is presupposed, the argument is closely reasoned, and the reader must work out the logical connections for himself. In the few places in which reference is made to graphical representations, it will undoubtedly be found helpful to construct the curves described so that the explanation in the text may be followed.

Being a history of ideas rather than of authors, this book does not present material of a merely antiquarian or anecdotal interest. Only in exceptional cases of historical interest will biographical observations be made. Likewise, references will be made only to the books whose ideas are discussed. Therefore, it may be desirable for the reader to use the book in conjunction with one or another of the older, carefully documented books in the field, in which many interesting references and extensive quotations will be found. A list of the more important of these books is given at the end of this text.

This book and its author have greatly benefited by the advice of three friends. Alvin Johnson and Adolph Lowe read the manuscript and made a number of important critical observations; and Hans Neisser's suggestions on many points, big and small, based on his extraordinary knowledge of the literature, have been a major contribution.

v

The manuscript in its original form was even shorter than the book is now. Mr. Arthur Goodman found a middle way between the author's inclination towards the greatest possible succinctness and the desirability of making it easy reading. The author's gratitude is also due to the publisher, for his interest, patience, and help.

EDUARD HEIMANN

New York
March, 1945

Table of Contents

I. Problem and Method

1. THE PROBLEM OF ECONOMICS

THE most conspicuous fact to strike the student of the history of economic theory is the recency of its origin. Economics is one of the youngest of the social sciences. Indeed, its history as a formalized body of economic knowledge begins only two hundred years ago.

To be sure, those human activities with which economics is concerned—the production, exchange, and distribution of goods —have taken place in every age; society cannot do without them. No doubt, too, men's thoughts have always been attracted to the consideration of these essential activities. However, it was long before the discovery was made that they can be organized in different ways. Until the special problem of organizing them arose, there was no need for a special science of economics. With the rise of this problem economic theory was developed to cope with it.

The eternal datum of economic life is the niggardliness of nature—including man's labor. Nature and human labor do not provide enough to satisfy all the wants of all men. Hence, man is forced to economize: he puts his labor and the resources of nature to what he regards as their best possible use and withholds them from uses that appear to him to be less important. In other words, he allocates his labor and resources in accordance with what he deems to be the relative importance of his needs.

There are some, it is true, who look forward to the day when the advance of technology will have abolished scarcity and ushered in an 'age of plenty.' To the extent that real plenty— abundance in relation to needs—is actually attained, we should indeed no longer be under the necessity of economizing. We do not economize with things that we vitally need but possess in excess of our needs, such as the air we breathe. However, most of those who envision an age of plenty mean to assert only that the basic needs of the people can be amply met, and this claim is not inconsistent with the demand that resources and labor be so organized as to give the satisfaction of these basic needs a priority over that of random or merely frivolous desires. Even in this loose sense, as matters now stand, the word 'plenty' would be applicable only to conditions that could be realized in one country, comprising little more than one-twentieth of mankind, and three-fourths of the rest would still be left in wretched poverty. At any rate, the main point is that scarcity and the consequent necessity of economizing prevail even after poverty is abolished, and we have to economize in order to abolish it.

Economizing implies two things: a standard for measuring needs, so that the 'greater' or 'more important' may be distinguished from the 'lesser' or 'less important'; and a suitable method of apportioning labor and resources in accordance with the results of this measurement.

The standard by which needs are measured may not always be immediately apparent. We often see people wasting their money and ruining themselves, in other words, acting 'uneconomically.' But we must not conclude that because their actions are not in accord with traditional or conventional standards they are not governed by any standard. The drunkard, for example, finds it more important to drink than to eat well and prefers to go hungry rather than deprive himself of the means of his chief satisfaction. Some standard of comparison for distinguishing 'better' from 'worse' is involved in every decision in which one need is given priority over another. To say that a person economizes is to say that he chooses among alternatives on the basis of a standard of comparison according to which his needs are commensurable. Different people or societies may have different standards, and the same person may change his standards from time to time; but in every act of deliberate choice some standard is presupposed as 'given.'

However, what is important is that standards today are arbitrary; no standard is generally recognized and accepted as 'objective,' i.e. as absolutely binding. This situation is a matter of grave concern. The fact that we do censure the 'uneconomic' use which the drunkard makes of his resources, although this use is economic in terms of his own standard of valuation, shows to what an extent something in our nature seems to demand an objective standard of excellence and to deprecate the arbitrary determination of values. Yet the absence of such an objective standard does not invalidate our thesis that some standard is presupposed in all economizing. And the blame for not providing a knowledge of objective value cannot be justly laid upon economics but rather upon that reality which it is the task of economics to reflect correctly. What the science of economics needs in its definition of economizing is some standard of value; and if it can construct its system even with the arbitrary standards actually prevailing, it certainly could do so with an objective standard.

For the individual, whether in Crusoe-like isolation or in society, economizing presents no special problem. He cannot help comparing his competing needs and establishing an order of priority among them. He will then use his money—or, if he is an isolated self-sufficient producer, his labor—for the things most important to him before turning to those less important to him. The order of importance will determine the order of purchase or production.

Now for any given money income and any set of commodity prices, there is a determinate limit to the number of needs that can be satisfied or to the extent to which they can be satisfied. But if we assume that a person can produce more or less by prolonging or shortening his workday, or that he can make more or less money by working longer or shorter hours, then the workday will end at the point at which he deems it more important to save some leisure and strength than to have more goods or money for consumption. Thus, a second factor must be taken into account, but it too presents no special problem for the individual. The leisure for the enjoyment of goods purchased or produced is itself a good and, as such, is commensurable with all the other goods which a person orders into a hierarchy. Each person makes decisions of this kind automatically as soon as the question of a choice arises; all his needs, whether for goods or for the leisure to enjoy them, are commensurable, and they are satisfied in the order of their importance. The ordering of needs and the allocation of the means to their satisfaction are one act—unproblematic, and in this sense 'natural.'

But the needs of different persons, organized in society on the basis of division of labor, are not commensurable in a way so immediately obvious. The problem of establishing a hierarchy of needs and of allocating means to their satisfaction remains, but there is no 'natural' solution to it. If A needs the products of B, at what point does B's leisure become preferable to A's consumption? In other words, how much shall B work to satisfy the needs of A? And if A and B need the products of C, who cannot fully satisfy the needs of both, how shall we decide whether it is more important that A's needs be satisfied, or B's, or those of both in equally limited amounts? None of the answers to these questions is more 'natural' than any other; they are all logically possible, and the choice of any one is arbitrary, i.e. rests on a decision that may not be approved by those whom it affects. Although the needs of an individual are to him obviously and immediately commensurable and in his view stand to one another in a given order of importance, society has no natural organ by which the needs of the individual members can be made commensurable and the means of satisfaction automatically allocated in proportion to their relative importance.

Society, however, cannot exist without the establishment of some order of priority among the needs of its members. In the absence of a 'natural' solution to this problem, each form of social organization that has been historically realized has provided its own solution—one determined by the special conditions of that society. Thus, both the hierarchy of needs and the allocation of means for their satisfaction are established in a manner that changes historically as everything social does. In every society certain functions are assigned to certain groups, and one's status is determined by the importance of his function in the hierarchy fixed by that society. But as different societies may esteem the same functions differently, the priest, the warrior, the producer, and the scholar, though they exist in all societies, may occupy different places in different types of society. The place assigned to each of these groups can be understood only in the context of the whole of a particular society and is determined by the total social and political organization. Thus, a hierarchy of persons, and consequently of their needs, which does not naturally exist, is established in each society and changes historically with the type of social organization.

Consider, for example, the medieval community headed by a lord and supported by his vassals and bondsmen in various grades of dependence. The entire social organization was such as to assign a distinguished position to the lord. His was the most important function, that of warfare, of protecting the community—a function from which the peasants were exempt because they had to produce the food. Since protection in war and government in peace were to be the concern of the lord, he became, in the eyes of the group, the symbolic representative of the whole community. As soon as this hierarchical structure is understood, through an inquiry into political and social history, the economic problem of such a society is solved implicitly. The standard for measuring any person's needs is given in his functional importance for the life of the feudal community as this is conceived by the community itself. That standard is codified in the law of feudal stratification, which assigns to each person a fixed status and function in the social order. The mechanism for allocating means to the satisfaction of needs is also provided in the very constitution of feudal society: government over a more or less unfree community involves authoritarian control of production, distribution, and consumption. In this sense, feudal society might be described as an authoritarian planned economy, on a very small scale, with an inadequate technique of social control. That is, feudal society must be explained in political terms, which include administrative techniques to regulate economic activities.[1]

A strictly communist society would differ in several respects from the one described above. In the first place, such a society would be organized on equalitarian principles. Furthermore, the technique of social control and of 'the administration of things' would be better perfected. And finally, the government, if democratic, would claim authority by virtue of the consent of the governed and not by divine right. Nevertheless, despite these differences the mechanism for the solution of the economic problem in a communist society would be the same as that in a feudal society in so far as both are planned economies. Even in an equalitarian society there is a hierarchy of needs: some needs of all persons are to be satisfied while other needs are regarded as of minor importance. The equality subsisting among the members of such a hypothetical communist society would be political and would be established by a purely political decision. Once this decision had been reached, however, the mechanism of the planned economy, as part of the functions of government, would make the necessary assignments of persons to jobs and allocations of means to ends, and would enforce its orders if necessary. In the communist form of planned economy political equality is presupposed, just as the feudal hierarchy is presupposed in the feudal form. But in both, the allocation of resources and labor is effected by legal command and enforced by sovereign power. If any one asks why people in one society receive equal and in the other unequal incomes, the answer is found by referring to the decision of the authority, and it is this too which settles the question of the mechanism of allocation. In a planned economy of this type there is no strictly economic problem—only a political and moral problem.

Hence, as long as the prevailing type of economic system was the authoritarian planned economy, there was no need for, or possibility of, a special science of economics. On the other hand, this arose when the authoritarian system became obsolete and was replaced by a 'free' economy. A free economy is one in which there is no central authority in charge of establishing the hierarchy of needs and of proportionally allocating available means.

The situation prevailing in such an economic system is most paradoxical. For a free economy is, after all, an economy, and as such, according to our definition of the term, it presupposes the establishment of a hierarchy of needs and of a method for the proportional allocation of means to their satisfaction. Yet all this is accomplished without a central authority in charge of operations!

Without the orderly functioning of production, distribution, and exchange, there would be famine and civil war, and society would not be able even to exist, much less to raise its standard of living, as modern society has done for more than a century. Accordingly, without an authority to establish order—in the economic sense—we should expect chaos to result, that is, the death of society and of most of its members. But instead we find that, under a free economy, mankind has not only survived but actually improved its economic condition. Hence, a free economy, far from being chaotic, is seen to constitute an order in which specialized functions interlock as under a plan. In the absence of a visible mechanism for organizing and integrating economic activities, the operation of a hidden, but nonetheless effective, mechanism for this purpose must be presumed. If a free economy proves to be possible at all, the question how it is possible must be answered. For this purpose a new science, economics, was developed; its task, to discover and analyze the hidden law of co-ordination and integration in a free economy.

The specific problem of economics can now be succinctly

defined. Since economic order is indispensable for the existence of society and seems to require a central authority to establish the relative importance of needs and to assign jobs accordingly, an economy without such an authority seems to be impossible. But as such an economy proves to have been not only possible but successful, economics is confronted with the problem of explaining this paradox and of opposing to the time-honored notion of order through authority the conception of order through liberty. This has been both the problem and the program of economics ever since the days of Quesnay and Adam Smith, its founders.

It follows that economic theory is the doctrine of the system of free enterprise, and originally of nothing else. It is a historical discipline, in the specific sense of the word, emerging at a certain moment and bound to be reabsorbed into a more comprehensive and complex structure of social science as the system of free enterprise is itself transformed and absorbed into a more centralized structure of economic society, with central and local controls in complicated combination. Recent developments in most countries show this tendency and a corresponding reduction in the role of economic theory, in comparison with the eminence it enjoyed in an age which claimed that virtually all economic problems are problems of economic theory, that is, of decentralized controls. It is, however, this decentralization which, in any economic order of the future, will limit authoritarian arbitrariness and will represent the element of liberty in that order.[2]

However, certain qualifications must be made if the concept of order through liberty is not to be misunderstood. In the first place, there can be no doubt that what economics must explain is the functioning of an order. The familiar charge that there is no order in a free economy but only an 'anarchy of production' is unfair, if not entirely false. Though the order may be far from perfect and may not even be a desirable one, it is still an order. There could be no organic or social life without that interlocking of specialized functions which we call 'order.' To be sure, there are different kinds and degrees of order: an economic order may be imperfect and in need of reorganization; various orders may be possible, and some may be deemed more desirable than others if they hold promise of functioning more smoothly or more justly. But even the widest difference between perfect and imperfect economic orders (which is analogous, on the organic level, to the difference between health and sickness), though an important consideration in judging various orders morally and in choosing among them, is nothing in comparison with the gulf that separates order from the absence of order— the abyss between life and death. It is unfortunately true that production in the great depression fell to 60 per cent of what it was at the peak of the preceding boom—reason enough for considering the economic system sick and for anxiously pondering remedies. But as long as some production continued, there was order. The fact that we continue to live and to discuss the disease of society indicates that society, however much weakened and imperiled, still survives; the concept of disease is relative to that of health, not that of death.

Thus, the term 'order,' as we use it to describe a free economy, has no apologetic connotation; it merely denotes the highly specific arrangement which makes possible any kind of life, organic or social, and which must be fully understood and appreciated before it can be reconstituted. After all, life, whether the life of an organism or of society, is anything but 'natural'; the only natural thing, if we are not careful to preserve life, is death. The existence of an order without an ordering authority is a phenomenon worthy of our wonder and inquiry, particularly since this order happens to be ours.

In the second place, the meaning of the term 'free' in the expression 'free economy' needs some qualification. The question may be raised: What of human freedom in such an economic system? It is true, of course, that the prophets and advocates of a free economy were inspired by the hope of promoting the ideal of human freedom. To what extent that hope has been fulfilled may best be understood and appreciated now as the decline of the free economic system brings with it the threat of the most oppressive tyranny. But to concede this much is not to say that the free economy is the perfect realization of human freedom or even the system most likely to promote it. In fact, no reference to the question of human freedom is implied in the use of the term 'free' to describe a form of economic organization. This term, though aptly suggestive of the ideal of human freedom, is used in a strictly technical sense in the expression 'free economy' to denote the absence of authority in establishing the hierarchy of needs and in proportionally allocating means to their satisfaction. Doubtless the exclusion of governmental authority from the economic scene, whatever other consequences it may have, eliminates the danger of tyranny from that quarter. But the question is still left open whether and to what extent this condition of freedom has promoted the goal of human self-realization, and no answer to this question is implied in the concept of a free economy.

These observations concerning order and freedom in a free economy can be combined. There must be order, and there should be liberty. Liberty without order is physically impossible; order without liberty is morally unbearable. To strike a just balance between these opposing principles is the task of any human organization. Astonishing, then, is the claim of those who advocate a free economy on the ground that it establishes order through liberty, by the operation of a hidden law of order in economic freedom. Though we may believe that neither the freedom in a free economy nor the order thereby established is satisfactory (even within the limits permitted by the frailty of man), the theme which this problem touches on is certainly the greatest in the life of society—inspiring even when it leads into the most intricate technicalities.

2. THE HISTORY OF ECONOMICS

Different methods have been followed in writing the history of economics.

One approach to be found in the literature on the subject is eclectic, that is, without any dominant, unifying principle of presentation. Different periods in the history of economics are treated from different points of view as the occasion seems to suggest them. Doubtless this method has its advantages. It offers opportunity for highly erudite treatment and may even provide the reader with a vivid impression of the various doctrines that have at one time or another occupied the center of interest.[3] But, lacking any logical structure of its own, such a way of presenting the subject can only add to the bewilderment with which the student views the jungle of conflicting schools and theories— for so the history of economics must then appear.

Another method that some historians of economics have followed in treating their subject is to describe the evolution of economic theory as the progress in analytic thinking—the technical growth in theory, as it were—that may be traced through all the divergent doctrines. Successive doctrines are then viewed as progressive expansions, clarifications, and refinements of one another in an evolution toward the ideal of a completely adequate science of economics.[4] There is, to be sure, a measure of truth in such a conception, but too often in the pursuit of this method the rich variety of theories is disregarded or their inner integrity is violated in order to make them fit into the procrustean pattern supposedly exhibited in history. The strictly limited point of view of the author may blind him to the fact most conspicuous to anyone who studies the history of economics without such preconceptions, namely, the rich diversity of points of view, on the one hand, and, on the other, the mutual inconsistency and irreducibility of conflicting theories (derived from conflicting presuppositions that are not made explicit), and the consequent futility of discussions concerning their adequacy. It is obvious that this difficulty is ignored rather than solved by the treatment under consideration.

A third method of approach is to reduce the variety of conflicting theories to the class interests of those who advance or defend them. Each doctrine is then interpreted as a rationalization of the interests of the economic class which it is supposed to serve, and the conflict of doctrines is taken to reflect the conflict of classes.[5] In this interpretation too there is a significant truth. Practical conclusions are often drawn from a given conception of society, as set forth in a theory; and there is no doubt that men are inclined to accept a theory when the practical conclusions derivable from it favor what they take to be their own interests. In this way, a theory may come to be used as a weapon —and is often, consciously or unconsciously, conceived as such— in the arguments that accompany the social and political struggle. But this is only part of the truth, and to present it as the whole truth is misleading. The scholarly integrity of Smith, Malthus, and Ricardo, and of many modern thinkers, prompted them to advance certain theories leading to practical conclusions in conflict with the class interests which they are supposed to have defended. On the other hand, Quesnay and Smith initiated opposing methods of dealing with the problem of economics, and the conflict between these methods has continued to the present day; to reduce either method to the class interests of the proponents, however, is to ignore the nature of this conflict (which is the central theme in the history of economics), because the two opposing schools represented the same bourgeois interest.

We propose to present the history of economics as a sequence of the methods employed in solving the problem of economics. In other words, our subject will be the methodology of economic theory as this has been historically conceived, whether implicitly or explicitly. Such an approach has the advantage of properly including within it the two approaches described above, while being more comprehensive than either one.

On the one hand, due attention is thereby given to the technical progress that may have been made in the transition from one method to another and to the sum of progress which may be our heritage from the past. It is a fact that methodological changes have occurred which were prompted solely by considerations of analytical expediency (e.g. logical consistency, precision, parsimony, unity, etc.) whenever the method hitherto employed was deemed inadequate. An example of such a change is the transition from the method of the classical school to that of the neo-classical school—a transition which, as we shall see, can be explained by a demonstration of the internal logic of the theory itself without any resort to the motives or interests of its proponents or indeed to any facts outside the field of analysis proper.

On the other hand, the wide variety of divergent theories in the history of economics—which makes an account of them in terms of mere technical progress in analytical thinking appear utterly inadequate—is attributable precisely to such extra-theoretical factors as the more or less subconscious motives of economists themselves or the *weltanschauung* of their age. If the peculiar combination of ideas and ideals which a man commonly employs to orient himself in life may properly be called his 'philosophy,' then method may be regarded as philosophy in epitome. Method reflects the prevailing philosophy of the age.

Two examples will make this clear. In the days before economics was developed as a distinct science, the world and the whole of history were generally conceived as subject to supernatural control or intervention: the hierarchical structure of society was ordained by Divine Providence, which had in view less the earthly welfare of man than the spiritual education of his immortal soul. Economics, however, took its rise in an age with a wholly different intellectual climate—that of natural science. The interest of natural science is factual, and its thinking is in terms of cause and effect. This difference in underlying philosophy accounts for the difference in method. The rise of the new method signified that the claims of traditional authorities to rule by supernatural sanction were disputed because scientific thinking is purely rational and does not recognize any authority beyond 'nature.' In other words, the change in method reflected the emergence of a bourgeois world from the world of feudal hierarchies.

Likewise, when later the socialist movement began to oppose the ideology of the bourgeois world, the socialist economists expressed their aspirations in a change of method. They were able to do so because a change was taking place generally in man's understanding of himself, and they incorporated this change, as it were, into their own theories. From natural science man turned to history as a methodological guide: if society and economy are conceived as a part of nature, the forms of society are thought to be relatively stable, as those of nature are; but if history serves as the guide, then the way is open to a fundamental change in the organization of society. Thus it can be seen that a change in methodology can have the most far-reaching practical implications.

Methodological innovations like these cannot be explained by an analysis of the internal logic of the theories themselves. However, the methodological approach to the history of economics, while including a treatment of the economic interests responsible for changes in methods, goes beyond and beneath such a restricted and superficial presentation of the subject. Methodological innovations do not simply reflect class interests and are not devised solely to serve them; changes in the method of economics are not of merely secondary growth. Man is the thinking animal; thinking, sound or unsound, accompanies every moment of his waking life. And man's thought is not merely a concomitant of his life; his thought actively participates in shaping his life, in giving it its character: Any change in man or society is reflected on all the interdependent planes of human existence; there is no 'independent variable' in the history of man. It is not because man's economic interests are new that he thinks in new ways; because man himself changes in history, his thinking and acting change accordingly, and his thinking helps to reshape his acting as his experiences in his new actions influence his thinking. The correlation which we propose to establish is not between economic interests and economic theories, but between changing forms of man's understanding of himself in his changing existence, on the one hand, and changing methods employed in economic thinking, on the other.

The methodological approach alone can often aid in disentangling what would otherwise be hopeless confusion. Differences of opinion often cannot be settled because the contending parties are not on the same plane of discussion; they use words differently or view the problem from different perspectives. Contradictory opinions may then be reduced to their methodological presuppositions and may thereby become reconcilable, or the issue may be resolved into the larger conflict of the two philosophies from which the opposing theories are derived. After all, the choice of a method largely determines the results to which it will lead; you cannot get out by reasoning what you have not put in by methodological presupposition. No science merely 'mirrors' reality as it is. A scientific problem must be formulated in terms of strict concepts, and to shape these tools of scientific research and use them in appropriate combinations is the most perplexing part of the scientist's job, just as, in mathematics, deriving equations is more difficult than solving them.

The most conspicuous example in the history of economics of the sway which method exercises over results is the cleavage between the schools of Quesnay and Smith. Both believed that there is a natural tendency in the world toward a pre-established harmony, and, accepting this presupposition in their method, concluded—as we have already briefly suggested and shall later show in detail—that an unregulated capitalist system would best permit the harmony of men's economic interests to be realized. But the followers of Smith conceived the law of natural harmony on the analogy of a mechanical law, and this preconception has prevented them to the present day from recognizing the possibility of functional disturbances and crises in the system.

Quesnay, on the other hand, started from a conception of economic laws modeled on those governing a biological organism, and accordingly his school was free to introduce the notion of sickness into the theory of the economic organism. Quesnay's method is the one adopted in the modern theory of economic fluctuations.

To be sure, the choice of a method does not necessarily imply all the results which those who use it may reach. Once a method has been chosen, there is still room for differences of opinion regarding its interpretation and implications. Methodological presuppositions are broad generalizations; they sketch the main outlines of the picture but leave the details indeterminate. This point is well illustrated in the development of Smith's school. Every follower of Smith believed that a laissez-faire economy is natural and that a rational man cannot but accept its rules and comply with them. Smith himself believed that these rules are easily followed because an impulse toward harmony has been implanted by Divine Providence in nature and man. But to the generation that followed Smith, experience seemed to show that the natural organization of economic life did not lead to the promised harmony. So Malthus reinterpreted nature pessimistically, asserting that nature is stingy and that man's natural impulse toward procreation exceeds the bounds of nature's gifts and should be deliberately kept in check so as to comply with the laws of nature. To this extent the fundamental methodological conception of a natural harmony left room for reinterpretation and was modified by experience. We can say that the methodological presupposition of a natural harmony was here used as a tentative hypothesis, to be modified when it could not be verified.

However, the same unfavorable experience which led to the pessimistic interpretation of nature by Malthus and Ricardo could, and did, lead to a different conclusion. One could also infer that nothing was wrong with the doctrine of natural harmony in economic life but that the existing organization was not yet a natural one and that the promised harmony could be realized only if the economic institutions inimical to it were abolished. This is the view of the socialist contemporaries of Malthus and Ricardo, and in our own day this position has been forcefully represented by Oppenheimer. There seems to be no way of deciding the issue logically.

A third way out of the difficulty is to attribute the economic disturbances not to wrong economic institutions, but to the interference of illegitimate influences from outside economic life. For surely harmony can be expected to result only if natural economic life is left alone. In reality, however, it is never left alone but swept by irrational passions, politics, wars, and institutional reforms; these are responsible for the fact that a natural harmony has not yet been realized. This has been the position of the Manchester school to the present day, as represented by Mises.

Thus, it is readily seen that if the methodological postulate of a natural harmony is accepted, everyone is free to select those economic institutions or outside influences which are distasteful to him and use them as a scapegoat to restore the belief in harmony.

Other examples could be cited to show the influence of method upon results. Like Malthus, Marx, also under the pressure of unfavorable experience, reinterpreted the concept of natural harmony, but in a different way, and with fundamentally different results. Marx reasoned that, as there is a natural tendency toward harmony and as there is no harmony in the present, it must and will be realized in the future: the present is so constituted as logically and necessarily to produce harmony out of its very discord, its 'inherent contradictions.' Here we have another methodological hypothesis which determines to a notable degree, and in a way anticipates, the results of the theory built upon its foundation. It would be ridiculous to deny Marx's acumen and insight; indeed, the relevance of his results has never been questioned even by his most bitter critics. Nevertheless, the dogmatic character of his method must be recognized. Those elements in the present economic situation which hold promise of promoting the ideal goal are inevitably emphasized, while those which are unfavorable are minimized with the assurance that history will dispose of them in due course. This proposition can neither be proved nor refuted; it is a dogmatic belief, the more so as the assurance of future harmony is immune to the danger of present verification.

There is, then, no way of avoiding the uncomfortable conviction that, as Lederer used to say, the propositions of economics are unverifiable and irrefutable. Statistics may provide considerable confirmation, but even statistical results are often subject to diverse interpretations, and, if their purport is unambiguous, their significance can be questioned by attributing the results to coincidence. Was the great depression due to strictly economic causes or, ultimately, to the aftermath of the First World War? No certain answer to this question is possible. The point has often been made that the propositions of physics are far more easily verified than those of the social sciences. For physics proceeds by isolating the crucial factors in the experiment so that whatever result is observed is attributable to the operation of a known change introduced into an otherwise unchanged context; whereas in the social world nothing can be isolated or held invariant, and any result is the product of many simultaneously conspiring factors—hence the difficulty in imputing events to their causes.

This does not mean that we should give up the search for causes. However, we need to keep in mind that there is no absolute certainty in science, just as there is no security in life. The hope that social science may some day enable us to conduct our lives 'scientifically,' i.e. automatically and unthinkingly, is as futile as it is immoral.[6] For it implies the anti-human hope that science will somehow relieve us of the responsibility for our decisions and that human life will become machine-like. The structure of the social sciences, as the condition of life itself, renders such hopes vain. But if free men can never be relieved by social science of moral responsibility in organizing their communal life, they still have to strive for as much intellectual clarity as they can possibly achieve: man needs all the enlightenment he can get. Though he may never have complete knowledge, whatever real knowledge he does have helps him to organize his life better than if he had none at all. The fact that man is not and can never be perfect is no reason for not striving after perfection —and knowledge is a part of perfection.

However, to attain as much real knowledge as possible requires the intellectual integrity that recognizes the inherent limitations of scientific inquiry and thereby protects us from the grandiose and hopeless ambition of attaining full and final knowledge. The beginning of intellectual integrity is veracity and modesty, and these are what a critical study of the history of economics teaches us.

II. Pre-History of Economics

1. ECONOMICS AS APPLIED ETHICS

FOR two thousand years thinking on social problems remained fundamentally unchanged. It was within this traditional system of thought that economics developed after the Renaissance until its emancipation in the eighteenth century.

The Greek and medieval Christian thinkers had philosophized about the *oikonomia*, that is, the problem of organizing the *oikos* or household, the community of those who co-operate under one roof. In Roman law the household, under the 'father of the family,' was the cell of social life, and the higher and more inclusive organizations both in ancient and medieval life were conceived on the analogy of the household: the city-state or the lord of the manor or the king of the realm was responsible for the welfare of the members of the community and, in return, entitled to their loyalty.

Thus, in their economic organization, the ancient and medieval communities were planned economies of the kind discussed in Chapter I. In such a conception of economic activity there was no room for a distinct science of economics, or indeed for any social or political science in the modern sense. To be sure, in both the ancient and the medieval world there was vigorous commercial life, considerable organization of money and credit, and much business for profit—in short, much of that kind of activity which constitutes the subject matter of modern economics. However, the Greek and medieval Christian thinkers did not concern themselves with these facts in isolation, but strove to understand how they might or might not fit into a healthy and durable organization of the whole of life.

To cite only the classical example: Aristotle,[1] by far the most 'modern' of the Greek thinkers, finds both money and the exchange it makes possible essential to the life of the community. It is proper, he says, that a man should sell the products of his farm or craftsmanship with some gain to himself; the value of his product must be such as to enable him to live in accordance with the standards of his estate. Moreover, Aristotle introduces the factual distinction, repeated by all economists ever since, between a thing's value in use and its value in exchange, and he describes money as a commodity that is originally coveted by everyone for its immediate uses and hence accepted as a medium of exchange, since everyone is sure that it can be passed on to someone else. But he insists that the acquisition of money must not be made an end in itself, as it is in the business of buying for selling, and, even more specifically, in the lending of money at interest. In these cases Aristotle characteristically speaks not of *oikonomia*, but of *chrematistiké*, the acquisitive system, which he regards as unsound. Thus, the modern name 'economics,' which has been taken over from the ancients, now denotes the exact opposite of what they meant by it. Aristotle's strictures show that what he was censuring was the common practice of his day, but also that it was not accepted by the leading thinkers; for they still looked to political authority to keep the acquisitive system under control, in accordance with the idea of *oikonomia*.

In sharp contrast to the ancient and medieval conception is the modern view that economics is an autonomous science. Social science today is all factual and technical, while the ancient and medieval conception from which it was derived was broadly philosophical, i.e. oriented toward the whole and directed toward the discovery of a method of organizing society wisely. It would have appeared absurd to Aristotle or Thomas Aquinas to discuss economic behavior outside its framework of general rights and duties and without a view toward securing a socially optimum result in the long run. Social science, in other words, was a field of applied ethics and is so to this day in Catholic doctrine

The modern economist, on the other hand, isolates the economic sphere and analyzes its instrinsic laws. The ancients did not, whereas the moderns do, assume that such an autonomous organization of the economic sphere is compatible with social and moral well-being.[2]

2. MERCANTILISM: SYSTEM OF ECONOMIC POLICY

The Renaissance marks a much deeper break in the history of the western world than is suggested by its name. The medieval conception of the world as a universal cosmos was shattered. The one empire gave way to a multiplicity of national territories and states; and the theory of the state, no longer a chapter in applied religious ethics, became an autonomous field of knowledge. This change reflected the aspirations of the national state for political autonomy: though no longer 'universal' in space, the state claimed to be 'absolute,' its sovereignty neither derived from nor subject to any authority higher than itself.

Nevertheless, this national state was not totalitarian in the modern sense. It rested its claim to authority not on mystical power or racial blood, but on reason or 'enlightenment'—a term which the age of the absolute state finally applied to itself. The state promoted the growth of what it called 'enlightened,' 'progressive,' 'rational' institutions wherever it could, not unlike the Russian autocracy today, although with different specific institutions as its goal.

The national state was, in a sense, the home in which bourgeois society and capitalist economy grew up. The modern state is prior to capitalism, a prerequisite, in fact, to its growth. It is highly questionable whether bourgeois rule and capitalism could have developed without the powerful protection, encouragement, and guidance of the state. For it was the autonomous state that took the lead in promoting that modern organization which made the development of capitalism possible. Local lords, establishing themselves as territorial princes, subdued their former peers and rivals, and, looking about for means of securing and fortifying their regimes, found in the struggling elements of the capitalist economy a potential foundation of power and source of revenue. What the state needed was an increase in the wealth of the people so that taxes could be levied for the maintenance of the bureaucracy and the army. Medieval organization had been decentralized because of inadequate techniques of production, transportation, and administration; the units were small and relatively unconnected. The modern state, on the other hand, functioned with a centralized administration, whose officials served in distant places in loyalty to the sovereign and in financial dependence upon him. The knights of the Middle Ages were equipped for warfare by the local units of which they were the lords; the new army of mercenaries—soon to be equipped with mechanical weapons, products of capitalist industry—were paid by the sovereign even when they were in distant places! Thus, the modern state needed money and could get it only by engaging in profitable commerce and industry or by encouraging people to do so and taxing them. Both methods were in fact employed. In this way, the national state helped to nurture the capitalist economy. |

The outstanding exception is the United States, where, in the absence of a feudal tradition, no state endowed with absolute power and administered by a permanent bureaucracy has ever taken root. It is here that liberalism became the original form of society, with capitalism naturally emerging as its economic organization. In comparison with conditions in the United States, the decisive part which the state played everywhere in Europe in setting up a capitalist economy is only the more conspicuous. The European tradition of loyal service, first to the lord as the symbol of the community, and later to the constitution as the foundation of the community, was unknown in the new country because the idea of loyalty to a master is utterly alien to the bourgeois world of contract, profit, and personal independence. Public service in the United States has not been a career, at least until quite recently, much less a family and group tradition. Or, to put it differently, the United States had no bureaucracy. At any rate, in Europe the modern state which grew out of feudalism used the hierarchical human relationships of feudalism for anti-feudal ends, which included the development of capitalism.

The British, American, and French revolutions mark the emancipation of the bourgeois from state tutelage once they felt strong enough to conduct their own business. The state which was overthrown in England and France was essentially feudal, not bourgeois. True, it had been instrumental in fostering capitalism, but it had not been capitalist in composition and ideology. It gave way to a bourgeois state, or at least, in England, to one which amalgamated the elements of the old and the new on an equal footing. In America foreign rule had been comparable to feudal rule.

It can readily be seen that capitalism is not necessarily free, i.e. unregulated. In its first phase it was dominated and regulated by the state. Yet it was already capitalism: a system of business enterprise for a profit to be realized in the market by the sale of products or merchandise. Indeed, commerce, and even some of the industries, among them the cotton industry, were on a more or less unregulated, competitive basis. Accordingly, we may say that the commercial revolution took place without the aid of the state. However, the much more far-reaching transformation of the system of production, that is, the absorption of the bulk of economic activities into the pattern of capitalism, could not be achieved without political guidance. The industrial revolution proper, although delayed until the last quarter of the eighteenth century, was heralded by the development of many technological innovations throughout two centuries. But in a system of completely regulated production, new enterprises and enterprises of new kinds must automatically come under the general regulations, unless specifically exempt and licensed. New products would not have found a market if none had been reserved for them, possibly conquered for them by the state. Nor would trained personnel, either managers or workers, have been available if the state had not cared to train them. And, what is most important, many new industrial processes were first tried out by the state in its own enterprises, principally to meet the demands of the army and the court, and were transferred to private hands only after the political upheaval. Thus, the leadership of the state in developing industry in its early stages cannot be doubted.

Of course, capitalism developed differently in each of the countries of Europe. In this brief survey we have tried to strike a mean between widely different extremes. In fact what the picture that we have presented portrays with some likeness is the early stages of French capitalism. England and Holland were more liberal, since their bourgeois economy was more fully developed and consequently their bourgeoisie was more influential. Austria and Germany, not to mention Spain, Italy, and Russia, were far behind. In England the prevailing form of business organization was the private corporation, the state often supplying part of the capital and granting monopoly rights and judicial and military authority in the colonies; in Germany and Austria the prevailing form was the state enterprise, with the participation of private capital. An apt characterization of the leading role of the state in economic history may be found in the remark made by Frederick the Great of Prussia as late as the second half of the eighteenth century to the effect that he had 'to drag the mob [meaning the bourgeoisie] to their profits by their noses and ears!'

Since the bourgeois economy was at first dependent on the guidance of the state, the interest of the leading thinkers of the age was chiefly centered in political problems, and economics was not yet constituted as a systematic branch of knowledge. Whereas the theory of the state was for the first time conceived as an autonomous field of thought and was emancipated from religion and philosophy, economics continued to be a part of political theory because economic activities were still largely dominated by the state. In other words, there was no system of economic theory; there was only economic policy.[3]

However, although never without reference to political principles and institutions, there was a rich, voluminous, and growing literature on economics, and an increasing tendency toward autonomy is noticeable from Bodin[4] through Mun[5] to Petty.[6] Even if the system of economics was not yet complete or self-contained, the larger outlines and elements of a system were beginning to become increasingly evident. This was the character of economics in the age of mercantilism, the first phase of capitalism, under the aegis of the absolute state.

The economic backwardness of Austria and Germany is responsible for their not contributing to the type of mercantilist literature that flourished in the West. Instead, these countries developed a special branch of that literature, known as Cameralism, a doctrine of which Veit Ludwig von Seckendorff,[7] Johann Joachim Becher,[8] and Philipp Wilhelm von Hornigk[9] are outstanding representatives. Whereas the word 'mercantilism' suggests bourgeois writings for bourgeois interests—even though not yet fully emancipated—the word 'cameralism' is derived from 'camera,' which, as in the form 'chamberlain,' denotes the royal treasury: the cameralists were public officials who gave advice on fiscal policy to their lords and fellow officials. Here we still find in its pristine form the pre-bourgeois idea of the lord's household as the directing center of all the economic activities in his territories. But the wide difference in intellectual climate between the cameralists and the mercantilists should not be permitted to obscure the fact that they represent two phases of the same development and advocate the same principle.[10]

It has already been mentioned that the state was interested in capitalism as a continually increasing source of revenue for the ever-hungry treasury. Money revenue was the goal of the economic activities which the state engaged in or suggested to private businessmen and of all the institutions which the state set up in order to direct private business into the desired channels.

It may appear superfluous to emphasize this; but it should be remembered that the new era superseded one which was largely without the use of money, and, what is even more important, that according to the underlying theory of mercantilism the state could secure an ever-increasing revenue only by developing the sources of public and private wealth. In other words, the doctrine and practice of mercantilism was eminently dynamic.[11]

Adam Smith's failure to understand this point invalidates his unusually bitter critique of mercantilism, which was generally accepted for a hundred years. His reasoning is correct on his own premises, but they were not those of the mercantilists. Money, he says, is nothing but the medium of exchange; as the wealth of nations consists of the goods exchanged, wealth increases when there are more goods to be exchanged. Without more goods, an increase in the quantity of money does nothing but drive up prices. If, with Smith's friend, the philosopher David Hume, we suppose that one dollar is added to every existing dollar, we shall find that though all prices are doubled, their respective ratios remain the same: if everyone pays twice as much for the things he buys, he also gets twice as much for the things he sells, so that nothing really is changed but the *level* of prices. This is the quantity theory of money, so called because it makes the quantity of money in circulation the determinant of the price level.

Now this theory was not unknown to the mercantilists. It had, in fact, been triumphantly discovered by Jean Bodin, the great political theorist, as the explanation of the price rise in the sixteenth century.[12] This, incidentally, was a major economic disturbance because all prices did not rise at the same time or in the same proportion, as indeed they never do. Bodin had traced the price rise to the influx of silver and gold, the money metals, from the New World.

Of course, Bodin was not the first man to develop a theory of money, just as the price rise of the sixteenth century was not the first disturbing event in the history of money. The depreciation of money in terms of commodities—which is tantamount to a general price rise in terms of that money—had been known throughout history to be the result of fraudulently taking metal out of circulating coins and substituting some inferior metal for it, a common practice of princes and republics in times of emergency, and much discussed, notably in the Middle Ages. The rise of prices in terms of a debased coinage can be explained as a result of the fact that a larger number of coins of a given denomination can be struck from a given quantity of the precious metal. Bodin's monetary problem was new, however, in that prices rose, not in terms of a money that had lost part of its metal weight, but in terms of the metal itself, which had become more abundant. Hence it was concluded that money has no intrinsic value but, like all other goods, a value influenced by its quantity. This conclusion coincides with Smith's.

But it does not follow, as Smith argued, that the mercantilist policy was mistaken in drawing more money into domestic circulation. His contention that the substance of wealth is not money but goods is perfectly compatible with the mercantilists' contention that, under the conditions of an expanding economy, money can act as a powerful agent in increasing the flow of goods. This is the core of the mercantilists' conception of money and the reason for their preoccupation with it.

Indeed, it was David Hume, Smith's comrade-in-arms in the struggle against the mercantilists, who, in those parts of his work on economics devoted to theory, provided the most penetrating analysis of the possible dynamic effects of an influx of money and thus unwittingly justified the practice of the mercantilists. Hume was, of course, heir to a long and gradually developed tradition from Bodin through Locke to Cantillon, all of whom, by contributing to the refinement of monetary theory, had helped to make possible its application to reality. The following interpretation of mercantilist monetary and trade policy can be said to be an application of their (and particularly Hume's) dynamic theory of money, which will be discussed later.

It is true that the mercantilists succumbed to the tendency of every discoverer to be one-sided and to exaggerate the scope of his discovery. The first phase of mercantilism in particular, to which the name 'Bullionism' is often applied, was dominated by an odd and theoretically absurd 'fear of goods,' and this continued far into the later phase. But in fairness to the mercantilists we must recognize the underlying motive of their doctrine by comparing conditions in the period of rising capitalism with those of the preceding age. Feudal wealth had been material and tangible, consisting in land, houses, and the like. Capitalist wealth appeared in the form of money, and though it is true that this original form must be abandoned in the process of production and the money invested in labor and materials, the continuance of trade depends on their reconversion sooner or later into the form of money. Money thus being for the first time the beginning and the end of all business, the mercantilists were justified in focusing their attention upon it. Money becomes business capital by being withheld from the purchase of consumers' goods. If it is, then an influx of this money into the loan market will lower the rate of interest rather than raise the prices of consumers' goods. A reduction in interest rates is, of course, to the benefit of all credit-seekers. All mercantilist writers from Malynes[13] through Child[14] to Petty emphasized the stimulating effect of a low interest rate on business activity, since the expansion of business depends on credit for new and larger transactions. It is interesting to note that the medieval sermons against usury—in the Middle Ages the principal content of the literature on economics—were echoed by these mercantilist opponents of medieval practices and organization. Malynes in particular, a business man like most of the others, was bitter in his opposition to financiers, whom he accused of making money artificially dear by drawing it into their 'unproductive' transactions and thus withholding it from 'legitimate' ends.

However, the expansion of business needed the stimulus not only of a low rate of interest but also of a rise in commodity prices. And prices would have fallen if it had not been for the influx of money into the commodity market. This point can be easily demonstrated. Suppose the quantity of goods increases as much as, or more than, that of money; then it is simply a problem in division to show that prices will remain stable or tend to fall. Now the quantity of goods in the market did increase during the period of early capitalism, not only because productivity was raised in existing establishments but because the old 'natural economy' of the household, which produced for its own consumption and needed no money medium, was now replaced by production for the market and purchases of goods in the market. Lest prices should fall, additional money was needed for the turnover of additional goods.

As a matter of fact, the influx of money was abundant enough even to raise prices. Moreover, the quickening of business activity characteristic of the period under consideration produced effects exactly like those of a money influx. A more rapid transfer of money from person to person increases the flow of money per unit of time and thus strengthens the effective demand for goods. John Locke, the philosopher and political theorist, was the first to call attention to this factor, the circulation velocity of money.[15]

A rise in prices stimulates business; a fall in prices discourages and stops it. When prices rise during the process of production, the price of the product exceeds the previously incurred cost of producing it by more than the expected margin. At the same time debts fixed in terms of money absorb a smaller part of prices and profits. Falling prices, on the other hand, bring unexpected losses and increase the relative burden of debts, to the benefits of creditors. Thus, an increase of money, by raising prices, can and did lead to an expansion of business activity and production. This is the familiar phenomenon known as a boom.

Our account, indeed, is too abstract to do full justice to the facts. In reality, there was in that age a psychological justification even for an idolatry of money such as the mercantilists practiced. Gold had always appeared to man as the visible embodiment of wealth, power, and splendor; and even the gods were pictured as risking their realms and their lives for it. But to strive after the precious metal did not occur to the common man; it was reserved for gods and demi-gods. Now suddenly gold came into the reach of anyone who could engage in business. An orgy of covetousness, but also an outburst of energy, ensued. Before calculating their prospective gains or losses, people had to be awakened to their opportunity; their lust for profit had to be aroused. The surest way of doing so was to put the symbolic prize on display. This is the real meaning of the mercantilists' preoccupation with money.

Their concern with foreign trade follows logically. A country endowed by nature with gold and silver mines can exploit them; in other countries foreign trade must take their place. The chief hope of the mercantilists was to gain gold and silver through foreign trade; their chief fear was of losing the precious metals through foreign trade. Together with domestic measures for the promotion of industry and commerce, the control of foreign trade was therefore the most urgent concern of all these writers.

A country obtains gold in payment for the balance of its exports over its imports; it has to pay out gold in payment for the balance of its imports over its exports. To increase exports and avoid imports was therefore the program of the mercantilists. Of course, the balance of trade includes only exports and imports proper, and not all the other assets and liabilities (service of debts, insurance premiums, freight charges, etc.) produced by transactions between countries. What ultimately matters is this 'balance of payments,' which includes the 'balance of trade.' A list of the items which figure in the balance of payments was given by Thomas Mun.[16]

In line with this foreign trade policy, navigation acts were passed in order to force the country's shipping services on foreign, particularly colonial, peoples and to prevent their ships from bringing foreign goods to domestic ports. The export-import balance was changed by the time-honored device of protective tariffs, which were now unified and concentrated at the border as an outer line of defense for the country's gold. Accordingly, the mercantilists' discussions were centered on the best method of constructing the tariff, although the correct procedure for securing a 'favorable' balance of trade by means of tariffs had already been stated by Bodin:[17] the imposition of prohibitive duties on the export of raw materials which could be processed at home and on the import of finished goods which could be manufactured at home; light duties on the import of raw materials not available at home and on the export of finished goods.

To be sure, even the mercantilists recognized that there could be too much gold in the country. Thomas Mun, a director of the East India Company, defended the export of a certain amount of gold for the company's business transactions on the ground that the gold was reimported with an accrued profit, while if kept at home it would only boost prices and thus make exports impossible. For in order to attract foreign orders, domestic products must be cheap. Capital export thus appeared as a legitimate means of policy. Petty, who was more radical, even recommended the sale of surplus gold abroad in order to prevent harm at home.

However, the opposite point of view with regard to this question was also expressed. Falling prices, it was said, favor exports but are otherwise undesirable since they turn the merchant's profit into loss. It is significant that in the discussions of the mercantilists these opposing doctrines stand side by side without any resolution. They can be reconciled only by a systematic analysis, which conceives of them as different special cases of a more comprehensive principle. But the discovery of this principle required a much broader outlook than that of the mercantilists and was left for the pre-classical theorists, particularly Cantillon and Hume.

Probably the most misleading doctrine of the mercantilists

was the oft-repeated proposition that a country can get rich only at the expense of other countries. In stressing this point, the mercantilists misunderstood the implications of their own theory, which, as we have seen, really assigned to accumulating gold a dynamic role in stimulating production. The accusations hurled against the mercantilists are justified to the extent that the mercantilists failed to see the mutual advantages of trade to both the parties involved. They always argued as if their task was to secure for their national economy the largest possible share of a fixed volume of trade. Thus they were misled into advocating a shortsighted policy of economic exploitation of foreign or colonial countries, since it plainly appeared preferable to them to exploit than to be exploited. However, the intrinsic implications of their own theory demonstrate that money is to be accumulated in order to develop the dynamic forces of trade —a doctrine that anticipated the teachings and the practices of Alexander Hamilton, himself a mercantilist, and of Friedrich List.

It has been said that mercantilism is the theory and ideological justification of commercial capitalism, whereas the value problem, which is the chief concern of the classical school of economists, emerged only when the transition to industrial capitalism raised the question of the distribution of the proceeds of industry among the classes participating in production. However, this interpretation is untenable. Although the English mercantilists may have been more commercial-minded than those of other countries, this fact should not be given exaggerated importance. Indeed, it was an Englishman, Mun, who blamed Spain for losing her 'treasure' by importing foreign goods rather than producing for her own needs. And in France, Colbert, after whom the entire system of mercantilism is often called 'Colbertism,' was definitely industrial-minded. Finally, all mercantilist writings deal with wages—an industrial problem, and even with labor-saving devices, which they uniformly recommend.

Both the export interest and the search for profits demand a low wage per unit of product. This does not necessarily mean a low rate of wages; whether or not wage rates should be high or low depends on the effect of high or low wages on the workers' productivity. A high wage would be cheaper to the employer—i.e. would cost him less per unit of product—if it increased the workers' strength and stimulated their effort at least proportionately. The contention that this is actually the effect of high wages is first found in the writings of Adam Smith and became a basic proposition in the program of nineteenth-century social reform. The mercantilists, however, stated the contrary: wages should be low in order to force the people to work more (Mun); the workers should be enabled to 'Live, Labor, and Generate,' but not more (Petty);[18] it is 'prudence to relieve but folly to cure' indigence (Mandeville)[19]—this is what a vocal chorus incessantly repeated. Petty went so far as to say, 'if you double wages, then he works but half so much as he could, or otherwise would.'[20] For 'it is observed by Clothiers, and others, who employ great numbers of poor people, when Corn is extremely plentiful, that the labor of the poor is proportionably dear; and scarce to be had at all (so licentious are they who labor only to eat, or rather to drink).'[21] This was probably true. The intensity of modern industrial work is utterly repellent to men who are unaccustomed to it, especially when it is imposed on them without their visibly sharing in its fruits; and a long coercive training seems to be required everywhere to adapt men to industry.

3. THE TRANSITION PERIOD[22]
a. Petty

There is no doubt that with Sir William Petty,[23] though he was a mercantilist in economic policy, a new line of theoretical thinking started, which was soon to become dominant. Petty was a pioneer in more than one field. He founded what the title of his book called *Political Arithmetick*, in which, instead of relying on 'intellectual argument,' he looked to 'Number, Weight, and

Measure' for sound advice to the rulers of the country on all matters of policy and tax assessment. He thus became one of the founders of the science of statistics. But he was far from repudiating 'intellectual argument'; he realized that it was needed to organize and interpret the statistical data. He had a searching mind and made the first attempt, at least in modern times, to explore the determining forces of income distribution; that is, in technical language, the relative values of the contributions of the 'factors of production' (land, labor, capital,) to the value of the product. He thereby became a pioneer in economic theory as well.

Taking as his starting point the old saying that labor and land are the sources of production, Petty separated their respective shares in contributing to the value of the product; he limited the wages of labor to the cost of the food necessary to sustain the worker—which was, in fact, the prevailing mode of calculating wages in his day—and the remainder of the value of the product he attributed to the land as rent. This ingenious method of determining rent was applied over and over again in the history of economic theory. Petty then made this food-determined wage a general standard of value by equating it with the amount of gold whose production takes as much labor-time as the production of the worker's food. In other words, according to Petty, equal amounts of labor-time involved in producing different commodities—and thus 'incorporated' in them, as it were —impart equal values to them, so that they would virtually exchange for each other. In support of this proposition he argued that if goods are not exchanged in terms of the equality of labor-time incorporated in them, the producer of one commodity receives less in exchange for it than he invested in producing it. He will then find it to his advantage directly to invest his labor in the production of the desired commodity, thereby diminishing the supply and raising the price of the commodity whose production he has abandoned and increasing the supply and reducing the price of the one to whose production he has turned, until equal amounts of labor are paid equally no matter where invested. For Petty, as later for Ricardo and Marx, labor-time thus became the common denominator of all values.

Petty did not recognize capital as an independent factor in production, or profit as the revenue specifically accruing to capital; he lumped together all revenue from property under the name of 'rent.' The rate of interest he derived from the rent on land, thus anticipating a thesis of which Turgot was to make use. Despite its logical inadequacy, this conception of rent and interest has at least the merit of emphasizing that, whatever the different origins of the two kinds of return on investments, incomes from loans and from land tend to be equalized, since the investor can withdraw his money from either one and invest it in the other if there is prospect of a greater yield. Moreover, Petty anticipated Ricardo's concept of differential rent—the incremental income accruing to lands by virtue of their proximity to the market. When production on lands more remote from the market becomes necessary to meet a growing demand, the higher cost of transportation must be covered by a higher price, which leaves a larger margin of rent to the lands nearer the market, where the cost of transportation is lower. Petty even saw that under these circumstances the older lands, situated near the market, would be cultivated with greater intensity, and he groped for an understanding of the rent phenomenon in this case; but here he was less successful.

If we add to all this his many penetrating analyses of monetary and tax problems, the harvest from Petty's writings is amazingly rich. He made a number of important contributions to the gradually forming system of economic theory—in particular, the suggestion that value is the determinant of price. As this proposition was to be the foundation of the classical system, it is possible to see in Petty, as Marx did, the real founder of modern economic theory. Ricardo's insistence that the problem of economics is the distribution of incomes supports this view. However, it is untenable if one accepts our conception of the economic problem: how does the system manage to function without a central authority to establish the order of needs and to assign jobs accordingly? Then it appears that, despite the ingenuity of Petty's contributions, he does not directly attack the central problem; the founders of economics are still Quesnay and Smith.

b. North and Locke

Throughout the period preceding the age of Quesnay and Smith, contributions to the growing system of economics became more impressive, paralleling the progressive emancipation of capitalism from state tutelage. In this respect the several generations' advantage which England enjoyed in leadership over its rivals is reflected in the progress of its literature on economics, which, long before the days of Smith, could no longer be classified as mercantilist.

As early as the end of the seventeenth century Sir Dudley North[24] had directed a devastating attack against the heart of the mercantilist doctrine—the theory of the balance of trade. North's attack was based not only on purely technical considerations but on the aggressively proclaimed conviction that the world is one, and international trade a matter of mutual, not unilateral, benefit. He was probably the first 'free-trader' in the nineteenth-century sense of the word, but with the special distinction of being the first to appreciate the fruitful possibilities of a distant future. North also seems to have been the first to suggest that capital—which he called 'stock'—is a separate factor of production and that profit is the income that accrues to it. He understood that only by being employed either for loans or as business capital could money earn a revenue, not by being kept in the form of money—an argument which hit the theory rather than the practice of the mercantilists.

To his contemporary, the philosopher and political theorist John Locke,[25] economic theory owes the first, if still hesitant and uncertain, enunciation of an improved form of the quantity theory of money. We have already mentioned Locke's doctrine that prices vary not only with the quantity of money but also with the velocity of its circulation. Locke also introduced into monetary theory the factor which is now called the 'volume of trade': an increase in the supply of goods *vis-à-vis* an unchanged demand for them in money makes for a fall of prices. Finally, he excluded from the effective quantity of money that portion which rests in hoards or treasures and is thus prevented from influencing the prices of goods. Though his successors formulated the theory more strictly, there was substantially little that remained to be added.

c. Cantillon

The climax of the pre-classical literature, which could easily have become the beginning of the classical literature—and was so regarded by Jevons, who rediscovered it after it had had a long period of complete oblivion—is a systematic treatise, the first of its kind, by an Irish-born British banker and international financier, Richard Cantillon.[26] This book, which was first published in a French version more than twenty years after the author's death at the hands of assassins,[27] immediately achieved great historical influence through the least commendable of its features. Cantillon was the first to teach, in excessive opposition to the mercantilist prejudice in favor of money and commerce, that the sole ultimate source of all wealth is land. Labor only transforms this natural wealth. In the system of the physiocrats this idea later obscured their own really immortal achievement, the theory of circulation, and assumed an importance which Cantillon doubtless did not intend it to have. For Cantillon himself—though in language none too clear—emphasized that capital too adds to the value of the product of labor and land and he divided the value of the product into three different 'rents'— or incomes— of which one goes to the landlord, one to the capitalist, and one to the laborer. But these are not the parts which justify the reputation of his book.

Elsewhere in the same book Cantillon gave a lucid account of the price mechanism, the theory of which was to become the center of the classical system of economics. He showed through examples how a rising or a falling demand for a commodity is reflected in a rising or a falling price, which thereby encourages or deters producers and thus regulates production as an authority invested with coercive power would otherwise have to do. Cantillon realized that a certain length of time is needed for such regulation—i. e. for the producers to change the disposition of their capital in response to the change in prices; but his successors have not always been aware of this fact. Cantillon's main thesis is that 'market price' (current price) fluctuates around a center to which he gave the name 'intrinsic price' (value) and which he said was determined by 'land and labor' (cost of production). There seems to be no doubt that Petty and North had had some notion of a self-regulatory economic system, and Locke in two separate essays even described the fluctuation of market price, on the one hand, and labor value as the foundation of price, on the other. But it was left for Cantillon to point out the decisive interaction of value and market price, which is the regulatory mechanism in an otherwise unregulated system.

Moreover, Cantillon made important contributions to the theory of money and international trade. Taking as the starting point of his analysis the assumed discovery of new mines of precious metals, he traced the way inflation spreads through the entire economic system of a country. Those connected with the mining of the precious metals are the first to receive additional purchasing power and are enabled to buy more goods, outbidding for them other people whose incomes the rising flood of money has not yet reached, such as landowners, who lease out their land, and workers, whose remuneration is fixed. Thus, the inflation changes the distribution of incomes until the additional money has been fully absorbed into a system of generally higher prices. The careful and realistic elaboration of this idea is an achievement in itself and may very well have suggested to Quesnay the study of the principle of circulation.

Cantillon added two significant remarks. In the first place, he realized that the effect of a rising quantity or velocity of money may be neutralized if transactions which had not involved the use of cash are now drawn into the monetary orbit—in other words, if the volume of trade is increased. And secondly, he compared an inflation of metal money with one of paper money and argued that because paper money rests on whatever confidence the people may have in the issuing authority, any fit of mistrust resulting in a situation in which people refuse to accept a money without an intrinsic value of its own would send the inflated price structure tumbling down. John Law's famous experiment in introducing a pure paper money into the French financial structure had ended in disaster a few years before—as Cantillon had predicted when he was invited to indorse Law's plan.

From the theory of money Cantillon derived the theory of self-regulating international trade. As prices rise in the country mining the precious metals, people prefer to buy the products of countries whose prices have not yet risen. Thus a depression is brought about at home, and money leaves the country to pay for the imports, until the point is reached at which domestic prices are again low enough to attract domestic buyers. Cantillon did not add what is implied in this theory, that the other countries attract their share of the precious metals through their additional exports resulting from their disadvantage in metals and their consequent advantage in prices, until the newly mined money is proportionately distributed among the trading countries. Instead, his explicit conclusion was a long-range historical speculation: the advantages of precious-metal mines are only transitory; the additional money spoils the country, makes it dependent on other countries for imports, and finally leaves the country altogether and passes on to another. It is true that in all this Cantillon was not quite original. Bodin had already described the mechanism by which the precious metals from America had been brought from Spain to France by the increase in Spanish prices relatively to those in France, and, like a typical French mercantilist, had welcomed this 'favorable' influence on the balance of trade. Cantillon's conclusion, on the other hand, was one of somewhat skeptical resignation to the ways of nature.

Cantillon's mastery in the field of monetary theory is further evidenced by the fact that he was able to explain local differences of price levels within the same country on much the same basis as he had explained the differences between the price levels of different countries. The question of local price differences was neglected for almost two hundred years after Cantillon until it was revived by Mises.[28] Prices, Cantillon said, are higher in the cities, particularly in the capital city of a country, than in the rural areas because these are usually indebted to the city, send money there, and thus produce a relative disparity in the distribution of money in favor of the city.

Cantillon followed Petty in taking as the determinant of the value of money the cost of its production, but he combined this theory with the quantity theory of money into a whole which is the special application of his general principle of value and price: the varying quantities of money in circulation determine the short-run fluctuations of the level of prices around a center determined by the cost of production of money. An application of this principle is provided by Cantillon's theory of the changes brought about by international trade, which we have already mentioned: the country mining precious metals loses its excess metal and lowers its inflated price level by paying for imports of goods that can be purchased from abroad at lower than domestic prices, and thus domestic prices are reduced to equality with those of the other countries. Cantillon even went on to show how the influx of money finally 'makes land and labor dearer,' that is, raises the cost of production and thereby the value of the product. This process tends to stabilize the inflated price structure. (We may leave out of account the repercussions in foreign trade and the large-range sociological influences resulting in possible decadence, which we have mentioned above.) Though Cantillon's analysis is not complete, his approach is that of Smith and Ricardo.

Finally, Cantillon's brief but profound observations on the nature and rate of interest deserve to be mentioned. 'Men in need must have at first tempted the Lenders by the attraction of profit; and this profit must have been in proportion to the needs of the Borrowers and to the fears and the avarice of the Lenders. This, it seems to me, was the original source of interest. But its constant practice in states appears to be founded on the profits which Entrepreneurs can make out of it.' ('Out of it' is doubtless miswritten for 'out of the loan'). This too is in no way a complete statement, but much of the work of later writers can be characterized as an elaboration of this suggestion. There is no doubt that the nearest rival to Smith—not to Quesnay—for the honor of being the co-founder of economics is Cantillon, Smith's predecessor by at least forty years.

d. Hume

Before Cantillon's book was discovered, David Hume,[29] Smith's older friend, had been given the credit for much brilliant thinking in economics. Now he must either share the credit with the older man, whose posthumous book was published only after Hume's own works—though of course written long before them —or must yield to Cantillon, if, as is likely, Hume had seen the unpublished manuscript during his travels in France, where it was kept for sixteen years. But even in this case, enough still remains to the credit of Hume to make him a remarkable and original economist too.

Hume has already been mentioned as a forceful opponent of mercantilism, who yet did more than anyone else before or after him to develop that dynamic interpretation of money which we have employed for an appreciation of the mercantilists' historic achievement. No one, on the one hand, has more rigorously stated the conclusion from the quantity theory of money that, 'if fixed,' the quantity of money in circulation has no bearing whatever on the welfare of the people, since it serves only to express all prices and salaries in proportionately greater or smaller figures, and any quantity of money can achieve the turnover of any quantity of goods. On the other hand, Hume has provided the best analysis of what happens if the quantity of money is not 'fixed,' that is, of the effects of inflation. Cantillon, it is true, had preceded him in this analysis, but had only drawn the conclusion that incomes are redistributed by the time-lag between the rise of some prices and incomes and that of others. Such a conclusion would suggest a rather unfavorable judgment of inflationary policy. Hume, however, found in this time-lag a cause for rejoicing, because it increases profits and provides a powerful stimulus to capitalists to expand production further. { He therefore concluded that a slow but constant increase in the quantity of money in circulation is advisable in order to provide a perpetual stimulant to business activity. ⟩This was actually the practice of the despised mercantilists. In reasoning thus, Hume surpassed his successors for more than a century. His conclusion is tantamount to the idea that permanent prosperity can be achieved through inflation.

In the theory of international trade too Hume went beyond Cantillon. The latter had argued that inflation and its consequent rise in prices lead to an increase in imports, make the country dependent on foreign supplies, and thereby initiate the process of the decline of domestic industry. As we have pointed out, this thesis is a long-range sociological speculation rather than an economic theory. In completing the latter, Hume was brought to the important conclusion that a country cannot lose its money by importing goods from abroad because the very loss of some of its money results in lower domestic prices, stops further imports, and may even turn them into exports and thus bring the precious metals back. This is the cap-stone in the theory of self-regulating international trade, and Hume gave it a particularly striking form.

Closely related is his doctrine of interest, which is remarkable for the wisdom with which he combined economic reasoning with historical and sociological analyses such as were demanded a hundred and a hundred and fifty years later by the historicist and institutionalist critics of orthodox theory. Less profound than Cantillon in analyzing the character of the phenomena, Hume was primarily interested in their mechanism: he did little to elucidate the nature of interest but did investigate its rate. His starting point again was his polemic against the mercantilists, who had believed that the way to lower interest and thus to stimulate business is to increase the supply of money. Hume's opposition to this view was based on his distinction between money spent on consumers' goods, the increase of which raises prices and wages, and money capital, the increase of which lowers interest. But here too Hume's strong sense for reality was not content with the mere separation of the two forms of money, as his classical successors were; he proceeded to study the interaction between money spent and money invested.

To this end, he first surveyed the factors on which the rate of interest depends, namely the intensity of the demand for loans, the magnitude of the supply of loan money, and the size of commercial profits (which, as Cantillon had already shown, is indicative of the profits to be realized from loans). In a commercial-minded country, Hume argued, frugality prevails, there are many lenders and few borrowers, and competition in commerce makes for low profits and consequently low interest rates; profligacy, on the other hand, which he associates with the preponderance of the landed gentry in a country, will manifest itself in a high rate of interest.

Finally, this penetrating insight was combined with the analysis —which we have outlined above—of the inflationary process resulting from the discovery of new mines. Hume contrasted two sociological types, the people of Spain, on the one hand, and those of Britain and France, on the other. In Spain interest was low only for a short time, while the new riches from America, coming in large accumulated sums, were loaned out. But people in Spain did not know how to turn money to commercial advantage and soon consumed the new wealth. In the end the usual high interest rates, with all that they imply, were restored. The inhabitants of Britain and France, on the other hand, knew how to benefit from Spanish squandering, attracted the metal in payment for their luxury exports to Spain, used it to stimulate domestic commercial activity, and were rewarded for their demonstration of all the capitalistic virtues by a low rate of interest. No socio-economic reasoning can be more brilliant than this.

III. The Founding of Economics[1]

1. ECONOMICS AS A SYSTEM OF NATURAL HARMONY

ANY order, economic or other, requires an ordering will. For thousands of years the ordering will had been that of political authority. As western man set out to destroy authority, the problem of economic order became more pressing. No solution to this problem was logically possible under the circumstances unless one assumed that order need not be artificially imposed by authority because it already exists 'naturally,' either actually or potentially, i.e. a natural law of harmony governs the activity of the cells of the economic body if it is left alone.

Natural law in its application to economic society was conceived in two forms, the one physical and the other biological. On the one hand, astronomy shows how the heavenly bodies move in accordance with a law that does not impel them from without, as a visible authoritarian power would do, but drives them from within their own nature. The 'harmony of the spheres' had long been an object of pious wonder and study; indeed, the desire to understand the operation of the divine law governing this phenomenon had given the decisive impetus to the development of modern physics from the Renaissance on. On the other hand, a younger sister science of physics was biology, which was conceived on the analogy of physics in so far as life is kept in self-perpetuating harmonious operation by some motor force implanted in it. Thus, if one claimed that economic society, because of the forces implanted in it by nature, would function better without authority, one could use either biology or physics as a model and guide.

Science, in the sense of the study of the laws of nature, had been developed by modern man and had enabled him to make those immense advances in technology and medicine which are the objects of his pride. Accordingly, when the problem of the economic organization of society had to be faced, the same well-tried tools of science suggested themselves which had been so successful in other fields. To subsume economic life under the categories of natural life seemed to be easy enough. Is not society a compound of individuals, each of whom is a natural being? Are not their needs natural, to be explained by physiology and psychology? And is not production a combination of forces in nature and man organized into processes in accordance with the laws taught by natural science? Finally, is not nature, including man and society, the creation of a benevolent Maker, who willed that His creatures should live in harmony with one another and gave them the faculties to do so?

This is the philosophy—called 'Deism'—from which the methods of economics were derived. According to the Deistic philosophy God's role has already been played in creating the natural order, and (whether or not we choose to give him credit for the faculties which we owe to his past act of creation) he can be safely left out of account as a factor in the present. He can no longer intervene in the natural order which he once created. He is, as has often been remarked, like an absolute monarch who, having once granted a republican constitution to his subjects, has by that act divested himself of all power and is now no longer free to rescind it or to interfere in any way with its interpretation or enforcement. What matters for the present is that man can and will create a harmonious world. The abdication of God in favor of man is presupposed in all modern systems of thought. Reliance on such godless systems, Christianity has all the while been predicting, can only lead to catastrophe, as must all the absolute presumptions of so frail a creature as man, who is always in danger of being unjust, most of all when he claims to be building the kingdom of eternal harmony.

It is true that harmony had never yet been realized. It was far from being realized even at the time the theorists described it. Their description was really meant as a program, an invitation to realize the ideal of harmonious human co-operation. Strictly speaking, they contradicted themselves in calling 'natural' a harmony that, by their own admission, did not yet exist. But the concept of the natural here approximately coincides with that of the rational, and both mean the essence rather than the given reality of the world. In other words, the theory requires a further refinement: the doctrine of natural law, heritage of two thousand years of philosophizing. The moral and legal doctrine of natural law may in this case be said to mean that man's insight into the workings of nature, which distinguish him from all other creatures, is required to complete the work of nature. Though the conditions of harmony are natural, it can be achieved only through an understanding of the laws of nature and by working in accordance with them. Ignorance and deceit have kept man in bondage for thousands of years. It is only now that he can free himself by his knowledge of natural law from his age-old superstitious reverence for artificial authorities and their artificial laws and can bring the law of man closer to its model, the law of nature.

In this proposition lies the political significance of the new doctrine. It is a revolutionary doctrine, though many of those who subscribed to it were not aware of this implication. The way was open for a restoration of the natural order through a revolution against existing authority once men became convinced that this order had been disrupted by those in power to serve their own greed. Medieval society, which had conceived of itself and its order as supernaturally ordained, superrationally established, now appeared unnatural and irrational; it had to give way before those who claimed to represent the scientific understanding of life and its natural harmony—the bourgeoisie.

In this way, the time-honored argument in favor of traditional authority was turned upside down. As long as man appeared as a frail creature under constant temptation to commit injustice, the peace and order of society, on which his physical and spiritual existence depends, could be guaranteed only by the strong hand of an independent authority; liberty for everyone to do as he pleased would result in chaos. If, however, there is in the nature of man, as in that of the stars, an inner impulse to contribute to universal harmony, then he can and must be made free; authority, by overriding the dictates of that inner impulse, would be destructive not only of liberty but of order as well. On the other hand, it must be obvious that individual liberty is physically possible only to the extent that it does lead to order, i.e. an organized interlocking of functions. Liberal democracy and laissez-faire economy are the two main examples of freedom established on the basis of this doctrine of pre-ordained harmony.

From this point of view, all preceding history was really only pre-history, an account of the changing errors and incessant sufferings through which mankind had had to pass until the dawn of enlightenment. From that moment history became progress: a development towards fuller harmony within the natural pattern and without further fundamental change. Indeed, progress, in the sense of development along predictable lines within a given pattern, is the opposite of history, the character of which is fundamental change. Once mankind has organized its life on the basis of the law of a free natural harmony and embarks on progress towards its ever fuller realization, further historical change in the direction of a new order is barred. Any attempt at a post-liberal order must be considered as beyond the bounds of nature and reason: these are immutable. This implication of the philosophy of natural harmony, which could not fail to become explicit in due time, constituted the chief defense of the once revolutionary economic system against its critics and adversaries, the socialists, who were to oppose the concept of historical change to the bourgeois concept of natural harmony.[2]

2. ECONOMICS AS BIOLOGY—QUESNAY[3]

Asked by the Dauphin what he would do if he were king, François Quesnay, court physician of Louis XV and Madame de Pompadour, is reported to have replied, 'Nothing.' Upon being further questioned who would then rule, he answered, 'The law.' The motto 'laissez faire—laissez passer,' which means freedom of business enterprise at home and international free trade, has been attributed to various members of his circle. It has given the name to an entire era. The world runs automatically, owing to the law implanted in it—this is the belief of the physiocrats.

Like all good theorists, the physiocrats were at great pains to define the institutional setting in which the economic law is supposed to work. This setting is, in their opinion, natural: it is the one institutional setting which does not thwart the operation of the inherent law of harmony but secures it. From our different point of view, this setting is historical, i.e. a transitory phase in the history of economic organization, and the validity of the laws governing the operation of a laissez-faire economy must be considered as limited; but this qualification only adds to the theory of the physiocrats the interest that must attach to anything that has the character of the concrete, the real, or the historical. The study of this setting is our first task, with a view towards making their immortal achievement technically intelligible.

For a while they called themselves 'Economists,' using the word as a proper name. When this ceased to be a distinctive designation, the name 'physiocrats,' which they had used at first but later abandoned, became customary. 'Physiocracy' means the supremacy of nature, and this in three senses. In the first place, the term denotes the philosophy and general political program of the era, i.e. Renaissance humanism. Secondly, it suggests the protest against mercantilism, which was a program for making commerce (and industry) supreme. The physiocrats wished to substitute the rule of agriculture (with possibly, according to some interpretations, mining). Finally this program was derived from the economic analysis of the physiocrats, which assigns a distinguished place to agriculture as the sole source of wealth.

The question of the ultimate source of wealth had been familiar to ancient and medieval speculation. A superficial answer had been given by the mercantilists, who did not look beyond the spoils of foreign trade. Petty had initiated a new line of reasoning by his analysis of labor and land as the two factors contributing to the value of the product. To the mercantilist prejudice Cantillon had then opposed the thesis that the land is the sole producer of wealth but had drawn no further conclusions. What distinguishes the physiocrats is that though they chose their starting point naively, they set an example of logical rigor by pursuing its theoretical implications strictly and fearlessly into the most remote conclusions.

To the physiocrats the supremacy of nature meant the exclusive productivity of the soil (agriculture and mining); mere manufacturing and processing labor they stigmatized as 'sterile.' Of course, they did not deny that industrial and other work is indispensable in that it converts the wealth extracted from nature into consumable form. But they preferred to ignore this fact in favor of the narrow consideration that only the extractive industries, working with nature, create new, additional nuclei of wealth, while processing labor only changes these nuclei from one form to another. In terms of the theory of value, this proposition was expressed in the statement that the sterile work of labor adds only its own value, i.e. the value of the things consumed in the process itself, but nothing more. The value added by labor includes not only the materials used in production and the wage representing the worker's food but also the manufacturer's profit; from the point of view of the process as a whole, all these appear as values consumed in, and for the purpose of, production, i.e. they constitute the cost of production. A real surplus over the value consumed in production, without which there could not be any new production, is found only in agriculture; it alone is truly 'productive.'

In addition to the productive and sterile classes of producers, the physiocrats distinguished the special class of landowners, whose presence makes the productive class tenant farmers, i.e. capitalist entrepreneurs who invest their capital in agricultural production and hire labor for it. The landowners were depicted as having originally cleared the soil for agriculture or as the heirs of those who had; this is their title to ownership and to a revenue from the land. Their present function is that of public servants and administrators—among them the king and his court. The physiocrats are emphatic in their insistence on the fact that this class is indispensable. They seem to have accepted unqualifiedly the pre-revolutionary organization of society and in particular the monarchy.

A society consisting of the productive, the sterile, and the landowning classes was then placed under observation as in an ideal experiment. The economic process in such a society was seen to be self-regulating and self-perpetuating, expressive of the law of nature in the economic body. The test of its success is that at the end of the process of production and distribution the original situation is restored: all classes have lived, worked, and consumed for one period and are ready to enter a second such period. This cyclical continuity is possible only if the whole economic process, abandoned to itself, makes the activities of the classes interlock and preserves the proportions between them that are required for this interlocking. In order to be able to produce and exchange their products, the three classes must begin each period with certain equipment for production— capital, in modern terminology—to be wholly or partly used up in the process, and the restoration of their original situation at the end of each cycle must also include the restoration to the producers of the capital expended in the process, so as to enable them to continue their work in the next period.

The discovery of the circular flow of goods, i.e. the demonstration that the process of production and exchange is self-renewed under these conditions, is the great achievement of the physiocrats, the starting point and one of the two principal themes of economics. The theory was inspired by the discovery, shortly before, of the circulation of the blood. The ambition of the physiocrats was to demonstrate the organic self-perpetuating nature of life in economic society as in the individual organism. As the blood in the body, in passing through the various organs, gives up certain ingredients and acquires others, proceeding in a strictly prescribed way and finally arriving at any one point with exactly the composition which it had on its last arrival there, so the wealth of society reproduces itself through production, exchange, and distribution in a strictly lawful, harmonious way. Economics thus appears as the physiology of economic society.

This thesis was demonstrated by the *Tableau Economique*, which had the form of a balance sheet, indicating the exchange of goods and money between various places in the system. In order to provide an accurate picture of this circulation, special numerical assumptions had to be made. At the beginning of the period—a new period using the capital inherited from the preceding analogous period—the net product of the productive class, to be distributed through the system, is, it was assumed, five billions. Two billions' worth of goods are the industrial products, still in the hands of the sterile class. In addition, there is a money capital of two billions in the hands of the productive class. Finally, there is the original capital of ten billions invested in the arable land, to be replaced at the rate of one-tenth a year. However, it is replaced within the productive class—through clearance, drainage, and the like—and therefore does not appear in any transfer.

The productive class transfers its money capital of two billions to the landowners as the rent due them on their original investment. They in turn use one billion to purchase agricultural products, leaving four billions to the producers, and the other billion to buy industrial products from the sterile class. This completes the account of the landowners.

The sterile class uses the one billion received from the landowners to buy food from the productive class, which now retains three billions of its products and has received back the two billions of money. Of the latter it uses one billion to purchase industrial products from the sterile class, partly consumption goods and partly tools for the cultivation of the land. Finally the sterile class uses this billion, which now describes its second circuit, to buy another billion's worth of goods from the productive class, e. g. raw materials. Thus the money is back at its starting point, and the sterile class is enabled to combine its own labor (reproduced by the consumption of one billion's worth of food) and the newly acquired one billion's worth of raw materials into two billions' worth of products, to be exchanged in the next period. Finally, two out of the original five billions are consumed by the producers themselves, as their own food and as seed, feed, etc. This completes the process. At the end, the original situation is restored, including the equipment of the two working classes with stocks of products and with money. This is the *Tableau Economique*.

From the social point of view the *Tableau* appears rather shocking. Although the physiocrats did not at all share the views of the mercantilists including Petty, on the wisdom of keeping the workers under the pressure of misery, the *Tableau* seems to block any understanding of the special problem of labor by lumping both employers and laborers together in the same account. However, what is much worse is that no less than two-fifths of the total income is appropriated by the landowners, whose services, if any, are administrative, not economic. Of course, the figures are chosen arbitrarily; but Quesnay took a special pride in the realism of his assumptions and, eager to glorify what he called the 'divine institution' of property, certainly had no reason to exaggerate the burden of property on the people.

On the nature of property, Anne Robert Jacques Turgot,[4] who was associated, but not identified, with Quesnay's school, differed from him, with practical consequences that became manifest only after their time. Turgot did not accept the doctrine of the divine origin of property but quite soberly traced it to the right of occupation, much as Smith did after him and Oppenheimer almost one hundred and fifty years later: those who had found no free land were under the necessity of accepting employment from landowners in return for a concession of part of their produce. And while the owner needs the farmer, who produces the food, the latter needs the owner only 'by virtue of human contracts and civil laws.' The divergence from Quesnay's scholasticism on this point, in the direction of realism and skepticism, is conspicuous.

But what is important in the doctrine of the physiocrats is not their social views but their theoretical approach. The contrast between this and the method of the mercantilists cannot be over-emphasized. The source of wealth is not the precious metal taken from foreign countries by way of war or of a favorable balance of trade, but the soil of the homeland. Consequently, the analysis of the physiocrats is in terms of goods rather than of money; the 'money veil' is removed for the first time to show the essential process beneath it. To be sure, money is given its proper place as a medium of exchange; what circulates is not only goods one way but money the other way. However, the dynamic effects of money, as suggested by mercantilist practice and by the theories of Cantillon and Hume, were lost sight of. The physiocrats inaugurated the practice of disregarding money as irrelevant: a practice that cannot fail to be dangerously misleading when it is followed, as it was later by the orthodox classical school, without regard to historical circumstances.

Still more important, the physiocrats replaced the partial dynamic analyses of the mercantilists by an all-inclusive static analysis, i.e. a description of the conditions of stable equilibrium and the tendencies making for it in the economic order. The fact that this analysis is all-inclusive makes it the first *system* in the history of economic theory, the real beginning of the science as a formalized body of knowledge. Some may indeed doubt the merit of static analysis, since life is always dynamic, and capitalism certainly is. But the first task for a laissez-faire theory was to prove the stability of the natural economic order by demonstrating its automatic reproduction. The first question was not whether the system could grow but whether it could live; only then could an all-inclusive analysis proceed to the problem of the conditions of stability in the balanced growth of the economic order. Unfortunately, economic theory has been slow in taking this second step; economists have been content to stay for too long—more than one and a half centuries, in fact—within the bounds of static analysis. It is not the physiocrats, however, who are to blame for this conservatism. Implicitly and explicitly they pointed beyond static analysis, as we shall demonstrate later in a summary contrast of the two founding schools of economics.

The paramount political conclusion to be drawn from an examination of the *Tableau* was the necessity of economic freedom. The order seemed to be self-adjusting and self-perpetuating and to require no outside interference. It is true that autonomy in the economic order was presupposed in the general assumption of a natural harmony, but this presupposition appeared to be warranted only now that the autonomous economic order could be proved to be stable. The revolutionary implications of the physiocratic theory could not fail to become apparent in a country as exploited by its bureaucracy as France was. It must always be kept in mind that Quesnay did not analyze an existing condition, but advocated a program. In a study of the meaning of theories rather than of the opinions of theorists, the question of the extent to which the physiocrats themselves realized the revolutionary implications of their doctrine can remain undecided. At any rate, it is not inconsistent that their reverence for the ancient regime should have led them to an appeal to the king to act as a really 'enlightened despot' and to set free the wholesome forces of nature in his realm. What the physiocrats advocated was a revolution from above—but a revolution.

Two examples may be singled out to demonstrate this point. One is the discussion of international free trade by members of the physiocratic school, particularly Paul Pierre le Mercier de la Rivière.[5] The physiocrats, it is true, never shared the exuberant hopes which inspired later free-traders, being more concerned with criticizing the thousands of mercantilist restrictions than with conjuring up visions of the wealth to be derived from the unfettering of international trade. Yet the polemic of Mercier de la Rivière against restrictions on trade is nothing short of brilliant (although not very original after the work of Cantillon and Hume), particularly when he insists that, should the mercantilist policy of the trade balance be successful and all money be concentrated in France, French exports would cease entirely, since no purchasing power would be left in the hands of the customers.

A second example of the hidden revolutionary trend in physiocratic thinking may be found in the strong democratic implications of their doctrine. All the writers of the school followed Quesnay's lead when he said that 'the division of society into different orders of citizens, some in supreme control of others, destroys the general interest and arouses dissension among the particular interests,' although it is never explained how this idea can be reconciled with the retention of the landowning, rent-receiving class.

That the physiocrats were not, however, advocates of all-around laissez-faire can be seen from the exception which they demanded in the case of interest on loans. They recommended that interest rates be fixed by the authorities, therein following the example of the hated mercantilists, and for the same reason— the protection of the debter-producer against the creditor-capitalist, whom Quesnay denounced as 'knowing neither king nor country.'

On this point too there was profound disagreement between Quesnay and the other great representative of the physiocratic school, Turgot. The latter advocated the free formation of interest rates on the ground that they only reflect the land rent, which is the real surplus of production. For, Turgot argued, instead of lending his money at interest, a man can always use it to purchase land and secure a rent; whether he does the one or the other depends on the relative advantage to be derived from each. He will buy land if the rent is higher than the interest he can expect to receive if he lends his money. If he buys land, the price of land is raised, and the percentage or yield of the given rent on this rising value will be reduced, while at the same time the withdrawal of money from the loan market will raise the interest on loans, until rent and interest are equalized. This doctrine of interconnection had been anticipated by Perry; formally, it is good classical reasoning, but upside down. For Turgot did not see that land has no original value at all; the value of land is derived from its rent by capitalizing it at the prevailing rate of interest so as to make the rent appear as the interest on the money invested in the purchase of the land. In other words, the rate of interest, far from being derived from land rent, is presupposed in the valuation of land.

But, whatever may be the source of interest, Turgot, in a later context, made a startling observation on its nature. Unless interest is paid, he reasoned, the capitalist will withdraw his money from the enterprise and disrupt production. Interest must therefore be inviolate. This argument was directed against Quesnay's recommendation that interest rates be fixed by the government. Even more, it was a strong and historically influential plea for free and unhampered capitalism, and in the history of economic theory it marks the discovery of interest as a cost factor, i.e. a sum the payment of which has an indispensable function in the maintenance of production. Rent, on the other hand, is not an indispensable part of the cost of production; it is a mere surplus and does not therefore have the significance that interest has. This distinction was clearly felt by Turgot though only Ricardo explicitly formulated it.

The physiocrats' single-minded concentration on land as the sole source of wealth led to the second political conclusion to be drawn from their theory. Their apparent prejudice in favor of the landowners, the rent-receiving class, proved to be quite the opposite when, with fearless logic, the implications of their theory were made explicit, and agriculture alone was found able to bear taxes. For a tax laid on the sterile class would cut into their livelihood, the equivalent of which is all they produce. Consequently, the tax has to be shifted, by way of higher prices on manufactured goods, to their agricultural purchasers, the only group which has a surplus and is in a position to bear the tax. The productive class, of course, must also be tax-exempt, since it has to yield its surplus as rent to the landowners. Thus, all taxes, wherever imposed, must finally fall on the agricultural surplus alone. However, to avoid the painful and confusing process of shifting the incidence of the tax through additions to or deductions from prices, the imposition of a single tax on land was recommended.

It is true that the single-tax program of Henry George, more than a century later, was not based on the assumption that agriculture is the sole source of wealth. George regarded rent simply as an unearned increment, to be taxed on grounds of social justice, on the basis of Ricardo's theory of differential rent. Nevertheless, George honored the physiocrats as his predecessors, and rightly so. Their suggestion for a single tax, aside from its results, marks an epoch in the history of economic theory in that it inaugurated the study of the shifting and incidence of taxes and contained a powerful plea for 'direct' as against 'indirect' taxation.

It was through their advocacy of the single tax on land that the physiocrats became tragically involved in the downfall of the *ancien régime*. Their rise to success and fame after 1758, when the *Tableau* first appeared, had been fabulous, but their fall was even more rapid. Opposition to their program was bitter from the outset. No less a person than Voltaire had sneered at their tax program, which would have left the rich rentier tax-exempt at the same time that it burdened the small freeholder. The Neapolitan abbé and diplomat, Ferdinando Galiani,[6] was an even more formidable critic because he was an economist of the first rank—one of those men who, like Cantillon and Hume, might easily have become the founder of the young science in competition with Smith. Galiani anticipated by one hundred years two important schools of thought—the neo-classical and the historical. His doctrine that value rests on utility and scarcity will be discussed later. It was his historical-institutionalist criticism of abstract theorizing which undermined the authority of the physiocrats on such matters as the free-trade and the single-tax programs. Galiani was not opposed in principle to the method of economic theory. Indeed, he himself was a master theoretician. But he was the first and most distinguished of a long series of writers to warn against theoretical oversimplification and the rash conclusions drawn from it for practical policy. He may be said to have generalized into a program of realistic theory what Cantillon and Hume as well as he himself had practiced in their monetary studies. He thus achieved a balance between abstract theorizing and historical analysis which neither orthodox theory nor the orthodox historical school proved capable of maintaining. No wonder that his influence weighed heavily against the physiocrats.

Meanwhile, the power of the physiocrats was still growing and reached its peak when Turgot became Minister of Finance in 1774, shortly before the death of the aged Quesnay. Turgot, a man of exceptional courage and purity of character, insisted on following out the physiocratic program and initiated that revolution from above which it called for. He abolished internal customs, eliminated guild regulations, and unified the tax system in the direction of the single tax on land. But he encountered furious resistance from those whose privileges were impaired, particularly the landed nobility, whom the political doctrine of the physiocrats had so lavishly extolled. In 1776 Turgot was overthrown.

This marked the abrupt and complete end of physiocracy. But it was also the end of the attempt at a revolution from above, which was the sole alternative to the real revolution, the revolution from below. In that same fateful year the American Revolution broke out, and in England, where the political revolution had taken place almost one hundred years before, there appeared the book which proclaimed the economic revolution and which, for a century and a half, utterly eclipsed the physiocrats—Adam Smith's *Wealth of Nations*.

3. Economics as Physics—Adam Smith[7]

Enough has already been said to show that Adam Smith cannot be regarded as an original genius from whose head the system of price theory sprang complete. Of Quesnay it can truly be said that he is solely responsible for the theory of the circular flow of goods; but Smith was heir to an already long and fertile tradition. He counted the considerably older Hume among his personal friends; when traveling in France he had access to the circle of the physiocrats and was in contact with Turgot and Galiani; he was prevented only by Quesnay's death from dedicating to him his *Wealth of Nations*. In some respects, notably in the theory of money, Smith's achievement falls distinctly short of that of Cantillon and Hume, and he thereby became responsible for a long-continued retrogression in monetary knowledge. In value theory he ignored the path which Galiani had already broken. Thus, Smith was by no means a pioneer.

Instead, Smith's achievement represents the crowning peak of the early development of economic theory. Through him economics reached maturity. One has only to compare his bulky treatise with the booklets of the much older Cantillon and of Smith's contemporary Turgot to be impressed by the way in which Smith provided a round picture of economic reality, rich in detail, full of life, and integrated into a system of theory as its organizing principle. None of his predecessors, for all their admirable achievements, and none of his school, for all its advances in analysis, can match him in richness of material and closeness to reality. If it is questionable whether the school he inaugurated can rightly be called 'classical,' there can be no doubt that Adam Smith is the classical economist.

The sixteen years which elapsed between Smith's *Theory of Moral Sentiments* and his *Wealth of Nations* witnessed a considerable change in his fundamental point of view. In the earlier book economic activities appeared in a distinctly unfavorable light. Smith the moralist argued that economic success beyond the level necessary for the satisfaction of one's physical wants does not add to a man's real happiness, and it is only vanity, the desire to be looked upon by one's fellow men with admiration and envy, that motivates the incessant accumulation of personal wealth. Smith strongly objected to the cynical proposition, stated half a century earlier by Bernard de Mandeville in his sensational *Fable of the Bees*,[8] that 'private vice'—meaning avarice and covetousness—is 'public virtue' in so far as it is a condition necessary for the operation of business. According to Smith the desire for admiration and envy is an inferior virtue, derived from the great virtue of sympathy, of sharing the feelings of others. Nevertheless, it is true that providence uses a roundabout way to prompt man to exert his efforts. In the book of Smith the economist, however, we read that, 'it is not from the benevolence of the butcher, brewer, and baker, that we expect our dinner, but from their regard for their own interest.' Here their interest is taken as legitimate and as incapable of being misunderstood. It is significant that this proposition is almost literally reproduced from Mandeville's *Fable of the Bees*. However, the difference between these two interpretations of self-interest does not affect the validity of the fundamental proposition of the *Wealth of Nations*, that man 'is led by an invisible hand to promote an end which was no part of his intention.' This is the classical formulation of the belief in preordained harmony, the condition of laissez-faire economy.

Yet Smith must not be regarded as simply a champion of capitalism. He did not believe that self-interest necessarily co- incides with the common good. He was bitter and violent in de- nouncing the self-interest of merchants and manufacturers, al- though he was more lenient with farmers and workers. 'Profit hunger,' he said, 'conflicts with public interest' in that it always aims at monopoly. The latter he defined as 'infamous covetous- ness . . . which does not shrink from terrorization and crime.' 'People of the same trade seldom convene without their enter- tainment ending in a conspiracy against the public or a scheme for an increase of price.' There are innumerable other passages to the same effect.

The contradiction between this view and the program of laissez-faire was resolved by the strongest emphasis on competi- tion as opposed to monopoly. If self-interest, left uncontrolled, asserts itself in monopoly, it has to be controlled by competition and directed into channels that serve the public interest. Monopoly raises price and to this end cuts output; competition lowers price and increases output. Smith's entire book is a plea for the enforcement of competition as the providential, or in this sense 'natural,' institution for the reconciliation of private and public interests. Indeed, Smith developed two different price theories, one for competition, the other for monopoly. Only the former is a part of his system; the latter is a foreign body. This bifurcation of price theory became prevalent in economics for more than one hundred and fifty years. Traditional economic theory is the system of competitive price theory.

Competitive price theory can be summarized in two proposi- tions. In the first place, price is determined by the ratio between demand and supply, and rises and falls with that ratio. Smith and his school had not yet made an analysis of demand. Accord- ing to them, demand is of a given magnitude at any moment and may change in time. The later understanding of demand as a schedule, i.e. as a readiness to take more goods at a lower and fewer goods at a higher price, was still unknown. Also considered as a datum in Smith's price theory is the short-run supply. Hence, the ratio rises when the demand happens to be higher or the supply lower, and it falls if the opposite holds true. It is this ratio which determines 'market price.'

In the second place, a rise in the price of the product increases the gain to be made by its sale and thereby encourages an increase of output. Falling prices, on the other hand, involve a loss to the producer or seller and make it psychologically and financially impossible to continue production on the former scale. Thus, the ups and downs of the market price, which reflect the fluctuations of demand for the commodity in question, stimulate a corresponding expansion or contraction of output. In this way, the former ratio of demand to supply is restored on a different level of absolute numbers, and the former price is restored. Price is, accordingly, the regulatory mechanism in a free, i.e. decentralized, economic system.

The 'normal' or 'natural' position around which price fluctuates is cost. Above cost there is profit; below cost there is loss. Cost is the sum total of what the producer has to pay out for labor, materials, tools, the rent of the land, and the use of capital (interest). If any of these factors is owned by the producer himself, he still has to compute the wage, the rent, the interest in favor of himself and charge it to the production account. If he fails to do so, he loses the wage or interest that he would have if he had lent his capital or sold his services. Cost is the natural position of price, inasmuch as price is drawn back to it by expansion or contraction of output, whenever the price rises over or falls under that equilibrium position. All this is, of course, the heritage from Cantillon.

However, it is essential to realize that the indispensable condition of natural price is competition. Rising price and profit are a signal for expansion of output, but not all producers will

be equally responsive to it. The signal will be followed by outsiders, who make less profit in their own field. It is they whom
the 'invisible hand' leads into the lure of profit, thereby destroy-
ing it. To be sure, the insider has the financial possibility of
expanding production by reinvestment of his abnormal profit,
but he will not necessarily so act as to cut his own profit if he
can avoid doing so. Whether or not he can depends on whether
or not he has a monopoly which would enable him to keep outsiders out. The result of monopoly is that price remains per-
manently above cost without starting the process of readjustment. Monopoly may rest on natural scarcity or on voluntary or
legal stipulation. The latter were the targets of Adam Smith.
Thus it can be seen that Smith's price theory—that price is
determined by the cost of production—holds only under conditions of competition. Monopoly price remains outside this
theory.

Behind price there is value: price is the manifestation of value.
From Aristotle down through the ages the distinction has been
made between two kinds of value—value in use and value in exchange. The latter coincides with natural price. Value in use,
according to Smith, is a precondition of exchange value; things
would not have exchange value if they had no value in use. But
value in use does not directly constitute value in exchange or
price. This is a crucial point in the history of economic theory.
Smith observed what was later called the 'economic paradox,'
i.e. that the most useful things, such as bread, are cheap, while
things comparatively less useful, such as diamonds, are expensive.
No one will pay a price, i.e. give up something useful to himself,
for an altogether useless thing; there will be exchange value and
price as soon as usefulness of any degree is established. The
degree of usefulness, however, will not determine price; to do
this will be left to the cost of production under the pressure
of competition. It remained for the so-called modern or subjective theory of value, developed one hundred years later, to
resolve the economic paradox by relating exchange value and

price to the degree of value in use. The procedure for doing this had already been suggested by Galiani[9] but was overlooked by Smith.

However, there are several ways of interpreting the proposition that price is determined by the cost of production. What is to be included in the cost of production? For more than one hundred years the defenders of capitalism have clung to an interpretation known as the general cost-of-production theory while the advocates of socialism have been proponents of the labor-value theory of costs. According to the former interpretation, the interest which the producer has to pay for the use of the capital (or the profit derived from it) is on an equal footing with the wage; both are accounted parts of the original costs of production. The labor-value theory of costs on the other hand, considers only the wage of labor an original cost and accounts profit or interest as a forced deduction from the total value of the product, which is the 'natural' reward of labor. Thus value theory became the main battleground of conflicting political aspirations in the field of economics. It is somewhat surprising that both versions of the cost theory may be found in the work of Adam Smith.

His normal understanding of the cost of production was in terms of the general-cost theory. It appears natural that a manufacturer should have his profit, the search for which is employed by the invisible hand as the stimulus to achieve the common good. In the general trend of Smith's argument the essential features of the laissez-faire system appear justified. But doubt creeps in when he comes to discuss the origin and nature of the capital income—a discussion based on the principle that the original cost is the 'toil and trouble' of the worker, and the original wage, the product. The share of capital in, or the deduction of profit from, the value of the product is explicitly traced to the desire of men 'to reap where they had not sown.' This statement is even stronger than the parallel passage in Turgot and became the starting point of the 'exploitation theory,' i.e. the theory that the capitalist robs the worker of a share of the product. But with Smith this remark is merely a passing expression of his general anti-capitalistic temper and is not of much consequence in his system.

It was in his fulminations against monopoly that his temper found its outlet in his theory. Some examples have already been given. What is striking is that though monopoly in general was his enemy, Smith was suspicious only of businessmen and much more lenient towards farmers and workers. Of farmers he said that it is only under the influence of businessmen that 'they forget the generosity which is natural to their status,' the spirit of capitalism thus infiltrating into the tradition-minded section of society. The attempt of the workers to defend themselves and to secure a better bargaining position by concerted action were at that time prosecuted as 'conspiracies' under the law, while employers' agreements, though illegal, were condoned. This situation aroused Smith's wrath. Owing to their small numbers, he said, employers can always use social gatherings to make business agreements to the detriment of the workers and the public. As a matter of fact, employers do find themselves 'in a tacit but uniform and permanent agreement.' Smith even went so far as to assert that the state should intervene and regulate labor conditions. Such intervention would always be just if it were done in the interest of the workers. In terms employed by later writers on the same subject, competition can work only where there is some equality of economic power; otherwise, special measures are required to establish that equality and make competition work. In a sense, all this can be subsumed under Smith's argument that there is an ever-present monopolistic tendency in business.

His suspicion of the motives and consequences of business finally found one more target in the joint stock companies—corporations, in the American terminology. He characterized them—correctly, but in an unfriendly manner—as doing business on 'other people's money' and suspected them of a propensity towards carelessness not to be found where people risk their own money. He therefore inferred that they would seldom be able to survive in competition with a really private business and that they would try to cover their inherent weakness by monopolistic practices and financial manipulations. Smith believed that only where mere routine suffices for successful management is there good reason for the corporate form of business organization. He knew of only four fields in which corporate organization is justified: banking—of the normal bill-discounting kind— insurance against fire and theft, the operation of canals, and the operation of waterworks, the last two representing what are called 'utilities' in modern terminology.

Smith's suspicions of the corporation and the dangers and inadequacies which he found in it constitute the substance of the objections currently raised by private business against public management. The bureaucrat, it is said, is careless because he has no personal interest in the outcome of his acts; he is capable of making only routine decisions and cannot safely be entrusted with important projects. What is overlooked in these objections —those of Smith as well as those of the modern critics of public management—is the stimulus which is provided by the interest in social standing, reputation, and influence and the financial interest in bonuses which are paid in proportion to the profits. Nevertheless, the dangers involved in the cumbersome nature of the big and necessarily bureaucratic organization do exist. The stimulus of working for oneself is found only in the Jeffersonian family farm and its urban equivalent, the small shop.

It must be said, however, that Smith's insight was limited by the historical circumstances of his age. He lived before the industrial revolution had reached its fulfilment. The psychological advantage of self-interest which the owner-manager had over the management of a large corporation was soon to be outweighed by the technological advantages which only a heavily capitalized enterprise can purchase. Only the rich firm can produce cheaply. This turn of events was unknown to Smith and was not anticipated by him. He was quite justified in attributing the existence of big business in his day to legal privilege and monopoly, and he expected that it would seldom survive in free competition with free men. Truly, to claim Smith as an advocate of 'free enterprise,' if this term is meant to include the monopoly corporation, is to betray an extraordinary measure either of ignorance or hypocrisy. In point of fact, Smith hoped that his liberalism, by making the individual's self-interest supreme, would lead not only to greater efficiency but also to a greater degree of economic equality.

The stern rule of free competition, on which Smith staked everything, found one of its most important applications in the field of international economic relations as the doctrine of free trade. Free trade leads to an international division of labor in which production always takes place only where conditions are most suitable for it. Each industry is concentrated in the country or countries offering the most favorable natural conditions for production; other countries, instead of producing the same product under less favorable conditions, i.e. at higher costs, can get the needed product more cheaply by importing it in exchange for domestic products which can be produced nowhere else under such favorable conditions. The result is that the needed products cost the country less capital and labor than if they were produced domestically, and more capital and labor is left for the production of other goods. Consequently, protection, by artificially raising prices and profits, diverts capital and labor from the most productive employment; the private profit of those who are protected does not then coincide with the public good, because foreign competition is excluded. Moreover, the fallacy of the mercantilist doctrine that one can gain only at the expense of someone else or of some other country is exposed by this theory.

But Smith was not blind, as later free-traders were, to the presuppositions and implications of laissez-faire. In his discussion of public finance (in the section on the financing of educational institutions) he deplored the crippling physical and intellectual effects of that same division of labor which he had praised so lavishly for its productivity. He demanded universal education to restore to the workers the fullness of understanding and development of which their specialized work deprived them. Moreover, he was aware that in the international division of labor, political disadvantages may be added to the human and social effects; a country may become economically dependent on its potential enemies and thereby weaken its strength for war. Smith was wise enough not to take the doctrine of free trade dogmatically. To be prepared for war, 'the noblest of all arts,' was in his eyes the principal duty of the state and one that would justify a certain measure of protection for the needed materials. The same sense for reality is exhibited in his recommendation that tariffs should be lowered gradually instead of being abolished at one stroke, in order to give the existing protected industries and their workers an opportunity to readjust themselves.

If, in the foregoing discussion, historical and sociological considerations have been introduced to qualify the results of pure economic reasoning, such considerations have an even more fundamental importance for economic theory in verifying its data, which reflect the conditions of the economic society in question. After all, supply and demand do not vary at random. The market process is determinate in time and as such is conditioned by historical and sociological factors. The supply of goods can vary only within the bounds of the supply of the factors of production. The latter, however, cannot simply be treated as a datum in the economic process; its size is determined largely by economic decisions, e.g. concerning how long the working day should be and how much is to be invested as capital. In other words, market and price fluctuate only within the bounds of a determinate structure, i.e. actual economic society.

The difficulty in appraising the work of Smith in this respect lies in the fact that his actual procedure was far different from and superior to his methodological program. His aim was to describe the natural circumstances in a natural society, freed from the arbitrary shackles of governmental and monopolistic power. What he actually described was not the natural society, which does not exist, but a historical society—that of his own day—imagined as freed of such 'unnatural shackles' and then interpreted as 'natural.' In his work we find a model of that integration of economic sociology and economic theory without which economic theory remains empty and formal. Because he believed that he was describing a natural society that had not yet been realized historically, Smith himself failed to see that the validity of his theory was limited to the historical conditions from which he had drawn its data.

The historical character of Smith's 'natural society' can best be seen in the type of man which he presupposed in all his reasoning, the 'economic man.' Smith's followers regarded the 'economic man' (as distinguished from the tradition-bound man) as 'natural' and even commonplace, while those who applied the historical-sociological yardstick to economic theory regarded him as a caricature of man, a type of human being that has never existed. That he is neither the one nor the other becomes obvious as soon as we try to define the term 'economic man.' The traditional definition is: the man who strives for maximum satisfaction with minimum sacrifice. But this definition is trivial and tautological; no other kind of man is thinkable. To the spendthrift an occasional debauch yields as much satisfaction as the miser derives from the sight of his unused money. As for the tradition-minded, they certainly derive satisfaction from the observation of customs and rites which give their lives color and significance. What is meant, then, by 'satisfaction' in the definition of 'economic man' is something narrower; not satisfaction as such, but a distinct kind of satisfaction: that which comes with the attainment of more goods rather than less. This restriction excludes the spendthrift as well as those who spurn the fruits of modern technology (e.g. Gandhi) and the Nazis, who eschew economic intercourse, however profitable, with people whom they deem unworthy. Wherever such 'extra-economic' types of behavior prevail, they prevent the adjustment of production to demand. In a free society the producer increases or decreases his output as the price of the product rises or falls in response to the fluctuations of demand. Thus, what is presupposed in such an economic system is a man motivated by the desire for a maximum quantitative return. This does not mean that the economic man must be an egoist, although he often is; the man who invests in his own business and the man in charge of a college or a hospital will both strive for a maximum quantitative return on the investment. What is important is that for the economic man quantitative considerations must prevail over traditional values or political passions. This is the kind of man presupposed in the economic order described by Smith as 'natural.'[10]

Given the economic man, the supply of goods will depend on the supply of the factors of production and the productivity of the methods of production. These are the data in the market process. In establishing a chain of causation between them, Smith was highly original, and particularly in taking as his starting point the growth of 'industrial arts' (technology) in the expanding market; for a larger market provides opportunity for a more intensive division of labor. A distinct series of effects follows: rising productivity, rising profit, rising savings and investments, rising wages, rising population, and rising productivity once again. This is the form of economic development in Smith's society of economic men.

Remarkable in this, from the point of view of method, is the extension of the validity of the law of price from the production of goods to the production of the factors themselves. It may be readily granted that the producer will be attracted towards those lines of production which offer the prospect of profit and deterred from those in which there is prospect of loss. But this does not imply, as Smith thought, that the supply of labor and capital too will vary with the rate of wages and of profits respectively. On the contrary, this chain of causation appears highly problematic, to judge from the history of economic doctrines and from economic history itself. In stating that the supply of the factors of production is determined by the same law of price which governs the supply of goods, Smith made the sociological data of the market process, including even the movement of population, dependent on price and income fluctuations. Thus, Smith's interpretation of historical change was strictly economic.

The two most problematic links in the chain of causation which Smith established are the determination of the capital supply and that of the labor supply. As to the former, Smith argued that a large demand for credits, for the expansion of profitable businesses, raises the interest rate. A rise in interest rates will, in turn, elicit from economic men the new savings needed for more loans. Hume had found that in a country of non-economic men, like Catholic Spain, the rate of interest was high because people who could afford to save preferred to spend their money for luxuries; in other words, they did not react in the proper way. Smith brushed this argument aside and introduced the theory, prevalent for at least a century, that the rate of savings depends on the rate of interest. This theory appears highly dubious today. The second, and even more serious, deficiency in Smith's theory is the assumed identity of saving and investment. That saved money should not seek and find investment but should merely be deposited in some private or institutional hoard appeared irrational and illegitimate in a society of economic men. Yet Smith's successor Malthus expressed dread of this very possibility, which was then forgotten for a hundred years.

The next step in Smith's chain of reasoning is even more illustrative of the kind of society in which and for which he wrote. To him increasing investment meant an increasing demand for labor. To Marx, on the other hand, increasing investment meant a decreasing demand for labor, because of the spread of labor-saving devices. However crude may be the generalization in either case, it is obvious that the two men had different types of technology in mind. Labor-saving devices were practically unknown to Smith. Handicraft supported by technical devices—this is the pre-industrial technique presupposed in his book.

The last step in the chain of causation, according to the reasoning of Smith, is that the rising demand for labor, expressed in a rising rate of wages, increases the exertions of the workers in the short run and the numbers of the laboring population in the long run. The short-run argument flatly contradicted the then traditional opinion, so convenient to exploiters, that the workers react to rising wage rates by proportionately diminishing the quantity or intensity of their work, as non-economic men, so as to limit their wage income to the strictly necessary and to take their share in rising productivity in the form of more leisure. Whether or not this was true at the beginning of capitalism, Smith now assumed that the workers also share the psychology natural to economic men, i.e. that the 'profit motive,' to use a later terminology, dominates all strata of society. In reality, a rising standard of living, combined with a shorter workday, has been labor's program ever since, while the productivity per worker has fluctuated, in contradiction to price theory, rising in the depression under the menace of unemployment and falling in the boom when jobs were plentiful.

The long-range aspect of Smith's argument concerning wages and labor brings us to his theory of population. Smith explicitly couched his argument in terms of price theory: rising demand—rising price—rising supply. This way of putting the matter has aroused much indignation on the part of those who protest that man is not a commodity produced under economic law to meet the rising demand for labor. Yet Smith's theory appears to be confirmed by the correlation between marriage and birth rates on the one hand and economic fluctuations on the other. What distinguishes Smith from his successors Malthus and Ricardo is that he saw no difficulty in the growth of population; he relied on the ensuing division of labor and the greater productivity to which it would give rise.

In this manner the circle of forces making for economic progress is closed and further progress assured. The philosophy of harmonious natural law substitutes the idea of strictly determined and balanced progress for the social transformation which we call 'history.' Apart from the special doubts already raised in the foregoing discussion of the adequacy of Smith's theory, one general observation on this point may be made. The state of industrial arts, according to Smith, develops exclusively under the influence of a growing market, which includes a growing population. Indeed, that technology does not develop independently is shown by the absence of labor-saving devices from his picture of economic society, although they did in fact exist. Thus, the state of technological development in any economic society is neatly geared to the available factors of production: the industrial arts are developed up to the point at which they fully absorb the supply of these factors. The full utilization of all the factors of production is secured through the free play of prices; a low wage, for example, makes the employment of labor more attractive as long as the supply of labor has not been fully absorbed. Accordingly, we may say that what Smith described, on the basis of his philosophy, is progress induced by the fluctuations in the prices of the factors of production; what he did not know is spontaneous progress, which may sweep the economic system and occasionally, as in times of crisis, destroy its balance.

4. Circular-Flow Theory vs. Price Theory

It is hazardous to characterize as mechanical the line of thought inaugurated by Smith and to oppose to it the biological type of thinking of Quesnay and his school, as we have done in the introductory section of this chapter. As a matter of fact, Smith himself seems quite explicitly to have ruled out such an interpretation and even to have suggested the contrary. For he not only criticized his French rivals for the rigidity as well as the narrowness of their doctrine but opposed to it his own belief in the self-healing tendencies both in man and society. Thus he claimed for himself precisely that approach by which we have characterized his rivals.

The essential difference between the history of thinkers and the history of thought is well illustrated in this case. It is not always true that what a thinker does coincides with what he thinks he does. At any rate, what he does cannot simply be ascertained from his own presentation of his view; these must be examined in the light of their consequences in the history of thought. Once a thought has been released by its author, it embarks upon a career of its own. Sometimes it becomes anonymous, and the seeds implanted in it germinate in history. It may even be abused and corrupted by those who later make use of it. But an effect different from what the author intended is not always traceable to the corruption of his thought; history may understand the logical implications of a thought better than its author. In 1803 Say translated Smith's system from the biological language which its author had used into the stricter form reminiscent of the laws of physics.[11] The question then is: did he thereby change the original meaning of Smith's doctrine? We do not think so.

In his criticism of Quesnay, Smith betrayed an overconfidence in the self-healing, self-regulating faculty of the economic process. Not once in his voluminous work is there any mention of internal disturbances that may arise in the working of the natural economic system. The price mechanism was described by Smith, and more succinctly by Say, as an infallible panacea. Suppose there is unemployment of labor and money capital; then, according to Smith's theory, the desperate competition of workers and capitalists to employ their resources productively will so lower wage and interest rates that the hiring of workers and the borrowing of money will again become attractive to producers. In other words, an economic depression arises only when wage and interest rates are too high; the price mechanism then reduces them to normalcy. It is true that Smith qualified his theory of wages, but only by introducing sociological, not economic, considerations. Thus he conceded that the free operation of the price mechanism does not always produce socially desirable results and recommended governmental intervention in the market on behalf of the workers. But what did not occur to him was that the technical regulation of the system by the price mechanism could ever fail to work.

However, no biological or physiological analogy can be found to illustrate such unfailing regularity. There is no state of health that is immune to infirmity, nor is there any panacea for failing health. Quesnay's presentation of the circular flow of goods, on the other hand, suggested that the self-regulation of economic society is liable to major and minor disturbances and needs the protection and encouragement of the doctor who watches it. His point was that health does not restore or perpetuate itself automatically. Only the laws of physics are unfailing.

In other words, Quesnay was concerned with the *how* and Smith with the *why* of the circular flow of goods. Quesnay described the automatism; Smith explained it. Description as such implies no claim that the functioning of the mechanism described is flawless; if anything, the contrary is implied. Yet it is doubtful whether science can ever do more than describe; explanation is simply description carried one step further back in the chain of causation. Of course, the ambition which inspires the attempt at explanation is different, and the explanation of the circular flow of goods by reference to the price mechanism was so logically convincing to Smith that he never cared to describe the total process regulated by so faultless a device. Quesnay, however, was not so sure; he tried to describe health instead of demonstrating why it cannot fail.

This point requires brief illustration. Not only did Quesnay, like Smith, warn against the oppression of the lower classes on the ground that this would harm the productivity of labor; he also argued, from the point of view of the circular flow of goods, that 'if those classes cannot consume enough, this would diminish the reproduction of goods and the income of the nation.' He likewise warned against the accumulation of money fortunes, or at least advocated that there should be equality of accumulation and recommended the liquidation of large fortunes, since otherwise 'the distribution of income would stop.' For the same reason he also recommended that the export of capital be prohibited, as the money is needed for a smooth circulation. And this idea was given a strikingly modern turn in his warning against 'sterile savings . . . which are withdrawn from circulation and distribution.'

Turgot too spoke of 'some disorder in the sequence of expenditures of the various classes of society.' Finally, when Quesnay's friend, the older Mirabeau, published the *Tableau* in 1760 in the appendix volume of his *Ami des Hommes*, he gave graphic illustrations not only of the normal circulation, but also of the results that would be produced by all sorts of disturbing influences. Health is the law of normality, but it is not inevitable. What the physiocrats discovered was the distinction between the normal and the disturbed flow of goods. This discovery makes them the path-breakers for the theory of the business cycle, although for a century and a half they found only occasional followers and were excluded from official economics.

IV. The Classical School: Rational Adaptation to Nature

THE Classical School of English economists,[1] represented on the continent by the Frenchman Say as the most influential of all its spokesmen, and comprising, in a sense, even Karl Marx, is characterized by the fact that all its members made use of the tools of analysis forged by Adam Smith. To be sure, there is not one among these economists who did not at some point in his reasoning come dangerously close to where Smith's system, instead of being enlarged, developed, and refined, has to be given up entirely; indeed, the German economist Thuenen went so far afield that one may doubt whether this highly original thinker can properly be classified in Smith's school at all. And even among its members considerable criticism of Smith and wide differences of opinion can be found. But what they have in common is the preservation of his methodological tools and presuppositions, however much these may have been modified and reinterpreted. In fact, it is primarily this continuity and reinterpretation of the tools of analysis that constitutes the history of the Classical School.

Part of this reinterpretation—though not all—was prompted by dismal experience. What chiefly distinguishes the members of the school from its founder is the change in general outlook and tone, from Smith's shining optimism and faith to the gloom of a 'dismal science,' as Thomas Carlyle called it. And there were good reasons for such gloom. It is true that progress had been made in all respects and with undreamt-of success. But it was not progress towards greater harmony. As the industrial revolution reached its full stride, beginning with the last quarter of the eighteenth century, it paved the way towards a solution of the problem of production only to raise a serious social problem. Self-interest and individual initiative took full advantage of the vast new technical possibilities but at the same time brought the full weight of concentrated economic power to bear upon competitors and employees. The abolition of regulation gave free rein to economic power. The result was the social crisis which ever since has been an integral part of the history of capitalism.

That economic power should assert itself in competition is far from being as natural as later generations, taught by past experience, have been inclined to believe. In fact, it is doubtful whether a social crisis would have arisen at all if it had not been for the intervention of the industrial revolution. For the small plant did enjoy an advantage in competition by virtue of the fact that all who worked there had a personal interest in its success. The actual competitive superiority of the large plant is due solely to its technological advantage, which only the command over large amounts of capital can secure. It is even true that size alone does not confer technological superiority in all fields; farming, for example, is an exception. Whether or not technological improvements give a competitive advantage to the large plant depends on the chance development of inventions in the various branches of production. Historically, however, the trend in industry proper did point towards larger plants, for technological reasons. The consequence was an accentuation of class divisions instead of the gradual leveling down which had been anticipated by Smith.

The social crisis was soon accompanied by the economic crisis, which, from 1817 on, became a periodically recurrent feature of capitalism. It is true that the crisis has only lately developed such towering proportions that it has become the dominant problem of present-day economic theory and policy. For a hundred years the crises were grave enough to harrow the minds of economists but not grave enough to disrupt generally the upward trend of production and living standards; otherwise we should not have had either a classical or a neo-classical school of economics. The early crises were limited in extent, and economists tried to deal with them casually, without giving up the fundamental propositions of their system; the problem of explaining the really abnormal character of the crises was left to outsiders and specialists. However, that this indifference was not characteristic of the entire classical school can be seen in the growing concern with which Malthus and Ricardo, its two leading members, studied the problem of the economic crisis.

The rise of social and economic crises could not, after all, be ignored by those who professed a doctrine founded on the optimistic belief in natural harmony. The members of Smith's school still continued to use his words, but with gradually changing meaning. Society was still presented as part of nature, but its promised harmony now appeared as less glorious, and man's reason had to come to the aid of nature before even this limited harmony could be realized. If human reason did not intervene, then one could not justly complain of the results.

This view implies a changed conception of nature itself. The immense difference between the eighteenth- and the nineteenth-century conceptions of nature is well known: for the 'Enlightenment' nature had been the rational subject of natural science; for Romanticism it was irrational, a subject for poetry and sentiment. The transformation of the conception of nature within the classical school of economics went only half as far. The world in which an invisible hand leads us to effect the good which was no part of our intention gradually became 'the best of all possible worlds,' which proved to be not a very good one. From Malthus's conception of the hostile forces of nature which frustrate man's efforts, Charles Darwin derived the idea of the struggle for survival, in which no trace of harmony remains. From the harmonious nature conceived by Smith we pass to the niggardly nature of Malthus's conception and on to the blind, indifferent, and in this sense irrational nature depicted by Ricardo. What unites these various conceptions is the belief in natural science; nature, whether good or bad, is sovereign, and man is subject to its iron law and has to adapt himself accordingly. The natural law of economic society, reinterpreted in this sense, remained the subject of economics.

A changed conception of reason is also implied in this reinterpretation of Smith's doctrine. Nature and reason coincided in his system; man, following the impulses of his own nature, could not fail to do what was beneficial to all. According to Malthus, on the other hand, man must curb his natural appetites and use reason and prudence to make the best possible arrangement for himself within the narrow limits set by a niggardly nature. The same motive, although less conspicuous, is found in Ricardo. In the doctrines of both, some modest hope is held out for man, but only if he makes good use of his reason to avoid the wrath of nature.

1. MALTHUS—REINTERPRETATION OF NATURE AND REASON

Two contributions make Thomas Robert Malthus[2] a great economist—one is to the theory of population and the other to the theory of the economic crisis. But for more than a century his name was associated almost exclusively with the theory of population, and, moreover, in a manner that was thought to be discreditable to him. The reason was partly the fury which the announcer of unpleasant facts, especially in the midst of exuberant hopes, invariably incurs, and partly the harsh form in which the young Malthus first introduced his objections. He himself admitted twenty years later that a sense of opposition had led him to overstress his point. At any rate, he continually qualified his position and made it more acceptable in each of the six editions of his work which were published in his lifetime.

Malthus was not the first to concern himself with the question of population; it had been a favorite topic in political and economic discussions for several centuries.[3] The absolute state, in its drive for power, needed men for the production of wealth and consequently engaged in a very active population policy.

Mercantilist writings on this subject are numerous. But dissenters had not been wholly absent, particularly in Italy. The earliest and one of the most impressive of these was Giovanni Botero,[4] who, more than two centuries before Malthus, opposed the limited nourishing power of the earth to the unlimited generative power of man. This is precisely the thesis of Malthus, although Botero, like other dissenters before Malthus, seems to have conceived the nourishing power of the earth as a fixed quantity. Antonio Genovesi[5] had criticized the ambitious population schemes of the statesmen of his day in the light of his observation that in every territory there must be an optimum population, depending on the fertility and natural endowment of that territory; on either side of this optimum people would live less well than they could. This is the most modern, and indeed the most scholarly, approach to the problem. Unfortunately, Genovesi did not elaborate his thesis, and Malthus's own discussion, owing to his polemical purpose, fell far short of it. Giammaria Ortes[6] had directly anticipated Malthus in asserting that the increase of the population tends to proceed in geometrical progression, at a constant rate of growth, so as to exceed the available food supply, and makes it necessary to resort to celibacy in order to avoid extreme misery and vice.

Without being so specific, the great Quesnay,[7] in a little known article, had written what could have been penned by Malthus: 'Population is always in excess of wealth, under good and bad governments alike, because propagation has no limits but those of subsistence and tends to pass beyond them.' His conclusion, however, was different from that of Malthus, and not in accordance with Quesnay's laissez-faire program, for he appealed to the state to 'regulate' population. In the English-speaking world the keen mind of Benjamin Franklin[8] had also grasped the fact that the increase of the population depends on the available means of subsistence, but Franklin had made this observation more concrete by opposing the more favorable conditions of the countryside to the less favorable conditions of the city, and the more favorable conditions of virgin America to the less favorable conditions of crowded Europe.

Quesnay's reservation regarding population tendencies gave way to the optimism that accompanied the growing belief in progress under the benevolent guidance of Providence. This belief is characteristically expressed in Smith's confidence that the growth of the population would be induced by the growth in productivity, which in turn would be facilitated by the growing numbers of people engaged in a more intensive division of labor. Yet such optimism must be regarded as conservative when compared with the exuberant hopes expressed in the writings of the British anarchist William Godwin[9] under the inspiration of the French philosopher Condorcet,[10] himself one of the most fervent apostles, and finally a victim, of the great revolution. These two revived the earlier revolutionary version of liberalism, which finds in faulty human institutions the obstacle to the harmonious working of nature and reason. They predicted that in an equalitarian society guided by scientific reason all men could be well-to-do even though they enormously multiplied their numbers. It is interesting that both suggested the theory of Malthus, that an increase in the population could not continue indefinitely because the production of food could not be indefinitely expanded; but they regarded the necessity for imposing some limit on the growth of population as far more remote than he did. They were confident that reason would have such complete sway over man that he would then cease propagating beyond the limits set by nature; and Malthus too recommended the exercise of prudence in this regard. The utopian dreams of Godwin and Condorcet culminated in the prediction that science would almost do away with death, so that generation would have to stop too. Malthus's sober realism revolted against such extravagances.

Malthus was daring indeed when he wrote—in a passage eliminated already in the second edition: 'A man who is born into a world already possessed, if he cannot get subsistence from his parents on whom he has a just demand, and if the society does not want his labor, has no claim of right to the smallest portion of food, and, in fact, has no business to be where he is. At Nature's mighty feast there is no vacant cover for him. She tells him to be gone.' And he drew the explicit conclusion—in all editions—that 'the poor are themselves the cause of their own poverty.' Though this doubtless was intended to exonerate capitalism from the charge that it was responsible for the condition of the poor, Malthus also wished to appeal to them to improve their lot by their own efforts.

In support of that provocative proposition Malthus argued: 'Through the animal and vegetable kingdoms Nature has scattered the seeds of life abroad with the most profuse and liberal hand; but has been comparatively sparing in the room and the nourishment necessary to rear them. The race of plants and the race of animals shrink under this great restrictive law, and the race of man cannot by any efforts of reason escape from it.' The generative power of human nature if unchecked is such, according to Malthus, as to double the number of the race every twenty-five years. This was the figure suggested by his study of population growth in the United States. The absolute figure is not important; what matters is the steady rate of growth. While his predecessors had contrasted man's unlimited generative power with the limited room and resources available to support him, none of them was specific about the latter; they all seem to have been under the impression that the land has a fixed capacity. Malthus, however, recognized that the capacity of land to support men can be augmented, but he contended that the rate of population growth outstrips the rate of growth in the productivity of land. He opposed to the geometrical progression in the increase of the population the arithmetical progression of 'production on land.' The latter, he said, can be increased only by the same absolute quantity during any given period, that is, at a relatively decreasing rate of growth, with a relatively declining fertility as production becomes more intensive. This is the so-called law of diminishing returns, more properly, of diminishing increments on the returns, which had already been widely discussed. The fact that Malthus adopted it as the basis of all economic reasoning indicates clearly how far the era of optimism had been superseded by one of pessimism. By way of illustrations, Malthus opposed to the geometrical series 1, 2, 4, 8, 16, etc., which he considered to represent the tendency of the population to increase, the arithmetical series 1, 2, 3, 4, 5, etc., which he took to represent the tendency of the crops to increase, as the land was more intensively cultivated by those growing numbers of people.[11]

In this conflict between the generative powers of man and the narrowness of the room assigned to him, disease, famine, war, and 'vice' are the 'positive checks' which, according to Malthus, keep the population within bounds. If a man wishes to avoid these evils, he must anticipate their work. The 'preventive check' is 'moral restraint,' i.e. the postponement of marriage. The later so-called neo-Malthusian practice of birth control Malthus classified as 'vice,' and he has been bitterly assailed for doing so. However, what matters for the economist is the fact that Malthus recommended that the poor restrict their numbers 'by restraining their passions within the bounds of reason' as the only way out of their misery.

He did not need to make this recommendation to the rich. Whether for biological or cultural reasons, those who could afford to have many children no longer did. Adam Smith had been one of the first to draw attention to this fact. On the other hand, Malthus did not believe in dividing the wealth of the rich among the poor because the margin of comfort thus created would immediately be filled by a further growth of population. However, from edition to edition he became more and more convinced that the preventive check did have some effect, as could be seen from a comparison of British birth rates and standards of living with those of primitive societies, of which Malthus was one of the first students. In his chief work, *Prin-*

ciples of Political Economy, published twenty-two years after
the first edition of his *Essay on Population*, he described how the
preventive check worked. What restrained men was their standard of living, i.e. 'their habits, or the amount of necessaries and
conveniences without which they would not consent to keep up
their numbers.' A man 'will acquire a taste for these conveniences, and his habits will be formed accordingly.' Cantillon,
with his usual perspicacity, had already thought along these
lines. He had given what amounts to a fairly optimistic picture
of the way in which the increase in population is regulated: the
marrying habits of the different classes are in conformity with
their living standards and designed to preserve them. In other
words, Cantillon understood that the rate of propagation is a
matter of deliberate decision. Malthus too arrived at this conclusion. Ricardo also, who had meanwhile incorporated Malthus's
population theory in his own wage theory, had preceded Malthus
in the recognition that living standards determine the rate of
propagation. Thus the increase of population does not tie the
wage to the level of physical subsistence; a higher wage, if the
standard of living it makes possible has become habitual through
the operation of the preventive check, determines a new psychological minimum of subsistence, 'without which they would not
consent to keep up their numbers.'

It is true that Malthus, by blaming the existing misery on the
unreasonable habits of the poor, wished to exculpate capitalism.
But it is no less true that he wished to point to the only way that
was immediately practicable for the poor to improve their condition, since he was convinced that the existing poor-relief measures could only aggravate the evil by relieving the poor of their
responsibility for their progeny and thus stimulating an even
more rapid increase in the population. It is significant that the
labor movements of all countries have made birth control a fixed
dogma of their program. Indeed, they have succeeded so well
in keeping down the population that they have raised the spectre
of race suicide, against which Malthus explicitly warned, remote

as such a possibility was in his day. Moreover, the supporters of
birth control use arguments they have learned from Malthus,
thus testifying to the formidable nature of the weapon that he
gave them. (It would be folly, of course, to attribute the rise of
living standards solely to the control of population.) It would
seem, then, that the real meaning of the Malthus-Ricardo doctrine is the advice to labor to raise wages by limiting the supply
of labor in the free market. This argument clearly goes beyond
mere special pleading for the class interests of the bourgeoisie.

In opposing his sober realism to the doctrinaire optimism of
his school, Malthus also became a heretic in his view on the
business depression following the Napoleonic wars. In his *Principles*, as well as in a series of letters to his friends and opponents,
Ricardo and Say, he reiterated with clarity, patience, and
tenacity, though with no favorable response from them, his conviction that 'the principles of saving, pushed to excess, would
destroy the motive to production. If every person were satisfied with the simplest food, the poorest clothing, and the meanest
houses, it is certain that no other sort of food, clothing, and
housing would be in existence . . . The two extremes [of too
little and too much saving] are obvious, and it follows that there
must be some intermediate point.' He vainly tried to convince
Ricardo of the fallacy of believing 'that every part of the income, whether entirely consumed or invested, will always produce an equal demand for goods, although not the same kind of
goods.' In modern terminology, Malthus denied that the saving
of money, which appears so profitable and virtuous to businessmen, would automatically find an outlet in investment, since the
very act of saving diminishes the demand for the goods to be
produced by investment.

And he drew practical conclusions from these considerations.
Though he found it highly desirable that workers should have
good wages, he said that he did not regard a rise in wages as the
way out, because this would raise the wage bill and the cost of
production and would thereby impair sales, exports, and employ-

ment. Some demand must be found that is outside the precarious market balance of cost and price. Malthus found two types of such demand, the unproductive demand of wealthy people, and public works. On the one hand, what is needed is a social class of people who are in the habit of spending their money for goods rather than of accumulating it like businessmen. Landowners are of this type, and Malthus regarded their presence in capitalist society as a godsend which saved the system from shipwreck. To denounce Malthus on this ground as a class advocate of the landed interests is to overlook the logic of his argument in order to make a trivial point. Its sociological implications are irrelevant. What Malthus was looking for was some form of income which was sure not to be saved, as profits would be, and on the other hand, would not enter into the cost of production, as wages do. Instead of private luxury, public luxury, had it been reputable in his eyes, would have served the same end. Public works, indeed, such as road building, are outside the market nexus, according to Malthus. He clearly saw that their effect upon the market is to strengthen the demand for goods without adding to their cost, thereby redressing the balance when demand slackens. For the producers of roads receive an income, while their own products are not for sale. This reasoning, of course, is much employed today.

The remedies suggested by Malthus were in themselves nothing new in the history of economics. One and two centuries before him mercantilist writers, among them Petty and Mandeville, had praised luxury as a stimulus to production, in opposition to Puritan parsimony. And many, even most, mercantilists had advocated public works to counteract the unemployment which might result from the introduction of labor-saving machines. But a whole world separates Malthus's systematic analysis from such partial and superficial speculations. The earlier writers were content to thrust on the omnipotent and paternal state the burden of anything otherwise intolerable.

The full meaning of Malthus's achievement, both intellectually and morally, can be appreciated only when it is realized that he had to break away from the established school of thought, of which he was an honored head, in order to do full justice to his problem. In the face of the objections constantly raised to his reasoning by his friends, who insisted that what he dreaded could not happen because of the operation of the interest and wage mechanism, he stood firm; that is, he saw that the price theory, on which his school had staked the existence of economics, was inadequate, and he turned to a type of reasoning which observed the aggregate economic magnitudes in their migration through the economic body, i.e. the theory of the circular flow of goods. What he discovered was, in Turgot's language, 'a disorder in distribution and expenditure,' something meaningless in his own school. He himself does not seem to have been aware of the connection between his own approach and that of the circular-flow theory, whose potentialities he made actual. He is, in fact, the first theorist of the economic crisis.

2. Ricardo—The System of Labor Value

Malthus's younger friend, David Ricardo,[12] eclipsed him for a hundred years. Indeed, as late as the twenties of the present century, Ricardo appeared to many as the greatest of all economists, and a number of essays were devoted to the study of his work. Such an impression could be justified on the ground that economics has no stronger—and more candid—thinker, no greater master in the art of reasoning from given assumptions. But we have since come to recognize that good judgment may be more important than logical acumen.

As Ricardo was the systematizer of his school, his work must be understood in the strict logic of its structure. Its center is occupied by value theory. Indeed, in Ricardo's system, value theory occupies an even more important position than it did in the system of Adam Smith, who, though engaging in a somewhat inconsistent discussion of value, was chiefly interested in the operation of the price mechanism. Ricardo took over Smith's price theory, based on the distinction between competition and monopoly, but refined the value theory. It was, in fact, greatly in need of refinement, because Smith's reduction of value to the cost of production was logically inconsistent. Costs are naturally heterogeneous and incommensurable. No sum total of the cost factors (land, capital, and the various kinds of labor) can be arrived at unless they are reduced to a common denominator. Money is not such a common denominator; to attempt to express the cost factors in terms of money is, in effect, only to face the value problem in another form. For in order to know how the factors of production can sell for money, we must first know what makes them and money commensurable. The commensurability of the factors which Smith naively wanted to add up is Ricardo's value problem.

Two logically possible solutions present themselves. The first is the reduction of the three kinds of cost factors to a fourth element underlying them all, utility, which is common to all cost factors and goods. This, the main road of later analysis, was, however, blocked for the time being by Smith's economic paradox, i.e. the apparent inverse proportion between value (price) and utility. The other solution is the reduction of two of the three factors to the third. This more elementary factor, from which the other two appear to be derived, is labor, and Ricardo's system is the labor-value theory, that is, the explanation of how labor value underlies the other factors of production and all economic relationships as their organizing principle.

The difficulties with which the labor value theory has had to struggle throughout its history are the following. In the first place, monopoly price is, by definition, different from labor-value price. The latter is cost price and prevails only under conditions of competition, while monopoly maintains price above the cost of production by keeping the supply limited. Hence Ricardo, like all the classical writers, placed monopoly price outside value theory in a category of its own. He claimed that such examples of monopoly price as those of old wines and paintings are too insignificant in economic life to impair materially the unity and strictness of the system. In other words, the problem of monopoly was removed rather than solved.

The second problem is that of rent, and it is with the solution of this problem that Ricardo's fame is connected. His solution rests on the law of diminishing returns to land, which, in a crude form, we have found already underlying Malthus's population law. The observation of the law of diminishing returns had, of course, been made even earlier. Immediately before Ricardo, Sir Edward West[13] had pointed to the chief application of this law in the field of agriculture: as the land is more intensively cultivated, the yield increases less in proportion to the cost, or each unit of the crop becomes dearer. Much earlier James Anderson[14] had made the same observation with regard to lands of different fertility: as cultivation spreads from the best to the less fertile lands with the growth of population, the cost of production rises. This application of the law of diminishing returns implicitly presupposes the former; it is only because more intensive cultivation of the best lands yields diminishing returns that less fertile lands must be employed. Malthus,[15] in his pamphlet on rent written in the same year as West's treatise, had come to a similar conclusion. However, none of these writers or their successors for more than two generations had provided so clear an account of the law of diminishing returns as Turgot[16] had done as early as 1768. He argued that the application of increasing amounts of labor to a given land, beginning with a low degree of intensity, would first bring increasing returns, then reach an optimum ratio of yield to labor, and beyond this produce smaller crops in proportion to the intensity of cultivation. Thus the curve described by the total schedule of production is a parabola. The reason for this is that with too little labor, the potential forces of natural growth are not fully employed, while at the optimum ratio land

and labor utilize each other fully; beyond this point there is a shortage of the forces of natural growth relatively to the input of labor. Ricardo added a third difference in cost, not in the production, but in the transportation of foodstuffs from the farm to the market. The cost of transportation depends upon the distance of the producing land from the market place. Here again cultivation spreads from the nearer to the more distant lands as the demand increases, and the increased costs of transportation raise the price of food at the place of consumption. In actual economic society the three practices that tend to increase the cost of production—the intensive cultivation of land and the use of less fertile land and land more remote from the market—may be found in all kinds of combinations.

The following is a much simplified version of a table given by Ricardo. I, II, and III are different pieces of land in the order of their diminishing fertility or increasing remoteness from the market.

The......unit of the crop costs	on I	on II	on III
first	5	6	7
second	6	7	8
third	7	8	9
fourth	8	etc.	etc.

On the (unrealistic) assumption that cultivation expands with perfect continuity from more to less favorable lands, all other things remaining equal, the following expansions or intensifications of production will be resorted to simultaneously on all three lands to meet an increasing demand: at the price 6, two units on land I, and one unit on II; at the price 7, three units on I, two units on II, and one unit on III; at the price 8, four units on I, etc. These price rises are prerequisite to the expansion or intensification, since they alone make it possible to cover the rising cost of production. However, at these rising prices, those units which are produced at a lower cost yield a net gain:

At the price	I	II	III
8	3 + 2 + 1	2 + 1	1
7	2 + 1	1	—
6	1	—	—

This gain is the differential rent, the word 'rent' denoting a surplus over cost, i.e. a revenue that is not required to make production possible.

It is clear from the last table that at the price 7, land III does not yield any rent; the cost of production is equal to the price of the product. Thus, 'rent does not enter into price.' On the other lands there is a residue: 3 on I and 1 on II. These produce some units of the crop at less than the price received; 'rent follows from price.' This is the proof of the labor-value theory in regard to land rent. It should be noted that the validity of Ricardo's theory of rent is not affected by the fact that a further growth of demand will cause land III to yield rent if there is no free land beyond land III. For if at the price 8 cultivation cannot be extended to less fertile or more remote lands, it can always be intensified. Accordingly, once all lands are cultivated, it is still true that no rent is yielded at the margin; not the marginal land, but the marginal units of the crop of each land, i.e. the fourth unit on I, the third on II, and the second on III are free of rent. It is not true, then, that the existence of rent on all lands disproves Ricardo's thesis.

But the thesis must be correctly understood, and Ricardo himself is to blame for its misinterpretation. In a strange relapse into physiocratic prejudices, he called the rent the payment for 'the original and indestructible forces of the earth.' However, if this were correct, we should not have a differential rent, but an absolute scarcity rent, i.e. a rent from every unit of production included in the price as a surplus over the highest cost. This is indeed the case of those particularly fertile lands which produce a distinguished wine that is sold at a price exceeding its (marginal) cost. Smith, who was still strongly under the influence of physiocratic prejudices, continually wavered between the thesis that rent does enter into price and the thesis that rent follows from price. Malthus too was uncertain on this point. A differential rent becomes scarcity rent only if a further intensification of production would not increase the crop at all, for in that case a rise in demand must be cut off by a rise in price. However, as long as this critical point has not yet been reached and production can still be increased—although only at an increasing cost—to meet a growing demand, the law of competitive price fixes the price at the cost of production. Under such circumstances, the only thing that has to be economized is labor. Thus, differential rent must be defined in terms of labor rather than of land; it is the payment for the saving of labor effected under favorable conditions of production.

If the same product is produced at different costs at different places, e.g. at rival factories, and is sold at the same price, a differential rent accrues wherever the cost of production is lower. When this advantage is due to special organizational or technological arrangements, price competition is bound to remove it. Land rent, however, is relatively fixed and attached to the particular land as long as the conditions of production do not change; hence, it counts as a return on the land, that is, as revenue to the landowner. Where the land is rented to capitalist farmers, as in Ricardo's England, the surplus over the profit included in cost attracts a multitude of bidders for so favorable an opportunity of investment and enables the owner to secure the payment of the rent from the tenants, leaving them only the profit which they could have had in other investments too. Ricardo reasoned that the existence of rent is not disproved by the fact that it may not be paid to the owner; in that case, the unpaid rent would only 'enable the tenants to live like lords.'

But it is only in a relative sense that the rent on a given piece of land can be said to be fixed. Conditions are naturally less variable in agriculture than in industry, but they vary nonetheless, notably in regard to the cost of transportation as an element of the price of foodstuffs—in other words, the rent of location. This is, of course, affected by improvements in methods of transportation. And even fertility is not something fixed and forever unchangeable; it varies historically with the technical improvement of methods of cultivation. This is why Ricardo hoped that improvements in agriculture would 'suspend' the strain of rising food prices and land rents on a rising population. But his main remedy was free trade, for this has the effect of inserting, as it were, intramarginal lands in the area under cultivation and thus of lowering prices and rents. Like Malthus, Ricardo underrated the progress of which both agriculture and transportation are capable; he placed too much emphasis on the law of diminishing returns. Still, it is true that we do resort to unfertile and distant lands instead of concentrating production of all foodstuffs on the most fertile lands or on those nearest the market. This proves that the law of diminishing returns raises the cost of larger crops on the more favored lands and enables the less favored lands to compete.

The third problem of the labor-value theory is capital profit. To all the classical economists this is identical with interest, because no interest can be regularly paid except out of profit; interest is profit passed on to the creditor, whose loan has made production possible. Ricardo did not inquire into the nature of capital and profit; he took them for granted and conceived of them in a manner later elaborated by Senior. He did, however, inquire into the compatibility of the theory of labor value with the existence of profit. His answer to this question is distinguished by candor rather than by success. Profit, said Ricardo, is, under certain qualifying conditions, an addition to labor value and rises and falls proportionately with it. Hence, price is not simply labor value but is proportional to it. But this reasoning is valid only if profit is calculated exclusively on working capital, i.e. that part of the total capital which is primarily represented by the wage fund. Thus, with a wage of 1000 and a profit rate of 10 per cent, the price would be 1100; with a wage of 2000 and with the same profit rate, the price would be 2200, etc. Where there is fixed capital invested in machines, buildings, etc., however, the situation is different. Suppose that the workers receive 1000 during the year that it takes them to build a certain machine. At a profit rate of 10 per cent their annual product sells for 1100. But if, in the second year, they tend this machine, the product of their two years of work sells for 2310, being composed of 1100 for fixed capital, 1000 for wages, and 10 per cent profit. (This price, it should be remembered, represents more than twice the quantity of goods produced in the first year, since the machine is more productive than the unaided workers.) Only at this price does the investment in the machine pay if capital elsewhere earns a profit of 10 per cent; at less than this price the competitive mechanism would restrict production and raise prices and profits. The result is that the presence of fixed capital prevents prices from being proportional to labor value. Ricardo's theory is less elaborate than, but essentially identical with, that of Karl Marx.

Ricardo extricated himself from the difficulty by asserting that the various branches of industrial production use fixed capital in approximately equal proportion to their working capital, so that the deflection of the price would be approximately the same everywhere, and one would still be able to say that prices corre spond to labor values. But such an explanation was bound to become increasingly inadequate as technical progress enlarged the capital equipment of some industries and left others lagging behind in equipment and efficiency. The progress of technology was, after all, unequal in the different branches of production. And in fact, in letters to his friends, Ricardo himself candidly and sadly confessed that he had failed in his labor-value theory because there are two factors that determine price, labor and the length of the period of investment, since interest on capital is paid in proportion to time.

Ricardo's power as a theorist is further demonstrated by his work in monetary theory. He continued the development of monetary theory from about the point at which Smith's predecessors had left it, without, however, going into the dynamic aspects of money suggested by Cantillon and Hume. He followed Cantillon in reconciling the cost-of-production theory of money, which Petty had suggested, with the traditional quantity theory: the value of money is determined by the cost of production of the money metal; equal quantities of labor incorporated in gold and in goods exchange for each other. This is brought about by the competition among owners of private capital for the most advantageous investments, that is, by the fluctuations in the quantities of goods and of money in opposite directions. Thus the quantity theory of money appears as the special application to money of the law of market price: the values of money, the reciprocal of price, varies inversely with the quantity, and it is through changes in gold production that the labor value of money is established or re-established.

On this basis the doctrine of economic liberalism could now be completed. The provision of the economic system with metal money could be left to private business operated under the profit motive. In this way the proportion of goods and money would be secured, and stable prices would be determined by labor value. However, Ricardo's practical sense rejected this conclusion. It was his experience as a banker that had first led him to economic studies, and it is in this field that his work yielded the most far-reaching practical results. England during the Napoleonic wars did not have gold coins in circulation; it did have an increasing number of notes circulating only at a discount from their nominal gold value after their conversion into gold had been suspended. Ricardo entered the public discussion of monetary policy with the emphatic declaration, suggested by the quantity theory of money, that the quantity of notes issued was responsible for their depreciation, since the legal right to convert them into gold had been suspended so that they were not reduced in quantity and did not circulate at their gold parity. In fact, the monetary situation in England at the time was that typical of almost all major wars. Ricardo, however, while deploring the instability of the new paper money, did not draw the facile conclusion that the thing to do was to abolish it and revert to a purely gold circulation. He had been impressed by the technical advantage, much more by the cheapness of paper money instead of heavy and costly gold coins. Convenience, cheapness, and stability, he said, could be united in a paper money redeemable in a fixed quantity of gold, on the one hand, and issued on delivery of gold, on the other, so as to prevent the paper money from either falling below or rising above its gold parity. He made the further qualification that only bullion, not coins, should be exchangeable for paper money; if the devaluation of the currency occurred, which would lead to an import balance, the bullion could be shipped abroad in payment for the imports.

In itself this arrangement is within the framework of economic liberalism in that the issuance and value of paper money is regulated by the free production of gold and silver and the arbitrary issuance of money by the government is prevented. Within the same framework, Ricardo went even one step further: he was emphatic in his insistence on the necessity for transferring the issuance of paper money from private hands to those of a special, strictly regulated, department of the government, in order to reserve to the public the large profit to be derived from making paper the equivalent of precious gold in a business without entrepreneurial risks. The bank acts, named for Sir Robert Peel, of the years 1819 and 1844, show strongly the marks of Ricardo's influence, except that they did permit the circulation of coins side by side with bank notes. A hundred years later, between the two world wars, many countries adopted the Ricardian principle of fixing their domestic paper currency at parity with the medium of international payments, but they went beyond Ricardo's recommendations in substituting assorted foreign exchanges for unminted metal as the currency reserve.

It is true, that today the circulation of paper money in the form of bank notes is no longer the primary problem of currency regulation, since checks against bank deposits have become the most important means of payment. Only if the ratio of bank deposits to gold were strictly fixed would the Ricardian automatism still work. But this ratio is in fact liable to wide fluctuations, shrinking when the banks have confidence in the soundness of the credits demanded of them, and increasing as confidence wanes. Hence, the price level is no longer automatically stabilized; although the value of bank notes and deposits is always equal to that of gold, it does not follow that the price level is determined by the value of gold. With a large production and influx of gold, governments may and do fix the value of gold too high—the price level too low—if they are ready to store away the surplus gold in order to stabilize prices, rather than let prices rise by minting the new gold for issuing banknotes against it. The meaning of the gold standard is thus lost, though the legal appearance is maintained, and Ricardo's doctrine becomes obsolete under these circumstances; for an inquiry into the respective volumes of money and credit has little explanatory value when these quantities are managed by the government. This point has been most clearly demonstrated by Keynes.[17] Of course, for practical purposes the analysis of these quantitative relationships is even more important under a managed than under a free currency system; one must know how to regulate those quantities. Such an investigation, hence, would leave considerable significance to the 'trade equation' of Irving Fisher,[18] according to which the price level is dependent on the volume of trade, on the one hand, and on the quantities and velocities of specie and credits, on the other. To be sure, in all this monetary policy we are far beyond anything Ricardo ever imagined. Yet no single theorist has left such a deep mark on any special field of knowledge and has so decisively influenced the training and methods of many generations of scholars as Ricardo has.

The theory of money leads directly to that of international trade, another field in which Ricardo made a major contribution.

The traditional proponents of free trade seem to have presupposed that special productive capacities are about equally distributed among the different countries of the world. But what if they are not? The answer in a universally competitive system would be that the factors of production are attracted to the countries in which the reward is higher because conditions are more favorable to production; in this way, the pressure in the old countries is relieved, and the new countries are brought under the operation of the law of diminishing returns, until equality is reached. But Ricardo knew this to be utopian, since neither labor nor capital move freely across borders, being liable to sentimental inhibitions, which, he said, it would grieve him to see weakened. An important corollary is the one which the German theorist Hermann made explicit:[19] in so far as international capital movements do occur, they are prompted by international differences of capital equipment and profit rates and tend to straighten them out. But the presupposition of the theory of international trade is that there is free competition of goods and money, but not of the factors of production, or only to a limited extent.

The solution is an application of the theory of money. From the generally less favored country, where costs and prices are higher, gold will be transferred to the others, to pay for a one-sided flow of imports. Far from endangering the position of the importing country, as nationalists invariably insist, this international movement of gold will restore equilibrium between the trading countries by lowering the price level of the importing country and raising that of the exporting country. To this extent the solution had already been given by Cantillon and Hume. However, even though one country is more favorably endowed than others for all branches of production, the degree of its superiority will not be the same in each branch; in some industries the superiority of the country over other countries will be greater than in other industries. As the price and cost levels of the countries engaging in international trade move closer to one another in the process of equalization described above, the less favored countries will first reach equality of cost in those industries in which they were least inferior, while the superior country will specialize in those branches of production in which it holds the largest advantage. 'Comparative cost,' according to Ricardo's famous doctrine, will thus decide the final division of labor among the trading countries. That this arrangement, by making the aggregate output larger, is to the benefit of all was later shown by C. F. Bastable. And Frank William Taussig[20] of Harvard University has drawn the conclusion that the less productive country can compete only when its wage level is depressed enough to compensate for its inferior productivity; then the price levels can be equal. On the basis of these lowered wages, those industries in the inferior country for which it is best endowed assert themselves in competition.

The principle of comparative costs, however, runs counter to the labor-value theory, since what is exchanged between countries is not equal quantities of labor. This fact is concealed in the market because these unequal quantities of labor are paid in equal amounts of money as a consequence of the redistribution of gold. The entire argument has become the most powerful theoretical support of the program for international free trade. On the other hand, the implied reference to the necessity of depressing prices and wages in the less favored countries in order that they may compete on the world market has become the chief argument of those who advocate protection and economic isolation.

The Hume-Ricardo theory of international trade was conceived in terms of a stable gold currency. Even before Ricardo, Henry Thornton[21] had adapted Hume's theory to conditions prevailing under a system of inconvertible paper money. The excessive issuance of such money raises prices, reduces exports, and stimulates imports, thereby also raising the foreign exchange rate until it adjusts itself to the new, lower value of domestic money, and the domestic price level, calculated in terms of the exchange rate, is on a par with the foreign price level. Gustav Cassel[22] calls this normal exchange rate 'purchasing power parity.' However, this parity is disturbed, as Thornton was also the first to point out, by international credit transactions; for these involve the purchase of currency of the debtor country by the creditor, or the sale of money of the creditor country by the debtor, to transfer the credit. This transfer leads, in a system of gold currency, to the shipment of gold, and in a paper system, to an increase in the international value of the debtor currency; in both cases, goods are attracted from the creditor country, and it is this transfer of goods which constitutes the real content and meaning of the transfer of the credit. During this process, then, the purchasing power parity is upset and the balance of trade disturbed in order that the mutual payments may be in balance; the same is true in the other direction for the period of the re-payment of the credit, or of the interest payment. Cantillon already showed that the payment of interest by rural debtors to urban creditors lowers the price level in the countryside. Thorn-ton's reasoning has been much refined, and statistically verified, by Frank D. Graham[23] of Princeton University and Jacob Viner[24] of the University of Chicago, after their master Taussig[25] had opened the way by arguing that an outflow of gold or a depreci-ation of paper must differently affect the prices of domestic, ex-port, and import goods in order that goods be transferred. All this clearly is within the framework of the Ricardian theory.

Ricardo's theory of the future of capitalism strictly follows from his principal doctrine when this is taken in conjunction with Malthus's theory of population. A theory based on the law of diminishing returns, as this takes effect under the pressure of growing population, is, of course, open to such doubts as attach to the law itself in view of the triumphant progress of technical knowledge. But if the production per worker diminishes and the price of food increases, the worker must still receive an undimin-ished real wage under the law which binds his wage to the sub-sistence minimum. Thus, nominal or money wages must rise; and profit, the motive force of capitalist production, squeezed be-tween rising wages, on the one hand, and rising rent, on the other, must needs decline. Sooner or later profit will become too low to encourage investment, and society will reach a stationary state in which capital and population can no longer expand because every available surplus has been appropriated by rent. Ricardo drew this picture coolly, as an inescapable fact of nature —a nature which certainly appeared to be lacking in that benevolence which the founders of economics had believed in. It is difficult, however, to see how the author of so pessimistic a theory of the future of capitalism could have been denounced, by generation after generation, as an apologist of capitalism.

That the charge is absurd can be seen from the chapter 'On Machinery' which Ricardo inserted in the third edition of his *Principles*, the last published during his lifetime. This chapter dismayed his admirers to such an extent that it has remained almost unknown in the vast Ricardo literature. Its purpose is to prove the possibility of technological unemployment in contradiction to his emphatic assurances in preceding editions that technical progress must benefit all classes by making the products of industry cheaper. But, Ricardo now added, though the workers will benefit as consumers, they may lose their jobs and be displaced by machines. His reasoning is complicated and based on very narrow assumptions, but it amounts to the thesis, disputed even today, that, in the words of one of his letters to a friend, 'a fixed capital cannot employ all the workers which it is designed to replace,' or, in other words, that a money fund used for the payment of wages will employ more workers than the same amount of money invested in a machine. That new savings can simultaneously open up new employment possibilities was explicitly admitted by Ricardo, but he correctly insisted that such savings are independent of technical changes and cannot be counted upon.

It is remarkable that the two great leaders of the Classical School should have come, in their later writings, to such skeptical conclusions about the system of free enterprise which they had set out to analyze and defend. Their objections were not the same, and certainly those of Malthus were more profound and comprehensive. Both estranged their friends and jeopardized their fame by lending their authority to such highly unpopular ideas. Nothing can be more honorable to two great seekers after truth than the last words of the last letter which Ricardo wrote, a few days before his death, to his friend and adversary: 'And now, my dear Malthus, I have done. Like other disputants, after much discussion, we each retain our own opinion. These discussions, however, never influence our friendship; I should not like you more than I do if you agreed in opinion with me.'

3. SPECIAL CONTRIBUTIONS
a. Say[26]

If Malthus and Ricardo far surpass the other members of the Classical School in independence and strength of thinking, a few of these others nonetheless require mention even in a brief survey. The first of them is Jean-Baptiste Say, French contemporary and correspondent of the two leading members of the school. Although he introduced the ideas of Smith on the continent, it is incorrect to regard him only as a popularizer. He was the systematizer of the accepted body of doctrines and added his own important contributions in at least two respects. His loyalty and modesty are responsible for the fact that to this day much of what really belongs to his credit is attributed to Adam Smith.

The first of Say's contributions is to the theory of value. Say was not impressed by the labor-value theory, possibly because he was suspicious of its revolutionary possibilities, and turned to the tradition of utility-value theory, which had been kept alive on the continent, through Galiani, for decades. In the most surprising among the many anticipations in the history of economics, Galiani[27] had developed the concept of utility value as opposed to that of cost value and, more specifically, labor value. To associate value with utility was nothing new, of course: Aristotle had been the first to do so and he had been followed by innumerable others. But the more one tried to achieve a strict formulation of the utility-value theory, the more one was impressed by the difficulty which was later to be given its classic expression in Smith's economic paradox: the cheapness of useful things and the dearness of almost useless things. It is this difficulty which, long before Smith formulated it, was boldly attacked and resolved by Galiani. He argued that value is a ratio of utility to scarcity. Air and water, under normal conditions, have no value because, though useful, they are not scarce; a bag of sand from the shores of Japan has no value because, though scarce, it is not useful. Or, more precisely, the degree of utility depends on the degree of satiation. A commodity, then, has no economic value in itself, independently of the present needs of its potential users; or, in the words of Galiani, who was a great wit: 'It is not utility alone, therefore, which governs prices: for God causes the men who carry on the trades of greatest utility to be born in large numbers, and so their value cannot be great, these being, so to speak, the bread and wine of men; but scholars and philosophers, who may be called the gems among talents, deservedly bear a very high price.'

Galiani, the critic of the physiocrats, had impressed Turgot; but his real successor, much older than himself, was the abbé and philosopher Etienne Bonnot de Condillac,[28] whose work on economics was published in the same year as the *Wealth of Nations*. He clearly understood that the whole system of economic theory must be unified in terms of value, the determinant of price. Condillac followed Galiani in holding that the value of a commodity depends on its utility in relation to the subjective needs of those who use it, increasing or decreasing as these needs become more or less intense. These variations in utility are then reduced to variations in degrees of scarcity: 'value increases with scarcity and diminishes with plenty.' In an exchange transaction, therefore, new value is created, because each partner exchanges what he has in superabundance—a commodity that has therefore comparatively less value to him—for what he needs but does not own—a commodity that has comparatively more value to him. Thus, Condillac restated the doctrine of Galiani. Their theory lacked only one major element of the marginal utility theory of value, namely, the notion of the margin. Condillac, himself a member of the physiocratic circle, employed his doctrine as a weapon against physiocratic prejudices: Whatever is productive of utility, whether in agriculture, industry, or commerce, has value.

Say put this idea to the same use, not only against the still surviving remnants of physiocracy in France, but also against the traces of that influence in the works of Smith and Malthus. Both had displayed an anachronistic inclination to assign a place of pre-eminence to agriculture and to differentiate between the 'productive' work of labor, visible in the physical product, and the 'unproductive' work of managers, technicians, and the like. Once value was seen to be determined by utility, all the cost factors were recognized as 'productive.' Each of the factors of production contributes some share to the value of the product, since each has some amount of utility. This reasoning led Say to the discovery that the entrepreneur (he was one himself) stands at the very center of the productive process; he is, as it were, the representative of the consumers whom he serves, combining in his own person their demands for all the factors to be utilized in the process of production. Each of the three factors of production—land, labor, and capital—thus earns its appropriate type of income—rent, wages, and interest. Profit is the entrepreneur's surplus over the interest. This conception of the productive process is superior to that of Ricardo. The latter had placed the capitalist, i.e. the investor of capital, at the center of the whole process, with the misleading consequence that successful production appeared as an automatic result of impersonal capital. However, what is actually needed for successful capitalist production is someone to anticipate the needs of the consumers and to direct production along these lines, namely, the entrepreneur. Say's presentation has become so completely identified with the Classical School that the more complicated and less realistic doctrines of the greater masters of the school have been absorbed by it.

Say's other contribution to economic theory is of still greater consequence. It is, in fact, the real keystone of 'harmony' thinking, unimpaired by the growing skepticism of the school—the climax in the optimistic trend of argument initiated by Smith. This is Say's theory of markets. According to Say, a general glut, general overproduction, a general fall of prices below cost—in short, a general economic crisis—is unthinkable in a system of free enterprise. For in such a system product is exchanged for product with money only serving as the medium of exchange. Every sale is potentially a purchase, for the seller receives the means of satisfying his own demands. Just as every demand elicits a supply, so supply itself creates a demand. What can happen, of course, is a disproportion of supply to demand in particular markets; the two need not necessarily coincide, since it is only in the aggregate that the supply of goods must be equal to, because identical with, the demand for goods. Localized disproportionality crises can thus occur, but there can be no general crisis, since any glut in a special market must be balanced by a shortage in others. However grave this crisis may be for those who have overrated the demand for their particular product, the disturbed situation produces its own remedy. The same reasoning, which is indeed typical of the classical school, was used by Ricardo in arguing that Malthus's dread of oversaving was unjustified: oversaving would be immediately remedied by a fall of the interest rate so low as to deter further saving and encourage consumption. This is an application of Say's law to the alternative uses of money—either for capital formation (saving) or for consumption (spending).

Say's entire thesis carries the teachings of Smith to their logical conclusion. We have already seen how Smith had protested against the physiocrats' anxiety over proportionality in the circular flow of goods: he had blamed them for ignoring the self-healing tendencies in the organism. Say also stressed the self-healing tendency—but it proves to be mechanical rather than biological because the law admits of no exception. Indeed, Say himself made explicit reference to Newtonian physics as the proper analogue of the science of economics. Smith had conceived of his studies as a direct contribution to the art of the statesman; he regarded his ardor for reform as perfectly consistent with his ambition to be scientific. Say, on the other hand, was the first in a long line of theorists to conceive of their work as purely 'objective,' detached reasoning by which causes are related to effects; they scrupulously refrain from giving advice. Economics is like physics, which equips the engineer with knowledge but leaves to him its proper application.

And yet there is a world of difference between Say's attitude of detachment and that adopted by modern theorists. Say's system was self-contained, progressive, crisis-proof; it left no room for the statesman's art or wisdom. Art and wisdom have to organize and reconcile things that are naturally unorganized and antithetical; what nature has made harmonious, however, must be left alone. It is important to realize that objective, autonomous economic theory, as a 'value-free' intellectual effort, is a reflection of 'harmony' thinking and would not have arisen in another intellectual climate. The objectivity of the Classical School did not repudiate the moral and political responsibility of the scholar; the classical economists presented to the world the one system that could live and prosper without intervention from man. They claimed that the organization of the capitalist system of production embodied an inherent wisdom; they did not disclaim wisdom but lifted Nature's wisdom—or that of Providence—above that of man. Once the belief in Nature's harmony and wisdom had been given up, however, the adoption of the same attitude of detachment connoted something else—indifference and irresponsibility. Once social science contented itself with merely describing class cleavages, depression, and potential civil war, and refused in the name of objectivity to teach wisdom and provide leadership, people were plunged into the despair from which there seems to be no way out but forcible reintegration by Fascism. For Fascism is the counsel of despair to which people turn when democracy loses its socially integrating power, renounces leadership and responsibility, and leaves the people with the fear of decay and civil war. The political dangers to democracy of irresponsibility on the part of its leaders had been clearly foreseen by Aristotle.

b. Thuenen[29]

It is extremely doubtful whether Johann Heinrich von Thuenen can be properly considered a member of the classical school. This lonely thinker, living all his life as an agriculturist on his estate in Northern Germany, is certainly not a member of any school in the sense of a group of scholars of common training and continual intercourse. Yet he is in the classical tradition in the sense that his starting point is Ricardian, though he arrived at results that are far from those of Ricardo. Thuenen is, in fact, a pioneer of modern economic theory, anticipating by decades one of its central doctrines.

His Ricardian starting point, which he probably found independently before becoming acquainted with Ricardo's writings, is the theory of rent. Because the intensification of agricultural production leads to rising costs, less favorable locations can be profitably cultivated. These new, less fertile or more remote lands must not, of course, be cultivated intensively; otherwise, production on them will not pay. Only extensive cultivation enables them to compete with the intensively cultivated more favored lands. Hence, the optimum intensiveness of cultivation for a given piece of land is determined by its fertility or its proximity to the market. The task of the agriculturist is to determine this optimum point, i.e. the number of units of labor that must be applied to one unit of the land in order to yield the maximum rent. Now, not only different lands but different crops need to be cultivated with different degrees of intensiveness. Consequently, there is a location best suited to each branch of agriculture, depending upon the intensiveness of cultivation required for the production of the crop. This point was demonstrated by Thuenen in the first volume of his 'Isolated State.' He assumed a land of homogeneous fertility with one city in the center, so that different locations would be distinguished only by differences in the cost of transporting the crop to the market. On this assumption, it is clear that the different branches of agriculture will situate themselves in concentric rings around the city in the order of decreasing intensiveness of cultivation, interrupted only in cases where the crop is bulky or perishable.

Through this doctrine Thuenen became the founder and undisputed head of the economic theory of agriculture, which he provided with the concepts and principles required for a systematic analysis. His approach to the problem of the best location of farms served as a model, eighty years later, for Alfred Weber's[30] analogous inquiry into the problem of the best location for industries. This, it was found, is determined by the weights of materials and products to be transported and by the location of materials and skilled labor. In both theories there is still much detail to be worked out, but the fundamental lines remain.

In the second volume of his book, Thuenen's interest shifted to the laws governing the distribution of incomes. He elaborated one point in the theory of rent which suggested to him an approach to other problems. The diminution of returns on a given piece of land is attributable to the fact that while one of the co-operating factors of production (labor) is increased in quantity, the other (land) remains stable; thus, beyond the optimum point, the combination of the two becomes less productive. This argument, however, is not necessarily limited to land and labor; it is applicable to any two factors in an analogous quantitative relationship, e.g. to an increasing labor force working with a given capital or to a given labor force more and more richly equipped with capital. The amount by which the additional unit of labor or capital increases the output becomes smaller as the total quantity of labor or capital grows beyond the optimum point. The additional product is the specific product of the additional unit of labor or capital, the change in effect being traceable to the change in cause; and it is—in modern terminology—this marginal product that determines the incomes of all the units of labor or capital employed. For there can be only one price for homogeneous units of any one commodity; otherwise, those units for which a higher price is demanded will be replaced by the cheaper units. On the other hand, price can neither exceed nor fall short of the cost of the marginal product; if the last unit of a factor of production costs the producer less than it brings him, then more units will be demanded and the price will rise; if the last unit of a factor costs him more than it brings him, the demand for that factor will shrink and the price will fall. This is Thuenen's law. Interest and wage rates are determined by the marginal productivity of capital and labor. This principle is virtually identical with the doctrine of John Bates Clark,[31] forty years later, and is the logical application of the modern marginal-utility theory to the problem of the distribution of incomes.

While Thuenen was engaged in developing his productivity theory in preparation for his second volume, which did not appear until twenty-four years after the first, the kindred idea of the utility of the factors of production, including capital, spread in Germany, partly under the influence of Say. The leading German academic economist of the period, Friedrich Benedict Wilhelm Hermann,[32] developed a fully elaborated theory of interest, which held that interest is the price paid for the employment of capital because of its utility as a factor of production. However, he was not familiar with Thuenen's idea of a schedule of returns on capital diminishing to the margin and thereby determining the rate of interest. In this, the decisive part of his theory, Thuenen's doctrine was paralleled by that of a long forgotten Irish theorist, Mountifort Longfield,[33] who independently hit upon the idea that the productivity of the unit of capital diminishes as more units are added; he thus arrived at a theory of the rate of interest and also applied the same idea to the wages of labor. And a generation before Longfield and Thuenen, James Maitland Earl of Lauderdale,[34] had maintained, against Smith, that capital is productive and had intimated that there must be, under certain conditions, a limit to the investment of capital—a margin, in modern terminology. Lauderdale, in fact, had explicitly referred to Condillac's utility concept in connection with his own productivity theory—a reference not found in either Longfield or Thuenen. Accordingly, Lauderdale may be said to be the British counterpart of Say, whom he excels, however, by his penetrating investigation into the diminishing productivity of an increasing capital equipment. Thus, Thuenen's work appears as the climax of a development of ideas that were, somehow, 'in the air.'

Thuenen was more interested in social justice under the conditions disclosed by his productivity theory than in the problem of economic value. These conditions alarmed him. On the one hand, all workers of equal skill receive equal wages; that is, each receives a wage equivalent to that earned by the marginal worker. On the other hand, though their skill is equal, their contributions to the total product, i.e. the units of the product produced by each, are unequal, diminishing to the marginal product of the marginal worker. In other words, each (except the marginal worker himself) is producing more than the marginal product and really deserves a wage exceeding that of the marginal worker by larger or smaller amounts. Why should the surplus of their product over their wage remain in the hands of the landlord, according to the theory of rent, or of the capitalist, according to the new and more general theory? Of course, Thuenen recognized, as Clark did too, that, theoretically, this argument can be reversed: a growing number of capital units co-operating with a given number of workers are exploited in the same manner. But Thuenen rightly did not consider this the way out of his difficulty. He proceeded to oppose a formula of the 'just wage' to that of the 'market wage.' The mean between subsistence—the Malthus-Ricardo level of wages—and the value of the average product per head is the worker's just share, Thuenen held, and leaves enough to the owner to continue in his business. Thus, both worker and owner gain from the rise in productivity and are interested in it.

This argument, of course, rests on an interpretation of the theory of rent and not on the theory itself. Indeed, interpretations even more radical than Thuenen's can be inferred from the theory, as well as the extremely conservative doctrine later arrived at by Clark. Thuenen, however, believed that he had discovered and proved in mathematically binding form the scientific solution of the vexing social problem of the just wage. Putting his theory into practice, he introduced a profit-sharing wage system on his prosperous estate. His tomb bears as its only inscription the formula $\sqrt{\mathrm{a.p.}}$ (the formula of the just wage), not as the sign that a final solution had been found to the enigma of social justice, but certainly as a worthy monument to an original and noble mind.

c. Senior

Nassau William Senior[35] is a theorist whose considerable merit and originality have been obscured for a century by the impression that his major contribution to economic theory is prompted by class bias. This impression is not quite unjustified, although Senior's work in general shows that he had a broad and flexible mind. However, what matters is the validity of a proposition and not the personal motives which may have inspired its formulation.

The doctrine in question concerns the nature of capital and interest and is known as the abstinence theory. It had been given passing consideration by many a theorist before Senior took it up. It is implied in Ricardo's thesis that capital formation and the growth of society will be stopped by the fall of profit resulting from the rise of rent; in other words, as Turgot had already seen, no capital can be formed unless there is a reasonable prospect of profit. This doctrine places capital side by side with labor in opposition to land, the revenue of which, according to Ricardo, is a mere surplus not needed for production. His view of capital, however, was logically untenable in a system founded on labor value, where capital was considered a special kind of labor—embodied labor, as it were. This inconsistency was made evident by Ricardo's failure to reconcile the existence of interest with the value theory. Hence, Senior made a significant contribution in suggesting that capital is formed by abstinence from immediate consumption; such abstinence requires compensation just as 'toil and trouble,' which is the essence of labor, deserves a reward. In order to form capital, a man must refrain from spending a part of his income, e.g. of his previous profit, and plow it back into production, either directly or through the medium of credit institutions. Senior ignored Malthus's problem of the outlet for saved money; but on the usual classical assumption that resources are always utilized to their full capacity, it is incontestable that capital formation requires the postponement of consumption. If employed for the purchase of consumers' goods, the money stimulates their production; if plowed back into production, it redirects the factors of production into the production of capital goods whose ultimate consumable fruits will become more plentiful, but available only later. The sacrifice which requires compensation is one of time.

After the failure of Ricardo's theory, it became clear that on the basis of the doctrine of labor value, the only logical explanation of interest or profit is that they are the fruit of exploitation; the worker is robbed of part of what he produces. If this conclusion is to be avoided, capital must be regarded as an independent original factor of production to be rewarded in the same way as labor is. This is precisely the contention of the abstinence theory of Senior. However, he looked upon his theory not only as an adequate explanation of the nature of profit, but as a refutation of the socialist critique of capitalism, for the abstinence theory provides a moral justification for private profit: it is the reward of 'abstinence.' It is true, and in fairness should be added, that if Senior held interest to be the indispensable condition of capital formation, he regarded interest accruing to the heir of capital property as unjustifiable, an unearned increment. In holding this view, Senior can certainly not be said to have been defending the practice of capitalism. Nevertheless, his theory was open not only to sneering quips about the modesty of the rich and the profligacy of those too poor to save a penny, but to the related objection that saving may not involve any sacrifice at all for the rich man; in fact, he may save even in the absence of interest. In this case, the abstinence theory can be maintained simply by introducing Ricardo's rent principle: saving need not involve sacrifice for all savers, but only for the 'marginal' small savers whose contribution society still needs; the intramarginal savers, who would save even in the absence of interest, would then receive the interest as a rent, an unearned increment.

Senior was too good a theorist not to realize that the reform of the theory of capital necessitated the reconstruction of the entire system of economic theory. Otherwise, the factors of production would appear, as they do in the work of Smith, side by side, without commensurability, and it was to overcome precisely this difficulty that the labor-value theory had been proposed. Senior consequently reasoned that it is not labor but scarcity which constitutes value; the scarcity of supplies is ultimately traceable to the scarcity of the two factors, labor and abstinence. Moreover, he made some progress in analyzing the nature of demand, which his classical predecessors had taken as a datum not capable of further analysis. According to Senior, utility constitutes demand as scarcity constitutes supply; that is, labor and capital are demanded on account of their utility. This view is in line with the productivity theories of Lauderdale, Longfield, and Thuenen, but Senior developed more comprehensively than any one of them the idea of diminishing increments of utility, not only in production, but in consumption as well. Indeed, his profit theory may really be a productivity theory rather than an abstinence theory; for there is profit accruing from the utility of inherited capital even after the death of the person who originally abstained from immediate consumption. Thus Senior's theory of capital remains somewhat uncertain. His reduction of value to scarcity finally enabled him to take a decisive step, again without following it up, towards unifying the two separate divisions of price theory, the competitive and the monopolistic. The scarcity of goods in free competition is determined by that of labor and abstinence; monopoly makes them still scarcer but is not altogether different from competition. Senior distinguished various degrees of monopoly power depending upon whether it is 'exclusive' or limited to special 'facilities' of production and whether or not there is a natural restriction of the supply.

It can thus be seen how great was his contribution toward the transformation of the classical into the neo-classical system of economic theory. But he did not go far enough; he held in his hands the elements of the new system, but he did not proceed to the task of composing them.

d. Mill

No one in the history of economics was more celebrated, even some time after his death, than John Stuart Mill,[36] and no one's fame has faded more completely. It is not that his fame was undeserved; but it was due to qualities of smooth formulation, elegant synthesis, and, above all, comprehensive and sympathetic understanding rather than to original contributions. Mill won fame through his book on logic before he became famous in the economic field, and through his essays in political science, *On Liberty* and *On Representative Government*, afterwards; the latter, indeed, have become classics of their type. He was a utilitarian who yet protested against the identification of utility with narrow interests, a classical liberal who was yet inclined to accept much socialist criticism. He summed up the doctrines of classical economics and proclaimed that there remained 'nothing in the theory of value for the present or any future writer to clear up' immediately before the disintegrating classical system crumbled to pieces.

From the point of view of the history of economic ideas, the one memorable event in his career was his (partial) recantation of the wage-fund theory, which had been an accepted part of classical doctrine and the cornerstone of liberal anti-interventionism. According to this theory, the wage of each worker is determined by dividing the total fund available for wage payments by the number of workers. Smith had taken this wage fund to be identical with the total capital. Malthus had identified it with the subsistence fund, which tends to lag behind the rising numbers of the population. Ricardo had narrowed the fund down to the circulating capital only, since the fixed capital invested in machines and equipment obviously is not used for wage payments; and Mill finally defined the fund as 'only circulating capital, and not even the whole of that, but the part which is expended in the direct purchase of labor,' thus anticipating Marx's concept of variable capital, although without the connotation that Marx attached to it. In the form finally given to the wage-fund theory by Mill, it had become a mere tautology: the wage fund is that part of the total capital which is paid in wages. Such a statement could have no sinister implications of its own; it is simply part of the classical economic theory of self-adjusting functional interrelations with which any interference from the outside would be futile. Thus, what rendered the wage-fund theory suspect in the eyes of many was that it could be, and indeed was, invoked to discourage trade-union demands for higher wages, and the workers were thereby placed in the position of having to wait for the growth of the wage fund through the increasing wealth of the capitalists.

In truth, however, to the extent that it set a limit to the amount by which wages could be increased, the wage-fund theory was not altogether wrong; except that it would be incorrect to regard the dependence of real wages on capital accumulation as absolutely rigid, since there is a flexible margin within which the total business capital can be apportioned between different alternative uses, and, as long as the capitalists themselves do not consume the entire profit, the size of the wage fund is likely to increase with increasing productivity. These objections to the narrow arithmetical interpretation of the theory were raised by the German theorists Hermann and, later, Lujo Brentano[37] in developing their productivity theory. The American economist Francis A. Walker[38] even went so far as to point out that the real demand for labor comes not from the capitalist but from the ultimate purchaser of the product; a rising demand for the product will increase profit and thus make for an expansion of employment in the industry producing the commodity for which the demand has increased. Thus, William Thomas Thornton,[39] who can claim to have caused Mill to recant the wage-fund theory, did not, in fact, say anything new. And none of those who raised objections to the theory could dispute the fact that the direct source of wage payments is a capital fund, more or less variable in size. All these objections, however, were inspired by the wish to remove what appeared to be an insuperable obstacle to social reform through intervention in the economic process, and so they could not fail to impress Mill. His recantation of the wage-fund theory, made in his review of Thornton's book and not followed up in the later editions of his main work, marks an epoch in the history of economic policy rather than in that of economic theory. Later the theory was revived and much refined by Boehm-Bawerk and Taussig.[40] They held that the limit of real wages is determined by the quantity of goods in the various stages of production and processing at the time when the labor contract is made; these are the goods which, gradually becoming available for consumption, can be bought by the money wages to be paid to the workers. The productivity of

labor and the size of the working population remain the ultimately determining factors, as in the Malthusian doctrine, of
which Mill remained an unwavering adherent throughout his
career.

Mill's real contribution to the theory of economic policy was
his thesis that although 'the laws of production partake of
the nature of physical truths . . . it is not so with the distribution
of wealth. That is a matter of human institution solely.' This
doctrine has been criticized to the present day on the ground that
wages and interest are not only incomes distributed but prices,
i.e. those of labor and capital respectively: hence, they belong
to production—as costs—as well as to distribution, and are accordingly governed by the laws of production, regardless of
'human institutions.' But such a criticism does not touch the
main point of Mill's thesis. For the persons or classes to whom
these funds shall be distributed are determined by social institutions; any change of personnel, whether in ownership or in
management, would change the distribution of incomes. To use
the terminology of John Bates Clark: with given functional incomes (total wage and interest incomes determined by the laws
of production), the personal (and class) incomes may still be
changed by transferring to different persons the functions which
draw incomes. In this way, the rigidity of the classical 'natural
order' and its 'iron law' can be broken through. Mill himself was
enabled by his own doctrine to recommend several types of intervention in the economic process. He proposed the confiscation of accruing land rent—a conclusion already drawn by his
father, James Mill,[41] from Ricardo's theory, which had shown
that rent was a surplus not needed for production. Mill further
advocated the abolition of inheritance, in accordance with the
reasoning of Senior, and the replacement of the wage system by
a system of co-operatives based on small properties, such as Mill
found prevalent in France; this plan also underlies the proposals
of the French so-called utopian socialists, which had much impressed him. Such a program is certainly not what one would

expect from a classical economist; rather, Mill should go down in history as a forerunner of liberal, anti-centralistic socialism.

e. The Manchester Doctrine

A theory as sophisticated, on the one hand, and as deeply involved with practical aspirations, on the other, as is classical economics could not fail to be popularized and vulgarized. Mere popularization would not have been enough; it would not have served its purpose because the masters of the classical school had been profoundly skeptical. In order to restore the original optimism of classical teachings, vulgarization was needed. It would not be necessary to mention this development if public discussion ever since had not constantly mistaken the vulgarized version for the classical doctrines themselves when, as is done every day, their authority is invoked.

This vulgarized theory is known to its opponents as the Manchester doctrine, after the British city from which an important current in it, the free-trade movement, took its start. The ultimate source of this movement was Smith and Ricardo—not Malthus. It achieved its greatest and most memorable success when its leaders Cobden and Bright helped to secure the abolition of the corn laws in 1846. Politically, the powerful British export interests allied themselves with the consumers to cheapen the cost of living and thereby the relative cost of production of export goods. Little less than a new golden age was expected of the spread of free trade: diminution of the importance of political borderlines; integration of the several national economies into one worldwide economic system, the constituent parts of which would be not the national economies, but the private business enterprises participating in production and trade; and world peace resulting from international intercourse and from the impossibility of waging war in conditions of ever-increasing mutual dependence.

The British free-traders were much embarrassed, however, by

the dismal parts of the 'dismal science,' and avidly seized upon the purified version of economics presented by the Frenchman, Frederic Bastiat.[42] In a sense, he is the 'classical' Manchester theorist. A brilliant writer, he achieved world fame with his parable of the candle-makers, who petition for protection against the unfair competition of the sun in order that the community may become richer by the enrichment of their industry. The tendency of his book is appropriately suggested by its title: *Economic Harmonies,*—in itself a protest against the gloomy prognostications of Malthus and Ricardo. In support of the principle of laissez-faire, he introduced the concept of service to the consumer as the explanation of every kind of income, thus replacing the morally neutral concept of the factors of production by a moral justification for any income whatsoever. Bastiat was not blind to the many hardships and sufferings entailed in the economic process, but he contended that they would best be remedied by the rapid and unfettered advance of capitalist production. This doctrine was applied in Germany to the 'so-called social question,' which the expansion of production on the basis of a rapid accumulation of capital was expected to solve.

Bastiat was charged with plagiarism by the American Henry Charles Carey,[43] who also wrote on economic harmony and achieved great influence in this country. Carey opposed to European pessimism the unbounded optimism of a vast and empty continent, without recognizing that it was the unique conditions of his country which seemed to enable it to smooth out the difficulties under which the Old World labored. His attack on the Ricardian theory of rent is well-known; historically the expansion of agriculture was achieved not by proceeding from more to less fertile lands, but the other way, e.g. from the hillside down to the richer soil in the valley, which may have been neglected at first because it required more initial clearing. But Mill correctly replied that all this was applicable only to a new country and that, in any case, what matters for the theory of rent is only the differences in cost of production among differ-

ent lands whose crops are in demand, irrespective of the historical order of cultivation. Carey and Bastiat drew the general
conclusion, necessary to their optimistic views, that there is no
serious population problem because the growing density of the
population will so increase its productive efficiency as to out-
weigh whatever tendency toward diminishing returns there may
be in nature.

A peculiar feature of Carey's system is his combination of a
doctrine of domestic laissez-faire with protectionism. He followed
Alexander Hamilton and List, but went beyond both in demanding protection as a permanent measure of economic nationalism;
for they had advocated protection only as a temporary 'educational' measure for newly founded, 'infant' industries in competition with the already established industries of the older countries.
Carey thus weakened the logic of his own laissez-faire doctrine
in giving expression to the aspirations of the American businessman. The combination of domestic laissez-faire with all-round
protection is, of course, the program popular with business all
over the world.

All this, however, because it is not peculiar to Carey, does
not indicate that he really is a figure of a caliber all his own. His
significance, recognized only by a few theorists outside the pale
of academic economics, lies in the fact that he widened his experience of his virgin country to a great vision—not sufficiently
transformed into a consistent and rigorous theory—of restored
liberty and the free association of working people. In a way he
revived Quesnay's doctrine of the supremacy of agriculture. It
is true that Carey did not claim any special dignity for the agriculturist; in fact, he insisted that a people composed only of
tillers of the soil is dull, and on this ground he demanded industrial diversification through protection. But he held that all industrial growth is determined and limited by the available sur-
pluses of agricultural products, just as Quesnay had compared
agriculture with the roots and trunk of the tree and industry
with the twigs. No European theorist outside the physiocratic

school had understood this strict dependence of industry upon agriculture. To Carey the architecture of the economic world seemed to be founded on a new principle, which Oppenheimer later called 'geocentric.' In the New World the absence of natural and historical restrictions would permit the people to flow freely to those places where they could enjoy prosperity and independence—a possibility closed to the peoples of the Old World. There would be no rent; and, though the absolute amounts of the incomes derived from property would grow, the lion's share of the increasing product would go to labor. Of course, this picture of a genuine social liberalism owed much to Adam Smith, but at that late period in the history of capitalism, such a vision could not have arisen anywhere but in America.

It is clear that Carey's doctrines, although apparently resembling those of the Manchester school in palliating the conditions of bourgeois society by representing them as ultimately harmonious, are actually in a different intellectual climate. Henry George, who based his economic doctrine on a different principle—the theory of rent—has something of Carey's spirit, but lacks his vision. No American theorist really followed Carey's lead.[44] His libertarian appeal was recognized and carried on only by Eugen Dühring and Oppenheimer[45] in Germany.

V. Critics and Reformers

THE criticism directed against classical economic theory was of three kinds: conservative, radical, and nationalist. What was common to all three was the protest against the thesis of a natural economic harmony or against the doctrine which that thesis later hardened into, namely that economic development, whether harmonious or not, is autonomous and natural. The differences among these three kinds of criticism were not clear at the outset. On the one hand, both the conservative and the radical critics were in common opposition to bourgeois capitalism, which, in its early stages, was the progressive, 'rational' force in society. On the other hand, the nationalist criticism of economic theory could ally itself with either conservative or radical elements; for the most part, however, the nationalists, following Carey, advocated domestic laissez-faire. The conservative critics, i.e. those who thought that modern industry requires guidance by the state, could not very well achieve a systematic economic theory of their own; the historical school, which later comprised the chief conservative critics, came closest to developing an adequate doctrine but only by dissolving economics into economic history. The radical critics alone, although originally under the influence of certain conservative doctrines, gradually developed in Marxism a systematic philosophy and economic theory and powerfully opposed it to the doctrines of liberalism. The main theme of both the conservative and the radical criticisms is the interconnection between the growing class division in the laissez-faire system, on the one hand, and the economic crises which periodically shook it, on the other.

1. SISMONDI

The work of Simonde de Sismondi[1] is a perfect example of the uncertain and hesitant beginnings of this criticism. Coming from the Classical School himself, he persisted in claiming loyalty to Adam Smith and maintained that it was Smith's successors who, by their abstract reasoning and their disregard of the human factor in the economic world, had arrived at absurd conclusions. He held that the adequacy of an economic theory can be judged only in the frame of the total historical situation from which it takes its data. He thus became one of the pioneers of humanitarian social reform and of the historical school. (He was, in fact, outstanding as a historian.)

His place in the history of economics is assured by virtue of the fact that he was one of the first theorists to discuss the economic crisis; indeed, many claim him as the first theorist of the crisis. Karl Marx in particular was emphatic on this point and even charged Malthus with having plagiarized the doctrines of Sismondi. It is true that Sismondi's *New Principles* appeared one year before Malthus's *Principles*, which contains his theory of the crisis and shows the strong influence of Sismondi's book. But since the publication of Malthus's letters to Ricardo, it has become evident that Malthus had formed his theory several years before Sismondi came from his native Switzerland to England to collect material for his book.

To Sismondi must be credited that still undeveloped form of the exploitation and underconsumption theory which people to this day mistake for Marx's elaborate formulation. According to this theory, the laborer's poverty places him at a disadvantage in bargaining with the employer and makes for a labor contract unfavorable to the former; and the resultant inadequate buying power of the masses sooner or later prevents sales from being profitable by causing a dropping off in effective demand. On the basis of this theory Sismondi elaborated the doctrine that there must be a necessary equilibrium between production and consumption in order for the economic process to continue; this necessary equilibrium was watched and preserved in medieval society but is upset by the inordinately rapid progress of production under modern conditions. Under capitalism the market is soon glutted with goods that have been produced in excess of effective demand. It was, in fact, against this theory of Sismondi that Say directed the devastating criticism of his law of markets, according to which the aggregate demand for goods is identical with the aggregate supply. Malthus had surmounted the difficulty by showing how saving can prevent potential demand from becoming actual; in other words, he had traced the disproportion between supply and demand to oversaving. Sismondi, however, never faced the real difficulty. All that he said was that purchasing power in the hands of the rich is used only to buy more luxuries; he failed to see that these require more labor too, or more skilled labor, into the training of which more labor enters.

However, he did point to a difficulty overlooked by Say: because of prevailing conditions, there is a tendency for both capital and labor to become immobilized so that they cannot be withdrawn from an unprofitable industry and transferred to another for whose products there is a rising demand. Under modern conditions of production, both skills and capital equipment tend to be specifically suited to particular industries and cannot be changed without great hardship. There is, to be sure, much merit in Sismondi's emphasis on these difficulties of readjustment necessitated by changes in consumer demand, which are so lightly glossed over by his adversaries. However, such problems are ever present in the economic system, and the immobility of labor and capital, therefore, cannot be the cause of the economic crisis, a sudden interruption of economic growth unique to the capitalist system.

Thus, Sismondi's emphasis is on the social ramifications of the economic system rather than on its structure. Of course, he was not the first to discuss this aspect of economics. The early socialists, and in particular Robert Owen, had anticipated much of the critique of capitalism and had pointed to the misery to which it dooms the workers. Sismondi's description of the class division between bourgeoisie and 'proletarians' is almost on a par with that of Marx, and in his theory of the growing concentration of production and wealth he is a true predecessor of Marx, if not the actual founder of the theory. Inadequate as his reasoning is, he was irrefutable whenever he confronted his adversaries with the facts which their superior reasoning chose to ignore. His insight is correct although he rationalized it incorrectly.

Since in his judgment the social problem coincides with that of the economic crisis, his remedy was social reform. However, this was not to be radical, for, true to the teachings of his master Smith, Sismondi insisted on the necessity of private property and a revenue from it. His doctrine of the equilibrium between production and consumption and its destruction by unregulated competition suggests his conservative leanings. These led him to recommend that industrial progress be held back and that the traditional forms of regulated production be preserved. But his recommendations were not of much consequence in history. Sismondi's lasting claim to glory is that he aroused the consciences of men.

2. List

Friedrich List[2] was an enthusiastic believer in progressive capitalism. His objection to the classical theory was that it was static rather than dynamic: instead of the equalization of profits and the natural quasi-automatic development depicted by classical theory, it is actually human endeavor that creates profit and progress. Specifically, List opposed nationalism as a dynamic force to the atomistic internationalism and automatism of Ricardo's theory.

But what is important is that List did not content himself with making a general protest against the doctrine of free trade; he attacked it at its root. In fact, his criticism reads almost as if it were Marxian in inspiration. He did not discuss the validity of the theory *per se* or engage in what he regarded as a purely academic dispute about correct or faulty reasoning. Rather, he blamed the doctrine of free trade on the ground that it was inspired by special interests posing as the general interest, in other words, that it was what Marx later called an ideology. List continually wavered between admiration for the classical school's instinctive understanding of its hidden political ambitions and the rage of the German patriot at the insolence with which it represented as good for the whole world economic policies which were designed to preserve British supremacy. He reproached them with having purposely ignored the difference in economic strength between the nations which they had invited to trade freely with one another on an equal footing. The precise parallel between this criticism and that leveled by Sismondi and later by Marx against the class consequences of domestic laissez-faire is striking indeed.[3]

Free trade seemingly diminishes the importance of international boundaries; it replaces political units by industries and individual firms as the elements to be knit into an international economic system on the basis of their natural costs. But industry is not a natural growth; it is the creation of living men who change in history. Accordingly, List developed a theory—taken over, it is true, from none other than Adam Smith the sociologist —of the normal stages of economic growth: first, the primitive beginnings of hunting and fishing, and then, one by one, in proper order, agriculture, industry, and world commerce are added. It is obvious that the units participating in such a development are political bodies, the nuclei of which are nations, and that not all contemporaneous nations are equally advanced in economic development. Yet their political and imperial strength depends on their economic maturity, and it is the fully developed country which derives political supremacy from economic supremacy. The affinity of this reasoning to that of mercantilism is clear.

It follows that the young and developing nations—in practice, Germany and the United States—will strive with all their power to develop industry, and that the old, established, already industrialized, and politically powerful countries—in practice, Great Britain alone—will try to prevent them from doing so. Under a system of free trade, such industries in the young country as are still in the experimental stage, looking for markets and for sources of materials, can be crushed by the competition of industries in the older country, which are in a position to sell at a lower price and to deny the younger industries access to materials. What List demanded was an 'educational' tariff on the products of infant industries designed to protect them for a limited period of time from the competition of industries not naturally more efficient but simply earlier in development. Free trade would freeze the monopoly enjoyed by the industries of the older countries; only 'educational' tariffs could secure genuine international competition. This doctrine had already been taught and put into practice by Alexander Hamilton[4] and had been further discussed by John Rae, a lonely thinker of great originality and constructive force.[5]

The argument is unanswerable. Mill, candid as ever, included it—with special reference to Rae—in the last codification to be made of the classical doctrine. In this context List appears fundamentally as a free-trader who advocated temporary measures of protection with a view toward ultimately integrating the fully developed faculties of all countries into a worldwide free-trade system. This interpretation is borne out by a number of important considerations. The motto on both of List's main works is 'Et la patrie et l'humanité.' The title of one of them, *The Natural System of Political Economy*, suggests his loyalty to the philosophical foundations of the classical doctrine. Moreover, according to List, the full development of the productive potentialities of a nation requires intellectual and political liberty as its precondition. Finally, the vision of a 'union of nations under the law' may be found in his second major work, the *National System of Political Economy.* List himself fled from the country of his birth because of political persecution; he lived and wrote both in France and in the United States, where he became a successful entrepreneur, before returning to his own country to resume his stormy and tragic career as a propagandist and a statesman, which he himself brought to a violent end.

Yet it is doubtful whether List personally regarded free trade among the nations of the world as the final outcome. Occasionally he was so inconsistent as to advocate the permanent preservation of his educational tariff. The idea of a union of nations may have been in his eyes the theoretical consummation of a process that does not allow of any conclusion in fact but is bound to continue indefinitely because it is a historical process. The outcome envisioned by List seems to have been a world of imperial powers, each based on economic supremacy in a self-sufficient and closely integrated bloc of countries and without much intercourse among the empires. But whatever may have been List's expectations regarding the outcome of the historical process, the logic of his argument in favor of temporary 'educational' protection with a view towards final free trade remains unaffected.

What is not in List's argument, and what he never intended to advocate, is all-round, paternal protectionism, which both friend and foe have thrust upon him. How contrary such a policy is to anything that he advocated can be seen from the fact that he refused protection to agriculture, in Germany or elsewhere, on the ground that it is an old and fully developed industry, as well as to all established industries. Underlying his theory is a fundamental confidence in the creative power of the capitalistic entrepreneur, who would be insulted by an offer of protection. In this view of the power and historical mission of capitalism, List again anticipated much of the Marxian doctrine.

For all his enormous influence, List had only one real successor, Eugen Dühring, who characteristically combined List's ideas with those of Carey. And only two generations after List his argument was further developed and given an entirely new bent by the Austrian foreign-trade theorist Richard Schueller.[6] Long before Schueller, the German theorist Hans von Mangoldt[7] had already taught that it is misleading to speak of the cost of production of an industry; its different enterprises have different costs. Hence, imports do not supplant all domestic production, as Ricardo's theory seems to imply, but only that part of it whose cost is higher than the price of the imported goods; imports and domestic production divide the domestic market between them, depending upon the cost differences of the individual enterprises. (This is an application of the modern idea of the schedule character of cost, which Mangoldt had been one of the first to develop, even independently of his predecessors; see Chapter VIII.) From this Schueller infers that tariff protection will be the more useful (and less harmful) the more new enterprises can produce at a cost near to the import price, so as to require only a moderate custom duty on imports.

This argument of Schueller's is still within the framework of the Ricardian system, as is List's idea of educational protection. Schueller, however, distinctly goes beyond the limits of this system and translates List's theory into those strict terms of economic reasoning to the use of which List himself never attained; for Schueller concludes from the concept of productive forces that there are unused potential forces in most countries, and generalizes this conclusion into the observation that it is more realistic, in trade discussions, to presuppose underemployment, and hence the possibility of increasing the volume of employment by a tariff policy along the lines indicated above. Thus, while the theory of free trade assumes full employment and infers that protection can only substitute a less efficient industry for a more productive one, the dynamic concept of protection would permit the enlargement of the total output and income. In his assumption of regular underemployment Schueller is a forerunner of the Keynesian system, and in particular his argument that foreign trade increases domestic employment has been revived in recent American and English discussions, which ignore the name of the pioneer.

3. EARLY SOCIALISTS

Among the early socialists there is only one group whose right to a place in a survey of economic doctrines is beyond doubt. This is a group of British writers, consisting of William Thompson,[8] John Gray,[9] Francis Bray,[10] and Thomas Hodgkin,[11] who drew socialist conclusions from the labor-value theory. As Professor Myrdal[12] rightly says, that this was done at all is less surprising than that it was not done by those responsible for the development of the labor-value theory itself. Yet a minor barrier had still to be removed, viz. Ricardo's doctrine that the value of a commodity does not consist in, but is only proportional to, the quantity of labor expended in its production. According to these socialist writers, then, value consists in nothing but labor, and the share of anybody but the worker himself in the value of the product is nothing but a gain of exploitation made possible by the superiority in bargaining position of the owner of land or capital over the propertyless worker. Marx, though he added much, is obviously in this tradition, and he acknowledges his indebtedness to his predecessors.

To a public educated in history and politics, the names of these writers are practically unknown; other names are popularly associated with the spectacular beginnings of socialism. In a way Marx himself belittled the achievements of the early socialists by calling their programs 'utopian.' Yet it was plainly unfair of him to apply this designation to those of his predecessors who had chosen the evolutionary approach which he himself then developed, and who differ with him only in the kind of evolution which they anticipated. Count Henri de Saint Simon[13] taught an evolutionary philosophy of history, which inspired the positivism of Auguste Comte, on the one hand, and the work of Rodbertus in Germany and of Proudhon in France, on the other.

Proudhon, in fact, merged this evolutionary philosophy with Hegelianism. All these, and in addition, the more utopian Robert Owen and Auguste Fourier, were extraordinary men, whose moral courage, eloquence, and initiative left a profound and lasting impression on social thinking.

The earliest of them is Robert Owen.[14] He, indeed, rightly deserves to be called a utopian in view of his communist settlements in England and the United States, founded in accordance with a philosophy that men are made and can be remade exclusively by their environment. Yet he was, at the same time, a very practical man. Before devoting himself and his fortune solely to the welfare of his workers, he had risen from poverty to become a captain of industry. Still more practical were his ideas for consumers' co-operatives and his finally victorious campaign for legislation protecting labor against the legally unlimited exploitation of early capitalism. His writings, although not scientific, are among the first to trace the economic crisis—there was one in 1815 whose repercussions fill the literature of the period—to the misery of the workers, that is, to their underconsumption. This mode of reasoning was shortly afterward adopted by Sismondi, who seems to have received from Owen a decisive stimulus in the study of the crisis.

Karl Rodbertus,[15] deeply convinced that capitalism cannot be made to work, but also strongly anti-revolutionary, inspired much German social legislation and state socialism. Like Sismondi, whose doctrines he took up, Rodbertus was a distinguished historian, and his penetrating analogy between capitalism and the various forms of serfdom in antiquity made him as famous as his warning that Rome was destroyed by the barbarians who had served in her army: in the same way, he contended, the industrial workers are in the service of the bourgeoisie. He was the first continental writer to give expression to the claims of the 'proletarians.' His theory of the falling wage quota in an increasing national income was derived as a corollary from the 'iron law of wages.' This law had been given a flexible formulation by Malthus and Ricardo: the level of wages tends to rise with the workers' minimum standard of living. But Rodbertus held that the income of the workers is inflexibly tied to the minimum of physical subsistence, and the increment accruing to the national income is reserved to the capitalists exclusively. This doctrine of the falling wage quota was an elaboration of Sismondi's theory and was used by both Rodbertus and Sismondi as an explanation of the deficiency of purchasing power which causes the economic crisis. However, this argument does not constitute an adequate theory unless it is supplemented by Malthus's or some other explanation of why the increasing income of the capitalists does not supply the needed purchasing power. Furthermore, Rodbertus's thesis fails to suggest any reason for economic fluctuations; at most what it can, and indeed was intended to, explain is permanent misery. But despite, or perhaps because of such shortcomings, this theory has become the accepted crisis theory of the socialists, and even Marx, though he rejected it, sometimes invoked it inadvertently. Rodbertus drew the practical conclusion that, as a minimum of necessary reform, the share of labor in the growing national income should be made proportional to that of the other incomes, rent and profit, in order to maintain sales. This obviously parallels Thuenen's wage reform.

From his explanation of the economic crisis, Rodbertus did draw one conclusion which was as original as it was historically influential; and, what is most important, the same conclusion can be drawn from the facts when these are regarded in the light of any theory other than that of Rodbertus. In the crisis, with markets glutted and goods unsalable, the capitalists try to sell in newly opened foreign markets. The desperate struggle for such outlets suggests the use of the military power of the national state to subjugate pre-industrial countries, secure their markets, and keep foreign competitors and their governments out. This is the famous economic theory of imperialism as the way out of the economic crisis. One must, however, distinguish between the theory as such and its derivation, by Rodbertus, from his underconsumption principle. What the theory presupposes is a surplus of goods which the domestic market cannot absorb; that is, it presupposes either an economic crisis or a monopoly, both of which involve a reduction of sales and underutilization of productive capacity. In such cases, however they may be analyzed by theory, the desire to secure sales outside the domestic market leads to economic imperialism. Rodbertus deserves the credit of having been the first to draw this conclusion.[16] He is the indubitable author of the theory of imperialism, although Marxians, because of Marx's bitter enmity towards Rodbertus, have been kept unaware of this fact.

Marx, who was extremely generous in the recognition of his debt to Ricardo and Sismondi, and viciously hostile to Malthus and Rodbertus, succeeded by his aspersions[17] in blotting out the memory of the great Proudhon for several generations. Only now is Pierre-Joseph Proudhon[18] gradually coming to be recognized as the proponent of the one really democratic alternative to the proletarian dictatorship and its Fascist counterpart. Hegel had glorified the conservative state as the one force powerful enough to unify a bourgeois society disintegrating in the social conflict and the economic crisis. Marx claimed to have 'put Hegel on his feet,' but this logically implies that the revolutionary state which Marx advocated was also to be a dictatorship. To the dictatorial way out of the crisis Proudhon opposed the idea of an organized equilibrium of forces directed toward a common goal—an idea liberal in its insistence on freedom protected by a system of checks and balances, but socialist in that this equilibrium is conceived not as automatic or natural but as deliberately constituted. Although Proudhon is the author of the famous indictment of private property as 'theft,' he was not a communist in any sense. What he, like all socialists, objected to is the 'right of escheat' (*droit d'aubaine*), which owners enjoy in dealing with non-owners, i.e. the right to exact an unearned tribute. His aim, however, was the rediscovery and restoration of the human meaning of property, its democratization rather than its socialization. A communist society, he thought, would be a new kind of class society, and, moreover, one without personal liberty. Another misapprehension concerning Proudhon is that he was an anarchist. It is true that he hated the state as it is, and, as an enthusiastic lover of liberty, wished to see the scope and functions of the state reduced. However, he was careful to develop the concept of the law as the means of defining and delimiting groups and their rights in such a way that the life of society can proceed on the basis of diversity in equality.

The economic measures he recommended for the attainment of this end are another application of the popular underconsumption theory. According to Proudhon, interest and rent are fruits of the 'right to tribute,' which threaten to keep the people in poverty and prevent the circular flow of goods. Profit, however, he regarded as the fruit of special effort and skill on the part of the entrepreneur. He rejected all schemes—such as had been suggested by Owen and Rodbertus, among others—for the distribution of goods among the workers in accordance with the amount of labor they have contributed to society. What Proudhon wanted was a system of free exchange and freely formed prices, and to this end he advocated the expansion of credit. The idea that credit is a revolutionizing principle because it emancipates purchasing power from the control of hereditary wealth and makes it accessible to any man capable of putting the money to good use had been a central feature of the thought of St. Simon; and the German Bruno Hildebrand,[19] one of the founders of the historical school, had opposed to List's theory of the stages of economic development the idea that primitive barter economy and the technically more convenient but socially inequitable money economy will be followed by a credit economy with equal opportunity for all—which, of course, presupposes that personal competence rather than collateral will be made the test of whether a man is worthy of receiving credit. Proudhon's scheme is in this line. He wanted a credit not convertible into metal money, the limited amount of which he thought is responsible for the emergence of interest, but a free credit that would lead to 'social liquidation,' the paying out of property rights, and the 'constitution of values' freed of the 'right to tribute.' Long despised, such projects have recently become respectable through Keynes's insistence that it is the rate of interest which keeps production down. Keynes himself, generous though he is towards many of his precursors, remains strangely unaware that the foremost place in his roll of honor ought to go to Proudhon.

VI. Economics as Historical Dialectic of Harmony

1. KARL MARX[1]

A FIGURE as towering in world history as that of Karl Marx is certainly not completely contained within the narrow confines of economics. Indeed, it is highly doubtful whether his principal significance as a thinker lies in this field. Moreover, his contributions to it are marred by the inadequate tools of analysis which he inherited from his predecessors; consequently, though his insights are penetrating, the reasoning by which he supports his arguments is often far from sound. Yet his contributions make him a very great economist, even if they cannot always be accepted on the grounds he offered for them. The presuppositions, which constitute the Marxian philosophy, we shall briefly describe before turning to his contributions to economics proper.

a. Marxian Philosophy[2]

The classical economists had contended that the natural order of capitalism, once established, would grow and develop but cannot and must not be changed. Marx took up the anti-revolutionary challenge of this philosophy and opposed to it his theory that society is subject to a law of historical transformation, in accordance with which those forces that have brought an order into being attempt to stabilize it by stifling the further growth of new forces threatening to undermine it, until these finally assert themselves and realize their aspirations. Hence, anyone who understands this law of historical transformation must ally himself with the new forces, so that the deadlock may be broken and the way opened to history, i.e. to fundamental, revolutionary social change.

The ultimate motive force of this entire process of social change is economic. The quest for a living, or for a better living, is a fundamental impulse of man, which overrides all other interests in case of conflict. In other words, at the basis of all historical change there is the logic of an autonomous gradual economic development, of progress in the methods and the organization of production. The social, legal, and political 'superstructure' built upon this economic foundation, however, has a tendency to persist even after its basis has begun to change; as a result, economic development is hampered. The history of this superstructure is thus one of periodic revolutions by which it is accommodated to the gradually accumulating results of the economic evolution that underlies it. The improvement of methods of production constitutes a transformation of the total pattern of production, requiring, in turn, a new type of man, with new qualities (skills, attitudes, etc.), and thereby revolutionizing the entire organization of society. The course of history is from medieval handicraft through bourgeois capitalism to proletarian socialism; or, in terms of the pattern of production, from individual independent work through dependent collective work to independent collective work; or, in (derived) terms of the forms of property, from general individual property through private property operated by the propertyless to universal collective property (Communism). This evolution is paralleled on all the reflected planes of the social superstructure and could be traced in the development of the forms of law, religion, science, art, etc. Moreover, the entire process is within the bounds of nature and partakes of the inexorable strictness of natural law; the Marxian doctrine is deterministic. Strangely this blind causal process has a goal, namely the ultimate liberation of mankind from all suffering that has its roots in social maladjustment. This goal is to be attained through the socialization of the means of production, which is the necessary objective of the working class—necessary both historically and morally.

This is a very brief sketch of the Marxian philosophy. Four elements are merged in it: the Hegelian dialectic; the economic interpretation of history; the teleological conception of history; and the scientific method. According to the doctrine of the dialectic, as this is applied to nature and history, every living being contains within itself the impulse to become something new and different, while still retaining its identity. This is an old element in the history of philosophy. It is dominant, for example, in the Christian doctrine of the transformation of achievement into pride and sin. In the same way, according to Marx, capitalism first unfetters the forces of production and then turns this achievement itself into a fetter and an instrument of injustice. The transformation takes place through the conflict between the old and the new, but there is nothing in the principle of the dialectic in itself which suggests that the process should or will stop at a goal. The economic interpretation of history, i.e. the idea that economic forces are basic to social life, was widely taught from the eighteenth century on, with remarkable clarity by James Madison in the tenth letter of the Federalist, though, of course, without the Marxian implications of dialectical change. Since the accumulation of wealth beyond that needed to maintain a satisfactory standard of living does not primarily serve for the improvement of living conditions but for the building up of power over men and things, the economic interpretation of history must be understood in terms of the social and economic power that great wealth confers. The Marxian interpretation of history, with its accent on injustice in the past and in the present, is closely akin to the pessimistic view of man held by the Hebrew prophets; but Marx expected man's liberation to be achieved by the working of the same economic motive, whereas man according to the Biblical understanding can be liberated only through spiritual regeneration. The idea of progress towards a goal (immanent teleology) is a watered-down form, appropriate to an age of naturalism, of the Biblical belief in a final transformation of the world into a Kingdom of peace and justice. The classical economists too had believed in progress—steady and unilinear—under the pressure of competition; by merging this notion with the principle of the dialectic, Marx conceived of progress as historical, i.e. as saltatory, catastrophic, revolutionary. Finally, the whole process of history, including the final change to socialism, was conceived as taking place in accordance with a law of nature.[3]

Marx took these disparate elements and wove them into a consistent, highly original, and impressive whole. Yet his doctrine has much in common with that of his classical predecessors. Both Marx and the classical economists believed that harmony is ultimately guaranteed by the operation of a natural causal law. Harmony is attainable, according to liberalism, in the world as it is presently constituted, i.e. under capitalism; according to Marx, harmony will be attained at the end of a causally determined process of continual strife, a process of which we have reached the penultimate stage. Although Marx ridiculed the doctrine of preordained harmony, he replaced it by the doctrine of a blind causal process the remote beginnings of which have been so arranged as to lead with causal necessity to final harmony, liberty, and peace. The forms of the final order are opposed to those of the liberal order because the process envisaged by Marx leads one stage beyond capitalism.[4]

These are the presuppositions with which Marx approached economics.

b. The End of the Labor-Value Theory

In his economic work,[5] Marx used the categories developed by Ricardo, to whom he constantly referred, although giving Ricardo's doctrine an altogether new turn. The labor-value theory had already been reinterpreted as a tool of socialist criticism, but this interpretation did not satisfy Marx. He opened

Capital with the famous deduction of the capitalist law of exploitation from the general law of the exchange of equal labor values developed by the classical economists. The paradox of capitalism is in the existence of unearned profit in a world of equivalent exchange; in other words, in the combination of the law of the exchange of equal labor values with the Malthus-Ricardo law of wages, according to which wages are determined, not by the product of labor, but by the amount of labor necessary to produce labor, i.e. the labor required to produce the worker's minimum standard of living. Marx resolved the paradox by distinguishing between the labor value of the product of labor (i.e. the amount of labor-time involved in producing it), on the one hand, and, on the other, the labor value of the worker's labor power, which the worker sells to the employer because the former has no means of production and nothing that he could produce and sell independently. The difference between the two values, which is due to the increase in the productivity of labor to the point where the worker can produce more than his minimum living standard, is the exploitation gain of the capitalist, called by Marx 'surplus value' in its relation to labor and wage, and 'profit' in its relation to the total capital invested in the business. The employer's wage capital thus brings him a return. Marx's explanation is that it is the employer's 'good luck' to be able to buy a commodity—labor—the use of which consists in the production of more labor-value than is needed for its own sustenance, which governs its value in exchange. In other words, labor is the one commodity whose value in use exceeds its value in exchange; therefore, he who buys labor on the market and uses it to produce exchangeable commodities gains for himself a surplus value. On the other hand, if the worker himself had access to the means of production, he would not sell his labor power for its equivalent; he would sell the product of his labor for its equivalent, which is higher, namely, the sum total of wage and surplus value. Employed by the capitalist, he works only part of the day for himself; the rest of the workday is unpaid.

Now the classical economists had proved their labor-value law of price by arguing that the cost of production must be replaced in full if consumers are to receive continuous service; if the cost of production is not replaced by the price, the supply of commodities is reduced until the price is raised to cost. Siegfried Budge[6] seems to have been the first to show that this law is abandoned by Marx. For, according to Marx, surplus value is not an element in the cost of production. The labor creating the surplus value has, it is true, been incorporated in the product, but by one who does not get the equivalent; whereas the one who does get the equivalent, the capitalist, has not given anything in return. Why, then, should the consumer give the equivalent of the surplus value to the capitalist? The law of equivalence thus becomes mysterious, devoid of economic meaning. For, according to classical reasoning, a mere surplus would attract competitors, increase production, and thus be finally eliminated.

Similarly, it may be asked why wages should be governed by the law of equivalence, which ties them to the minimum standard of living, instead of rising with increasing productivity. In answering this question, Marx invoked the doctrine of the industrial reserve army. Just as Malthus's natural law of over-population keeps wages down in Ricardo's system, so Marx's historical law of capitalism's surplus population serves the same end and thus explains the preservation of profit. If wages rise, profit is impaired, the stimulus to the accumulation of capital is reduced, and the fund from which capital is accumulated is depleted; the growing population does not find employment, and the competition of the unemployed brings down the wages of the employed and restores profit. However, what this ingenious theory fails to take into consideration is the fact that, as the productivity of labor rises, wages can rise without encroaching on profit and lessening the inducement to production. Oppenheimer,[7] who developed this line of reasoning, inferred that the workers can build their own co-operative enterprises from their rising wages without making capitalism prematurely inoperative.

Capital, according to Marx, is not a factor of production but only the means of exploitation. Its physical form is the means of production on which the propertyless are employed. The means of production, of course, are in turn products of labor, and are bought for their labor values from their capitalist producers, who pocket the profit resulting from the difference between the labor value of the finished machines and the exchange value of the labor employed in making the machines. The user of the machine thus derives no profit from the machine itself; that profit has already been skimmed off by the capitalist producer of the machine. The capitalist uses the machine only as the means of employing and exploiting workers. Thus, the material part of his capital—that part which is invested in machines, tools, equipment, etc.—does not bring him any return; Marx called this capital 'constant' because it merely transfers its value to the product but does not increase in value in the process. On the other hand, the wage capital, which Marx called 'variable,' earns a surplus value by employing labor at its exchange value. The service of the material capital consists in making the employment of labor by the wage capital technically possible.

As capital is accumulated out of the profits of the successful capitalists, they are enabled to expand production and at the same time to produce more efficiently with the larger investment of capital. Technical progress tends to increase the amount of capital equipment per worker and thereby to increase the productivity of labor. In other words, as the total capital increases, a rising share of it must be material, i.e. constant, capital; and the capacity of a capital of a given magnitude to employ labor decreases correspondingly. With the progress of technology, the share of wage capital in total capital becomes smaller. Hence, with an unchanged rate of exploitation (the ratio between paid and unpaid labor-time, or between wages and surplus value) the rate of profit, which is the ratio between the surplus value and the total capital, decreases because the surplus value, derived from the employment of labor, becomes a smaller percentage of the growing total capital. And it is, of course, exclusively the rate of profit—what his money brings him—that interests the capitalist.

This is the Marxian version of the law of the falling rate of profit—a law that was regarded as an important element in the classical doctrine. Smith had explained it simply as the result of the fact that capital accumulates more rapidly than the population increases. Ricardo and Mill had derived it from the law of diminishing returns. Marx lays the greatest stress on this law; it serves him as the demonstration of the inescapable self-destruction of capitalism in a final crisis in which production and employment break down for lack of profit.

It should be noted, however, that this law is predicated on the assumption of an unchanged rate of exploitation. What escaped Marx, as several critics have observed, is that this assumption implies that wages rise with the rising productivity of labor. However, such a rise in wages is contrary to Marx's assumption that they are determined by, and kept down to, the exchange value of labor power, the minimum standard of living. Here, as elsewhere, Marx fell into the pitfall of his own labor-value concept, which obscures the fact that different quantities of the product correspond to the same quantity of labor in different conditions of productivity; for the labor-value theory, they still appear as equal quantities of labor value. If productivity rises and the amount of wages remains the same, i.e. equal to the exchange value of labor power, the labor value of the wage falls and the rate of exploitation rises. Under such circumstances, a fall in the rate of profit is no longer necessarily deducible; what happens is simply that the capital employed is used to exploit relatively fewer workers more intensively. To be sure, the rate of profit can still fall; the capitalist may be unable, for reasons arising out of the circumstances of the capitalist market, to sell his product at a price that will 'realize' the money value of the labor surplus incorporated in the product. But this is another matter, to be discussed later.

The further question arises why capitalists should introduce less profitable, although more productive, methods. Marx's answer is that the individual producer who is first to do so has an extra profit as long as his competitors do not follow suit and as long as he sells approximately at a price determined by the cost of his competitors while his cost is lower. Only when they do follow suit, under the pressure of his superior competition, or when they are eliminated by him, will the new, lower level of costs determine price and will the general rate of profit become lower. It is the stimulus of temporary extra profits that lures capital to its self-destruction—a fascinating doctrine of dialectic.

But this doctrine can, at the same time, be used to invalidate part of the labor-value theory itself. According to Marx, it is anonymous 'society' that equips the worker with the means and techniques of production. The 'socially necessary labor-time,' which determines the value of a commodity, is not fixed by the lazy, the weak, the incompetent, or the inadequately equipped; it is the average time necessary to produce the commodity under the normal conditions of production at a given time in a given society. Being a function of the productivity of labor, it is considered to be part of an anonymous historical process. Hence, as productivity rises, the increase in the product of the average worker in a given period of time appears as exclusively his, and a deduction in favor of the capitalist appears as exploitation. However, the description given by Marx of the actual process by which productivity is increased shows that the introduction of labor-saving machines is brought about, not by anonymous 'society' or even by the workers themselves, but by the individual capitalist. Practically all improvements in production are brought about in this way. Why, then, does the labor-value theory not impute value to this productive achievement of the capitalist?

The doctrine of value is brought to its completion in the third volume of *Capital*, which, like the second, was published by

Marx's friend and collaborator Friedrich Engels[8] from notes left by the author. The problem treated here is the relation between profit and price. On the one hand, competition tends to equalize profits. On the other hand, the profit in any branch of production depends on the percentage of the total capital constituted by wage capital, since the labor value of the product includes the surplus value (from which profit is derived) in proportion not to the total capital, but only to that part of the total capital which is paid in wages. Now the capacity of capital to exploit labor, i.e. to realize a surplus value and hence a profit, varies inversely with the degree of mechanization and thus differs in different branches of production, depending upon the extent to which labor-saving machinery has been introduced. But the degree of mechanization of a particular industry is, of course, a purely chance result of the development of technology: the textile industry is relatively little developed technologically in comparison, for example, with the electric-power industry. Marx's solution to the problem is parallel to Ricardo's but more ambitious. According to Marx, the competition for profitable investments causes capital to flow into those branches of production in which labor costs constitute a relatively higher percentage of total costs, i. e. to transfer from highly mechanized and therefore little profitable to less progressive industries employing more labor per unit of capital, until equality of profit rates in all industries is attained, as prices and profits rise in the former and fall in the latter group. The prices which contain equal profit rates are called 'production prices.' These prices deviate from values, being lower where values would include more than the average rate of profit and higher where the opposite holds true. The result is a redistribution of surplus values in proportion to the capital invested.

This logically necessary completion of the labor value theory has been criticized by Boehm-Bawerk[9] and others as a capitulation to classical theory, a reinstatement of the classical thesis that prices are determined by the cost of production, with interest in proportion to invested capital—instead of to wage capital only —included under costs. Prices are no longer labor values. But for the labor-value theory to be vindicated, it is not necessary that prices simply coincide with labor values. If Marx succeeded in drawing a line of logical derivation from the value principle to 'production prices,' if his logical principle leads to the explanation of observed facts, then his theory is vindicated. It has been said, on the other hand, by Joan Robinson[10] and Schumpeter[11] that because competition tends to equalize profits, we need not bother about the way this result is brought about in the Marxian theory; it is simply a fact that capital seeks investment wherever this is attractive. But this argument obscures the real issue, which is whether profit can be explained as withheld labor value; in other words, the argument obscures the gravest objection to the labor-value theory.

The capitalists of the highly mechanized industries receive, in production prices, a profit which is not produced entirely by the workers in their industries, while the capitalists in those industries employing more labor per unit of capital do not get the full profit produced by their workers. What is implied by Marx's solution is that the profit produced by the second group of workers is transferred from their capitalists to those of the first group by the tendency of the competition of capitals for favorable investments to equalize profits. Now this transfer can be effected only in the sphere of consumption: those who consume the products of the second group purchase goods for less than they are worth; those who consume the products of the first group purchase goods for more than they are worth. If the same consumers purchase the products of both groups, in the long run their savings and losses will cancel each other out, and the total gain of exploitation will be unchanged. But actually the class division between consumers practically parallels that between producers; the capitalists and the workers consume different types of products. The mechanism of transfer described above would work only if the two classes participated in equal proportions in the consumption of both groups of products. If the share of the workers in the consumption of the second group of goods is larger than their share in the first, they will receive a refund, as consumers, of part of what they have been robbed of as producers; the capitalists, as consumers of the first group of goods, will have to pay out of previous profits part of the profits of the capitalist-producers in that group. On the other hand, if the workers are the principal consumers of the goods whose prices exceed their values, and the capitalists of the goods whose value exceeds their price, the exploitation of the workers as consumers will be added to their exploitation as producers. In the former case, the labor-value theory is invalidated. In the latter case, although the assumed situation fits the political purpose of Marxism, the labor-value theory is also shown to be inadequate: the margin between the exchange value of labor power and the value of the product is not the only source of profit; profit is produced not only by the process of production, at the expense of the workers, but also by the process of distribution or circulation, at the expense of the consumers.

Thus Marx's attempt to prove by economic theory that the workers are exploited by the capitalists must be accounted a failure. Only the moral, not the economic idea of exploitation can be maintained. And the collapse of the theory of labor value had far-reaching consequences for economic theory in general. But it is strangely anti-climactic to observe that the main parts of Marx's work are not thereby affected, simply because they do not really rest on the foundation of labor value.

c. Theory of the Development

The main parts of the Marxian system are derived from his doctrine of the trend towards large-scale production, which in his terminology is designated as accumulation and change of the composition of capital. This trend involves the concentration of production and wealth, the destruction of small-scale, independent enterprises, and general proletarianization, all of which Marx's prediction has made the focal points of any realistic economic discussion ever since. According to this theory, the capitalist system of production is inexorably transformed in pattern, increased in productivity, and undermined in stability as the rate of profit falls. This trend was pictured not only as the way to the self-destruction of capitalism but at the same time as the way towards the final solution of the economic problem: the planned economy. The individual enterprises grow in size and comprise under one management more and more specialized activities formerly organized as separate businesses and industries, whose relative sizes had been determined by the market. The market thus diminishes, and as profit falls until production stops in the economic crisis, the only way out is the planned, profitless unification of the whole system of production.

But it is not the capitalists who bring this change about; they continue to operate their private businesses and to seek for profit to the very end. The force which the dialectic of history trains for the task of replacing capitalism is the working class, i.e. the organized exploited wage-workers. They are trained both negatively and positively. Negatively, the increasing misery created by the mechanization of production and the decreasing capacity of capital to employ labor profitably makes the workers revolutionary. Positively, they are trained for socialism by their new collective work, their disciplined, planned co-operation in large-scale production. These experiences combine to produce in them the will to socialism, the historical mission of which is to institute common ownership of all workers in all means of production, and, on this basis, planned, unified management. In the 'social revolution'—which is not an economic revolution but the social and political result of it—the paths of economic and social development meet: the system of production is ready for collective planned management, and the new social force, the proletariat, is ready to take it over to this end.

Now what a doctrine with these tremendous social implications requires to support it is certainly not the theory of labor value; it is immaterial whether profit is a deduction from labor value or the cost of an independent service of impersonal capital. What the doctrine presupposes is nothing but the fact of the search for profit which, at any rate, is dominant in capitalism, and a universal tendency toward large-scale production, which every theory recognizes as superior in competition if it saves costs, and towards an aggravating economic crisis, however this may be explained. But regardless of the validity of Marx's proofs, he was the first to state both the theory of the concentration and breakdown of production and the theory of the rise of the proletariat, and he did so with such force that they have appeared Marxian ever since.

However, certain critical observations must be made regarding both theories. In the first place, although large-scale production has generally reduced costs and proved superior in competition, there are significant exceptions; an increased capitalization does not always render a business more efficient. Marx failed to consider fully all the circumstances in which labor-saving devices may be added. It is not always true that the introduction of a labor-saving device has the effect of superseding workers formerly employed; it may take the place of workers who would otherwise have been employed for a larger output. Adding such a device to the equipment of a small plant is like adding a number of workers to it; the business becomes a capital enterprise without a labor problem. Electrification, for example, has this effect, particularly on small-scale farms. What Marx had exclusively in mind is the case in which the labor force does grow, but not in proportion to the fixed capital. This case also involves labor-saving and alone meets Marx's conditions. A third case, in which fixed capital is cheapened by technological progress and the wage capital's share in the total capital is thereby increased, was recognized by Marx, but he claimed that it was not prevalent; yet today it has become very significant. The trend of the development as a whole is doubtful, and there is no logical necessity for an unbroken tendency toward large-scale production of the kind envisaged by Marx.

In the second place, as far as this tendency does prevail, it is not accompanied by that increase in the numbers and the unity of the proletariat which Marx had predicted. The number and functions of the workers do not increase with rising productivity. It is the new middle classes who take over an increasing number of functions: more engineers to supervise the growing machinery, more accountants to compute costs, more middlemen to distribute the larger output of increasingly concentrated production. Late capitalist society, while confirming Marx's prediction about its concentration and instability, refutes his prediction about the growing uniformity of economic functions and the consequent proletarian unification of the people.

In the third place, the theory of the increasing misery of the proletariat, however vital it may be for Marx's political program, is inadequately supported. Increasing misery would be the lot of the proletariat only if an absolute shrinkage were to occur in the capacity of increasing capital to employ labor, or, in the event of a growth in population, if that capacity were to grow more slowly than the number of the workers. Marx sometimes seems to make this assertion. However, it implies continually growing unemployment throughout the history of capitalism, which is contrary to the facts. For the most part Marx conceded that accumulation of capital in general increases employment, although more slowly than the capital increases. Nevertheless, he concluded that 'accumulation of wealth at one pole is . . . at the same time accumulation of misery, agony of toil, slavery . . . at the opposite pole'—a necessary conclusion if the workers are to be revolutionized by capitalism. The 'relative' interpretation of the doctrine, also suggested by Marx and elaborated by many Marxists, is that the standard of living of the proletariat rises, but more slowly than that of the capitalists. But this interpretation does not serve the revolutionary political program of Marxism. The 'absolute' interpretation, on the other hand, according to which more and more workers continually lose their jobs, does not serve the positive political program of Marxism, the establishment of socialism; for according to Marx it is not through unemployment but only through disciplined communal work that the workers can be trained in communal thinking and planning. Finally, experience shows that the standard of living of the workers has gradually risen, although this tendency has been periodically interrupted by unemployment; and, despite the vast literature on the subject, the problem of 'relative misery' remains undecided. Experience does show that the working masses of capitalism have received considerable training in collective work and socialist sentiment, but this has not generally been accompanied by revolutionary aspirations on their part.

d. Theory of the Business Cycle

Marx's greatest achievement as an economist is undoubtedly his contribution to the theory of the crisis. In this respect he surpasses both Quesnay and Malthus. Quesnay had made the theory of the crisis possible; Marx made it actual. Nor does it detract from Malthus's achievement to say that what he described was the crisis proper, but not that rhythmic cycle of prosperity and depression which history shows to be the form in which the industrial-capitalist system grows. Indeed, Marx was the first theorist to understand the significance of the fact discovered by Clément Juglar, that the real problem is the business cycle, the rhythmic fluctuations of employment, output, and income; previously the crisis had been conceived as a mere interruption of an otherwise steady movement upward.

There are, it is true, three or four different theories of the economic crisis in *Capital*, not all of them equally elaborated. In Marx's total system it is easiest to derive the theory of the crisis from his law of the falling rate of profit. Before the final doom of capitalism, crises are temporary and give way to short-lived booms if the tendency for profits to fall is temporarily checked and reserved; thus capitalism is given a new lease on life. The temporary upward movement of profits is induced by technical improvements, the introduction of which, as we have seen, creates a short-run increase in profits for the first enterprises to use them. Profits are increased in particular by those technological improvements which cheapen the cost of living of the workers and thereby reduce the exchange value of their labor power, leaving a larger surplus to the capitalist. However, there is a wide difference between this theoretical conception of the business cycle, which takes account only of the diminishing capacity of capital to employ labor, and the actual business cycle, which involves, in addition, the idleness of capital and the contraction of output. To the extent that these aspects of the business cycle are ignored, the theory is inadequate, and, at any rate, with the invalidation of the law of the falling rate of profit, the business-cycle theory based upon it also becomes untenable.

Marx's theory of the industrial reserve army is far superior as a description of the process by which employment increases and then falls off. This theory anticipates Keynes's thesis that full employment, far from being the rule, as the classical economists believed, is the exception, achieved only in extraordinary circumstances; the rule is underemployment. Yet Marx's theory of the industrial reserve army does not really provide an adequate explanation of the business crisis. According to Marx, as capital accumulates and output is increased, the rise of wages encroaches on profits and leads to the slackening of accumulation until profits are restored. Here again, there is a surplus of labor, but not of capital, and the theory does not make provision for that contraction of output which is characteristic of the actual business cycle; labor, according to this theory, becomes superabundant because there is a shortage of capital. And, as we have pointed out above, another objection to this theory is that an increase in wages may be offset by the rise in the productivity of labor instead of by a fall in the rate of profit.

Marx's great contribution to the theory of the business cycle is in the tradition of Quesnay, whose 'Tableau' Marx praised as 'incontestably the most brilliant idea' in economics. His own contribution to the elaboration of this idea is no less brilliant. He replaced Quesnay's special organization of economic society, which was predicated on Quesnay's special theory of the surplus, by a really ingenious division of the total production of society into two sections: the production of producers' goods and that of consumers' goods. The value of the product of each section includes, of course, the value of the used-up materials and machinery, the value of the labor employed (wages), and the surplus value (profit). The problem is to find the equilibrium conditions which will insure a smooth and continuous exchange of machines and materials produced in department I and needed in department II and of consumption goods produced by II and needed in I. In a purely stationary circular-flow economy, that is, on the assumption that a social capital of a given magnitude produces the same quantity of value in commodities each year and that the capitalists consume the surplus in full and do not accumulate new capital—a condition which Marx designates as 'simple reproduction'—the value of the wages and surplus in department I must be equal to the value of the material capital to be replaced in department II, since the material capital to be replaced in department I is produced there and the goods to be consumed by the wage workers and the capitalists of department II are also produced in their own department. If this equation obtains, then the system can go on producing indefinitely. However, if part of the surplus value of both departments is accumulated by the capitalists and reconverted into additional capital—a condition which Marx designated as 'reproduction on an enlarged scale'—this simple equation must be replaced by one considerably more complicated, since in both departments less consumption goods and more production goods are now in demand. To meet this increase in the demand for production goods, department I must be enlarged more rapidly than department II so that the increasing consumption demand of the workers and the decreasing consumption demand of accumulating capitalists in department I may be equal to the demand for replacements and the accumulation of tools and materials in department II. Hence, a smaller part of the profit must be accumulated in department II than in department I, in a definite proportion determined by the size and composition of the capitals invested in the two departments. (The situation would again be modified if capitalists of department II used their money to contribute towards the accumulation of capital in department I.) Such are the equilibrium conditions in the circular flow of goods, developed in the famous equation tables at the end of the second volume of *Capital*.

Equilibrium in capitalism is supposed to be secured by price fluctuations. Marx showed that even in the simplest conditions disturbances may arise from the intervention of money in the circular flow of goods. Fixed capital is gradually written off over a period of years and then suddenly replaced by the expenditure of the accumulated depreciation funds. In a smoothly working system, the annual replacements would be equal to the annual depreciation allowances; but if the age-composition of existing machinery is unequal or if business conditions suggest a speeding up or a postponement of renewals, orders for replacement will exceed depreciation allowances in some years and fall short of them in other years. This discontinuity in the expenditure of depreciation allowances for capital replacements disturbs the smooth course of business activity and is responsible for fluctuations in employment and income. For, the piling up of depreciation funds is a 'sale without purchase,' as is any saving, and needs to be balanced in the same year by a replacement, which is a 'purchase without sale,' as is any investment. All this holds true even in the case of 'simple reproduction' and anticipates some famous quips by Keynes about sinking funds as a drag on the circulation of purchasing power. It can be seen that this line of argument is in accord with Malthus's general approach to the problem; however, Malthus had no theory of the structure of capital.

Unfortunately, Marx's equations, as Marxists themselves concede, are arithmetically incorrect. The numbers representing different amounts of capital designate labor values. Now, as we have already seen, values do not coincide with prices. Hence, in Marx's discussion of the market process, the capital values must be transformed into prices in order for the equations to be valid. Ladislaus von Bortkiewicz[12] has corrected them accordingly by determining the 'production prices' at which the rates of profit are equal. However, not only has he been led, in the process, through highly complicated exponential equations, but his conclusions are subject to the same criticism which we have already made of the whole procedure of transforming values into production prices. In addition he has had to give up the indispensable condition that the total gain of exploitation must only be redistributed but not changed in aggregate volume.

What follows from Marx's discussion is that if the free economy depends upon securing such complicated conditions of proportionality, disproportions are most likely to occur. Now it is essential to grasp the significance of these disproportions. Say's disproportionality theory was designed to prove the impossibility of a general crisis and to reduce whatever disturbances there might be to purely local difficulties. Moreover, since every glut in one place is balanced by a shortage in another, it is relatively easy for the factors of production to be shifted to those sections where they are needed. For this reason, the disproportionality crisis, if it is a crisis at all, is not only localized but temporary, and is by no means as catastrophic as the doctrine of the dialectic, not to speak of the political program of Marxism, would have it. Those Marxists (among them Hilferding) who hold to a disproportionality theory are, hence, denounced as renegades by the 'true' followers of Marx, who praise the sturdy theory of the falling rate of profit as the only 'true' revolutionary doctrine and relegate the proportionality equations to the status of exercises in hypothetico-deductive reasoning which could be useful only in a system of socialist planning.

But such a view is wrong. The two types of disproportion are

entirely different. In Say's system, the disproportion between supplies and demands occurs in a market in which industries compete in mere juxtaposition. In Marx's system, with its ingenious
division between producers' goods and consumers' goods industries, the disproportion occurs between two departments of
production, which are not only in competition for factors of
production and purchasing power, but in positive correlation,
because the production of consumers' goods presupposes the
previous production of producers' goods, and the production of
the latter logically implies the future production of the former—
neither can exist without the other. In other words, the disproportion posited by Marx is not simple, like that of Say, but
is integrated into the theory of underconsumption. The pressure
on wages, however this may be explained, and the accumulation
of capital out of profits, which is forced on the entrepreneurs by
the danger of competition from large-scale enterprises, hold consumption at a minimum, while the production of producers'
goods is speeded up until they no longer have any outlet.

A necessary disproportion resulting from underconsumption
is a sufficiently strong indictment of capitalism to satisfy any
socialist sentiment. Yet it is remarkable that this theory, although
it is indeed a theory of capital, is not a theory of labor value;
Marx's disproportionality theory presupposes only the fact of
profit but no special explanation of it. Orthodox Marxists still
cling to the antiquated and discredited labor theory of value;
but others are free to make full use of Marx's brilliant analyses
without feeling themselves bound by sectarian or other considerations to accept at the same time a theory whose correctness or
incorrectness in no way affects the validity of Marx's central
thesis.

2. THE MARXIST SCHOOL

The vitality of the original Marxian doctrine and the realistic
quality of his vision assert themselves even in the vitriolic discussion of his disciples concerning the correct interpretation of the

master's theories and their correct application to changing circumstances. It is significant of this discussion that the one doctrine exempt from it is the theory of labor value. To this day, it is held as a dogma of socialism, although no less a person than the martyred first leader of the German Communist Party, Karl Liebknecht,[13] did resolutely jettison the theory of labor value and built his system on the basis of modern value theory.

In other words, what really makes a man a Communist is not that he accepts the theory of labor value, but that he subscribes to the social doctrine according to which society is divided into two warring classes, the bourgeoisie and the proletariat, and to the political doctrine according to which the bourgeois state is to be replaced by a proletarian dictatorship over the bourgeoisie and finally by a harmonious classless society of proletarians after the 'withering away' of the state. (The social doctrine is partially, and the political doctrine completely, outside the scope of this book.) What makes a right-wing socialist, as opposed to a Communist, is the confidence that no hazardous and violent action will be required to bring this happy condition about.

The basic difference between the two schools of Marxist thought is philosophical. What we have said concerning the Marxian philosophy requires some qualification. It is true that a law of inexorable causal necessity is supposed to govern the growth of socialism as of anything else in history. But in his more specific discussions of practical issues, Marx was most emphatic in his insistence on the heavy responsibility of the revolutionists themselves in bringing about the wished-for consummation: there is no guarantee of ultimate success. Whether they succeed or fail in their endeavor will depend on their devotion and courage—they are free. Obviously, freedom and necessity cannot be reconciled in scientific logic but only on the transcendent plane of religious experience: it is a fundamental fact of human experience that man is both in the hands of God and responsible to Him. This dialectical equilibrium, which is really the intention of the original Marxian doctrine, has been broken by his successors; hence the cleavage between them.

The deterministic school—interpreting the doctrine of materialism in its narrow sense—believes that the natural and inevitable development of capitalism must lead to an all-proletarian society. Meanwhile, the workers must be educated, organized, and prepared for the day when they will have to take over the heritage of a system that has run its course and has become inoperative in the final crisis. The idealist-voluntaristic wing of Marxism, on the other hand, relies on revolutionary action to bring about the transition to socialism. Even though the capitalist system becomes economically inoperative, it may be so strongly entrenched politically in the armed organization of the bourgeois state that it can no longer be dislodged except by the most carefully planned and directed violent action. One cannot afford to wait until men and conditions are 'ripe'; they are the materials for the deliberate transformation of society into the all-proletarian pattern.

Within the right wing another cleavage developed, that between the orthodox, who looked forward to a democratic transition to a socialist society of proletarians, and the 'revisionists,' who denied that capitalism will ever make society completely proletarian and advocated the reconstitution of the working class as a special pressure group within capitalist democracy. The revisionists, however, did not develop any positive political program. On the other hand, the orthodox dream of an all-proletarian socialist society is dead, since late capitalist society is anything but all-proletarian. The only hope for the future can be in the gradual democratization of Communism.

The occasion for this hope arises from the menace of Fascism, which can be understood politically as the violent reintegration of crisis-stricken capitalist society in an anti-proletarian pattern. Fascism directs its appeal to all those whom Communism proposes to annihilate, both capitalist bourgeoisie and middle-class workers. Fascist political philosophy accepts much of the orthodox Communist criticism of bourgeois society and laissez-faire, including the indictment of liberty as a 'bourgeois pastime.' Fascism too finds in dictatorship the only solution to the crisis, but opposes a nationalist or racial dictatorship to the proletarian dictatorship. The Fascist philosophy implies the abandonment of the fundamental principles of spiritual perfection—whether this is achieved through religious experience or as the culmination of a preordained natural process—in favor of the doctrine that men are naturally divided into eternally hostile camps and interlocked in everlasting strife, in a world which knows no supreme spiritual standards of justice and peace. In view of this menace, a reform in the theory and practice of both capitalist democracy and Marxism appears possible. The central position of right-wing Marxism should facilitate such a development if it were not for the formidable enmity, for historical reasons, between the two wings.

In their discussions of economic theory the differences of opinion between the left and the right wings of Marxism were of minor significance and were arbitrarily inflated for political purposes. These differences, as we have already suggested, chiefly concern the theory of the business cycle, of which the Marxian disproportionality theory has been wrongly identified with reformism. Rudolf Hilferding,[14] who ended his life when the Vichy French handed him over to the Nazis, was the ablest of the Marxian economists. He elaborated the suggestions of Marx, not as a theory of disproportionality in general, but of one specific disproportion. The extra profits which accrue to those pioneering in technical progress must be largest in those branches of production in which the degree of mechanization is greatest and in which productivity increases the most. Hence, extra profits lead to overexpansion in the heavy industries, the leaders in both prosperity and depression. Hilferding put his argument more spectacularly by connecting it with the discredited Marxian law of the falling rate of profit, but this is unessential for his thesis, which presupposes nothing but a condition of disproportion: increasing employment in the heavy industries on orders for new machines induces an increasing demand for consumers' goods, while a falling off of employment in the heavy industries induces a falling off of demand for consumers' goods.

Hilferding's *Finanzkapital*, which is based on the somewhat exaggerated proposition that the concentration of industrial capital is prompted and controlled by the banks, the real masters of late capitalism, is a book in the grand style of Marxism—realistic, impassioned, and dogmatic. Its three main topics are, of course, monopoly, the business cycle, and tariffs. It had always been an objection to the theory of labor value that there are some prices, namely those fixed by monopoly, which are not determined by labor costs. As we have seen, monopoly price is, by definition, different from labor-value price, which prevails only under conditions of competition. Hilferding attempted to reconcile the existence of monopoly prices with the theory of labor value by showing how, within the frame of Marx's value theory, a redistribution of profits takes place among the industries in addition to that already described by Marx: monopoly price is at the expense of unmonopolized industries, which have to content themselves with less than the average rate of profit when buying monopolized materials. However, Hilferding admitted, in passing, that the ultimate consumers, regardless of what class they belong to, may also have to contribute to monopoly gains, and he made no attempt to reconcile this fact with the dogma of labor value.

The most impressive personality and the ablest economist of Western Communism is Rosa Luxemburg,[15] who, together with Liebknecht, was murdered by the forerunners of the Nazi storm troopers. Like too many others who have contributed to the strange and voluminous literature of Marxism, she took the magic proportionality formulas of Marx's second volume as a starting point for a speculative proof that capitalism must collapse because these conditions of equilibrium cannot be satisfied. She denied that consumption can increase at all in the process of capital accumulation—although, according to Marx, wage capital too is accumulated, but in continually decreasing proportion to the amount of fixed capital accumulated—and arrived at the conclusion that in a closed capitalist system, accumulation is impossible. The fact that capitalism has lived and grown can be explained only by the sale of goods unsalable within the capitalist economy to buyers outside the closed and glutted market. Capitalism can survive only as long as there are such buyers either in the home country or abroad; the system must expand or die, yet in expanding it destroys itself because the pre-capitalist markets are now absorbed into the orbit of capitalism. When this happens, the whole system will come to an end.

It is frequently objected that the sale of surplus products outside the domestic market will not solve the problem because these exports either bring more money into the capitalist country, and thereby cause inflation, or more import goods—and these even in a quantity greater than that of the goods exported, since the colonial markets are exploited—so that the excess goods return, but in a changed form. Yet this change of form may solve the domestic problem if consumers' goods are exchanged for such colonial raw materials as are useful for the expansion of production, which is the material form of the process of capital accumulation. The true objection to Luxemburg's doctrine is that it is based on the false presupposition that capital accumulation precludes any increase in consumption. Nevertheless, the theory that capitalism is forced into imperialist expansion has become classic through Rosa Luxemburg and through an earlier book by John Atkinson Hobson,[16] based on a popular, non-Marxian underconsumption theory. It is true that this thesis can be deduced by any modern theory from its doctrines of the crisis and of monopoly, which always include reference to the reduction of domestic sales and the consequent urge to the conquest of foreign markets. It is also true that Rosa Luxemburg was quite aware of Rodbertus's priority. However, she and Hobson have most effectively proclaimed and explained the theory of economic imperialism.

3. THE THEORY OF LIBERAL SOCIALISM: FRANZ OPPENHEIMER

The work of Franz Oppenheimer[17] does not properly come under the general heading of this chapter. The connecting link between him and Marxian socialism is not dialectics, but the theory of labor value as this was used by the socialists to criticize the capitalist system. In other words, Oppenheimer was a socialist in that he regarded profit as the gain of exploitation, to be proved as such by pure economic reasoning; but this reasoning is not Marxian: it follows the lead provided by suggestions of Turgot and Smith. Oppenheimer was a liberal in that he regarded as the source of exploitation not private property and the market, as Marx did, but monopoly. But Oppenheimer gave to the term 'monopoly' a far wider connotation than Marx did. The seat of monopoly is landed property. Oppenheimer's theory is thus 'geo-centrist' as opposed to the 'industry-centrism' of Ricardo and Marx. He derived his geo-centrism from the doctrines of Quesnay and Carey. The social liberalism of Carey is based on the idea of free land,—as the liberal socialism of his disciple Eugen Dühring[18] and of Oppenheimer himself is based on the idea that landed property is unfree. The landed property of feudalism, transformed into a capitalist monopoly, survives in capitalism and prevents the mechanism of the market from functioning naturally; if landed property were abolished, the operation of the market economy would produce a society of the free and equal with co-operatives in charge of large enterprises. These are the propositions which Oppenheimer's reasoning is intended to demonstrate. With a strong and original foundation in both economic theory and sociology, he revived militant, rationalistic liberalism.

In a society of equals a man appropriates only as much land

as he and his immediate family can use and till. As cultivation becomes more intensive, the unit of property per man becomes even smaller. If an employed man is dissatisfied with his condition, he can take unappropriated land and make himself independent. It is only in a slave society that it is reasonable for a man who belongs to the ruling class to appropriate more land than he can take care of by himself. Thus, a conquering tribe which reduces the conquered natives to slavery builds the state upon the foundation of private landed property monopolized by the ruling class and cultivated by the dispossessed. But when slavery is abolished, private property in land still persists, and the large estates remain in the hands of their owners; the important sociological difference between genuine bourgeois property, the result of personal work done, and the transformed feudal property, the land monopoly resulting from violent expropriation, is ignored. Hence, those rendered propertyless must seek employment on someone else's private property, landed or industrial, and will find employment only if they consent to accept a deduction from the product of their labors in favor of the proprietor. This deduction is the tribute of monopoly. In this manner, a 'class monopoly' is established in which all owners of land or capital share—a monopoly that can be broken only by opening up the unused private land to the public so that every man can establish himself as an independent, self-sufficient farmer or industrial producer. Statistical investigation shows that today even in many old countries, and much more in the United States and in the world at large, there is plenty of unused land—but privately owned. Marx too had explicitly stated the view that where the land is not appropriated, no capital property can be established, without, unfortunately, following up his own suggestions. And before him, Smith had described the American colonies as the country of free access to the land. Thus both Smith and Marx anticipated the frontier theory, which, in a sense, underlies Oppenheimer's system of thought.

Oppenheimer acknowledged his indebtedness to America's

Henry George,[19] who shared his ambition to restore the free-dom of the people through the freedom of the land. But the theoretical difference between the two points of view is wide indeed. Like all agrarian socialists, George directed his attack against the ground rent, which, making use of Ricardo's theory, he denounced as an unearned increment. He found the most spectacular illustration of his theory in the mushroom growth of American cities, which, without any effort on the part of the owners, suddenly added tremendous increases in rent to the lands of those fortunate enough to have selected the potentially favorable locations. He made a strong case in favor of the con-fiscation of all ground rent—not only of the rent accruing to present owners and their successors but even of the rent which accrued to past owners. However, he overlooked the fact that in purchasing the land, the present owners had to pay the capital-ized value of the rent which at that time accrued to the previ-ous owners; hence, the rent of the present owners is only the interest on the capital invested in the purchase of the land, and the whole of the present rent really accrues to the benefit of the previous owners, whose identity can no longer be ascertained. Oppenheimer rejected this limited and unequitable reform. According to him, the private appropriation of the land is re-sponsible not only for the rent which accrues to favored lands but for the profit on capital; both are the gain of a class monopoly.

It is interesting to note that Oppenheimer's theory of monop-oly is based on the theory of labor value—the only instance in the history of economics, since the principle of labor value, as the cost of production, is generally assumed to preclude the explanation of monopoly price, which exceeds the cost of pro-duction. However, what Oppenheimer calls 'monopoly' is not monopoly proper, i.e. monopoly in sale for the purpose of raising prices, but what is now called 'monopsony,' i.e. the monopoly of purchase for the purpose of forcing prices down. How far the seller monopolist can raise prices depends on the reaction of buyers, their purchasing power and tastes—'subjective' factors which are taken in consideration in the theory of 'subjective' value. But Oppenheimer justifiably claimed to have based his monopoly theory on the 'objective' concept of labor value. The time-honored argument employed to prove that products are exchanged among free producers in proportion to the labor-time spent in their production is that only under these conditions are incomes equal; as long as incomes are unequal in the different branches of production, producers in free competition will switch to those branches in which incomes are higher. Since the value of the product is such that the incomes of free producers are equal, the class monopoly enjoyed by the owners of land and capital will force down the wages of dependent workers from the value of the product to the minimum standard of living and will reserve to the monopoly as profit the difference between value and wage.

From these considerations the difference between the theory of Marx and that of Oppenheimer becomes evident. According to Marx, wage is the normal and legitimate exchange value of labor power without any deduction. According to Oppenheimer, wage is a price depressed from the value of the product by the pressure of the class monopoly. According to Marx, profit, then, is a normal and necessary income in the free market; according to Oppenheimer, only in a monopolized market; his point is that the mechanism of the market under capitalism is subject to the distorting influence of the monopoly of landed property. Marx had contended that profit is the result of the fact that labor produces more value than its own exchange value, and the purchaser of labor thus receives more value than he gives. It was Oppenheimer's view that profit is the gain of monopoly. From this comparison it can be seen that Oppenheimer's solution is far superior. The specific objections to Marx's theory of exploitation are not applicable to Oppenheimer's.

However, the difficulty in this, as in any, theory of labor value lies in the fact that profits are equal although capitals invested in different industries have different capacities for exploiting labor. As a way out of this difficulty Oppenheimer takes recourse to the concept of class monopoly: the share of any person in the monopoly is proportional to the specific value of the means of production which he owns. This solution is parallel to that of Marx, who uses the analogy of the joint stock corporation to explain the final distribution of profit in equal rates throughout the capitalist system. But here again Oppenheimer's solution is superior, since his concept of class monopoly is fundamental to his whole theory, whereas Marx had to resort to the introduction of an analogy. Yet there is one specific difficulty in Oppenheimer's solution. The value of the land cannot, without generating a vicious circle, figure in the formation of the rate of interest, because the value of land is determined by capitalizing the ground rent at the prevailing rate of interest. This is the obstacle which Turgot had failed to overcome. Oppenheimer withdrew to Ricardo's position that land as such yields only the differential rent, and it is from the value of the capital equipment that landed property derives its share in the profit of the class monopoly. But even so, mere reference to the class monopoly does not constitute an explanation of the mechanism which equalizes unequal profits. Such an explanation is not found in Oppenheimer's system of thought beyond the already familiar assurance that competition so distributes capital among the different branches of production as to make all profits equal. Thus Oppenheimer's theory does not escape the fatal weakness of every theory of labor value; it is open to the same fundamental objection that attaches to Marx's version and indeed must attach to any version: no theory of labor value can explain the fact that profits are proportional to the total capital invested rather than to the number of workers exploited.

Yet this objection to his reasoning does not prove that Oppenheimer's basic thesis is wrong. The uncovering of fundamental facts in the sociological organization of economic life cannot fail to affect the results of economic reasoning. Oppenheimer held that because large tracts of land are privately owned, those without property leave the land for the freedom of the cities, thus making wages lower and profits higher than they would otherwise be. He proved that this huge migration is not from the densely populated peasant areas, but from the thinly settled areas of large landed estates in eastern Germany, southern Italy, Ireland, and Poland, to the industrial areas of these same countries and to America. This theory needs some modification in order to be applicable to the United States, where the prevalent one-crop system deprives the small landowner of that economic independence which in Oppenheimer's view is the peculiar virtue of small holdings.

The overcrowding of the cities and the consequent distortion of the structure of incomes from its natural form—in a word, capitalism—are thus brought about by a reserve army different from the permanent, self-perpetuating reserve army postulated in the Marxian theory. The industrial reserve army of capitalism is nourished by the 'surplus population' of the feudal areas—those who cannot stand the social and economic pressure of the country-side—and is thus merely a transitional phenomenon bound to disappear as soon as these areas have been completely depopulated or reorganized as freeholds. And since it is this reserve army that sets the profit mechanism in motion, capitalism itself will vanish with it. Meanwhile, the existence of the reserve army, the result of a distortion of natural economic forces, leads to further distortions that culminate in the economic crisis. For the entrepreneurs use the reserve army to increase their output in order to maintain aggregate profits as the rate of profit declines. Thus, the market is ruined by an action that seems rational from the point of view of the private producer, although in fact the fall in prices is a signal to all that production must be curtailed. However, this argument is not cogent because even in the absence of a reserve army the individual producer faced with a falling income per unit of his product can increase his output through the prolongation of his workday. On the other hand, it is doubtful whether capitalist producers do increase their output in the face of falling prices, except in the isolated instance of farmers. And if output were increased, the crisis might be remedied instead of aggravated. Finally, Oppenheimer described only a possible reaction to falling prices; he did not explain why prices fall. Yet the story of the reserve army is not thereby refuted.

4. IS THE THEORY OF EXPLOITATION REFUTED?

The labor-value theory in all its versions is untenable. It cannot provide a solution to the increasingly important problem of the seller's monopoly, which raises prices above labor costs. Nor, as we have seen, do the prices of goods sold in international trade represent equivalent amounts of labor-time. And prices and profits cannot be explained on the basis of the theory of labor value.

In the socialist economic system of our own day, on the other hand, profit appears as a legitimate form of income. Indeed, it is demanded of the managers of socialist enterprises as a test of their ability. In terms of economic theory the fact of socialist profit can no more be explained by the contention that this income is needed to provide a fund for the accumulation of social capital, than can the fact of private profit under capitalism be explained as a fund for private accumulation. What matters from the point of view of economic theory is not the use to which profit is put but the existence of profit. After all, a fund for capital accumulation in a socialist system could be collected through taxes even in the absence of profit. But what is contrary to the assumptions of socialist theory is that the existence of profit in a system without capitalist private property should be natural and legitimate.

Hence, capitalism cannot be defined in terms of the existence of profit or socialism in terms of the absence of profit. The difference between the two systems is not economic but social. Capital exists and profit arises in both systems; capital belongs, and profit accrues, to a separate class of private owners in the capitalist system and to the entire community—however this may be organized

—in the socialist system. This difference in the distribution of incomes involves a difference in incentives between the two economic systems and thus may lead to a difference in efficiency and stability, i.e. among other things, a difference in the size of the output. But there is a complete parallelism between the capitalist and the socialist systems with regard to economic functions. Construing the organized socialist community as a corporation, one can say that as a worker the citizen gets his wage and as a shareholder his dividend; his total income is then the full value of his product, although he, or the organs of the corporation acting for him, may decide not to distribute the profit but to save and reinvest it immediately, as in a capitalist system. That the worker-citizen receives the full value of his product reveals the economic nature of a system which distinguishes two income streams even though they flow to the same recipient; it is the economic function that distinguishes them even where the distinction implies no corresponding distinction in the social classes of the recipients. What the distinction between the two streams of income does imply is that capital fulfils a specific economic function of its own. This, it will be remembered, is precisely the thesis of Senior; and the problem of a rate of profit independent of the technological capacity of capital for the employment of manual labor is automatically solved. Senior himself, of course, had conceived his theory as a refutation of socialism. The exactly parallel structure of socialism and capitalism with regard to economic functions seems to have suggested itself vaguely to Mill, but was clearly expressed only later by Friedrich von Wieser.

The result is a real anti-climax to the bitter debates concerning labor value and exploitation. According to Marx or Oppenheimer, the worker is exploited because, and as long as, he does not own the means of production. But the same inference can be drawn from the theory of Senior, or indeed from that of any 'bourgeois' economist (i.e. one who holds that capital makes a positive contribution to the total value of the product): if the worker does not own the capital, he receives only the wage; if he does own the capital, he also receives the profit. The two opposed economic theories lead to the same social result.

On the other hand, it should be evident from the existence of profit in Socialist Russia that a vindication of capitalism is not necessarily implied in the thesis that profit is the equivalent of the value of the contribution made by capital to the total value of the product. Indeed, from this thesis the precise contrary may properly be inferred. Why should the contribution of impersonal capital become anyone's personal income? With regard to land rent this conclusion has often been drawn. (Of course, the nationalization of land is far from the nationalization of farms or houses.) It is true that land is not produced and capital is, in the sense that individual saving sets factors of production free to produce capital goods rather than goods for immediate individual consumption. All orthodox reasoning rests on the assumption of a direct connection between individual saving and the conditions for the expansion of production and draws a conclusion favorable to private ownership. But, in the first place, the argument reaches less far than is generally believed, as can be seen from Senior's and Mill's opposition to private inheritance. In the second place, there is no logical reason why only private persons should save. The moral question of exploitation and the political question of the choice between capitalism and socialism are independent of the economic question of the function and origin of capital, although both Senior and Marx believed the contrary.

Economic theory is thus deprived of much of the impassioned and sensational interest which the discussion of fundamental decisions concerning the social system naturally arouses. Economics is a purely technical branch of knowledge, and all those who are sincerely interested in its problems should be able to concur in the results of their reasoning without fear that they may be trapped into accepting a decision concerning the organization of society which they would not otherwise have accepted. It is a myth typical of this age that the answer to the technical problem of the productivity of capital must determine the political decision between capitalism and socialism—that in fact there is no genuine political decision to be made. Once this myth is exploded we are free to realize that the fundamental political decision between capitalism and socialism is a moral problem.

VII. Historicism and Institutionalism

THE Historical School never achieved a quite clear formulation of its doctrine. The one thing that can be said of this school with certainty is that it represents a reaction against classical theory. The members of the Historical School criticized the classical theorists for their narrow approach to economic life, based upon a crude hedonistic psychology, and especially for their contention that this approach leads to strict laws. The method of the classical economists is deductive: by reasoning from a limited number of premises, they claim strict validity for their logical conclusions. They take as the premise of their reasoning the basic human motive of self-interest, but in its narrow, pecuniary form; all the classical economists explicitly accept the utilitarian philosophy and base their method upon it. However, according to the Historical School, the experience of history provides abundant evidence of the great richness and diversity of human motives, traditions, and forms of economic organization and confutes the argument of the classical economists that there is a natural law of economic life. The Historical School called the classical method 'mechanical' and opposed to it an 'organic' method that takes account of the manifold forms and conditions of economic growth. The program of the Historical School called for an inductive method in accordance with which the individual causes of any phenomenon are first investigated in order to provide the data for generalizations, so far as there can be any. The name of the school was inspired by the success of the historical method in the fields of law and language, and it is significant that the German branch of this school also liked to call itself 'ethical' to denote its critical attitude towards utilitarianism.

It is strange, however, that the founders of the so-called Older Historical School, Wilhelm Roscher,[1] Bruno Hildebrand,[2] and Karl Knies,[3] though engaging in a spirited discussion of these methodological principles, remained on the plane of theory in their own scholarly work. All they did towards putting their declared principles into practice was to intersperse their theoretical studies with historical material for illustration, much in the manner of Adam Smith before them and Karl Marx after them; Ricardo was the main target of their criticism. Moreover, both the older writers and the younger school, which centered around Gustav von Schmoller[4] and Lujo Brentano,[5] often fell into the danger of blaming the errors and inconsistencies of classical economists solely on their method, although no one would ever have denied that for the logical conclusions of deductive reasoning to be adequate to the facts the careful selection and verification of the premises is a vital and easily overlooked prerequisite. It was only the Younger Historical School that turned its back on economic theory and launched those monumental studies in economic history which opened new horizons of knowledge and understanding and need no methodological justification. Schmoller, Brentano, Georg Friedrich Knapp,[6] and Karl Buecher[7] are the leading historians of the older generation, and even they were surpassed by Max Weber[8] and Werner Sombart[9] in the younger generation. In England the movement was paralleled by the work of William Cunningham[10] and J. W. Ashley.[11] The methodological controversy between Schmoller and Carl Menger,[12] the spokesman of neo-classical orthodoxy, long conducted with verve and even with some bitterness, gradually came to an end for lack of a real problem when it was recognized that the two points of view complement each other.

The members of the Historical School were united in their insistence upon the need for measures of governmental intervention in the economic system. Their opposition to the policy of laissez-faire follows from their methodological position; in the absence of a natural law—whether of harmony or not—that governs the economic order, the way is open for the deliberate intervention of the government in shaping the economic process to the desired social ends. And such intervention is rendered necessary by the unfortunate consequences of adhering to the principle of laissez-faire in conformity with the doctrine of natural harmony. In Germany the school proudly accepted the name 'socialists of the chair' bestowed on them by the members of the Manchester School, and it was a powerful force in inquiring into social conditions and in stimulating social legislation. Likewise the works of Emile Levasseur[13] on labor in France and even more of Sidney and Beatrice Webb[14] on labor and trade unionism in England have become classics.

The influence of the school in general was on the conservative side, although many of its famous teachers, particularly Brentano and Max Weber, were sturdy liberals, who insisted that progress can be achieved by relying rather on reason than on tradition. Schmoller, the most influential member of the group, placed great emphasis on the plasticity of economic life and studied the state archives in order to demonstrate the blessings of an enlightened and benevolent bureaucracy. It alone could guide and mould the forces of society and secure for the people a justice that could never be achieved by the pursuit of a policy of laissez-faire. Friedrich List, though of different philosophical and political inclinations, was cited as an authority against free trade and, despite his declared intentions to the contrary, in favor of all-round protection. Social conservatism became the German reaction to classical liberalism and found a scholarly basis in the teachings of the historians. The climax of this movement was reached when Knapp wrote not an economic theory, but a *State Theory of Money*. According to the very first sentence of his book, 'money is a creature of the legal order.' Thus the way was blocked for the study of the economic function and properties of money, although many brilliant observations were made concerning the regulation of money by the authorities.[15] The illusion that the government has the power to control money contributed towards the spectacular blunders of the German post-war inflation and was thereby effectively blasted. Schmoller himself lamented on his deathbed that the younger generation—educated by him—no longer knew the theory of free trade, that is, the doctrine of the more or less autonomous process of economic life.

As a matter of fact, the Historical School seriously erred in denying the existence of what it called mechanical laws of economic life and in insisting that man is motivated by ethical and other impulses different from what he conceives to be his own interests. Social groups are driven by selfish interests, economic and other (although it is generally overlooked that these, naturally vague, become determinate only in the light of the total set of values, and may be sublimated to a certain extent). Man almost never acts against what he conceives to be his true interests and usually interprets these narrowly. In the second place, and still more important, economic reality presents itself as a complex of determinate prices that bear to one another calculable, i.e. arithmetical, relations: the cost of satisfying any impulse is, in a system of money prices, mathematically commensurable with the cost of satisfying every other impulse. Whatever may be the motives leading to the decision concerning which impulse shall be satisfied, the result influences the decisions of other people and the economic system as a whole only through a change in money prices, which are numerical indices of the relative weights of different choices. These are the hard facts of economic life recognized by the classical economists, and the Historical School was simply being unrealistic in denouncing the 'materialism' of classical economic theory. Max Weber more than any one else was aware of this.

There were other members of the Historical School who did not disdain economic theory. The business-cycle theory of Arthur Spiethoff[16] is a fully developed theory arising from the very center of the school. It is true that Spiethoff follows the inductive line of research laid down by his school and more specifically the program of business-cycle research devised by the French statistician Clément Juglar,[17] who must be honored as the first man to investigate the cyclical movement of booms and depressions as opposed to the mere interruption of a steady movement by crises. But generalization led Spiethoff to theoretical interpretation. He emerged from decades of study of the historical and statistical material with what soon became one of the classical types of business-cycle theory. He attributes the upswing to technological innovations and the opening of new markets, and the downswing to the disproportion between the value of 'real capital'—machines and other equipment—and the money capital available to buy it. Since machines are used and are fit to be used over an extended period of time, it is difficult to estimate the demand for them before the production of real capital has already been encouraged beyond the proper measure; on the other hand, the formation of money capital out of savings is slowed down by the rise of wages in the later phase of the boom. Hence, the prices of the products of the heavy industries fall, and this leads to a disturbance of the whole system.

This theory, which suggests as the immediate cause of the economic crisis not underconsumption, but overconsumption at the end of the boom, is incomplete. Spiethoff's theory of the business cycle is not, and is not intended to be, a comprehensive system of thought embracing the whole of economic reality, but is simply an attempt at an explanation of one phase of economic life. No reference is made to the larger framework in which a disproportion can occur between the value of real capital and the amount of money capital without being corrected by the free play of prices. Spiethoff frankly states that the upswing requires additional workers and additional money capital. Where do they come from? In the traditional system depicted by classical theory there is no idle capital and there are no idle workers because interest and wages rise or fall to the point at which all the factors of production are absorbed. Spiethoff attributed the crisis to a disproportion between the value of real capital and the money capital available for its purchase. But why does not a rise in the rate of interest elicit enough additional money capital, and why does not the fall in the price of the real capital in relation to that of consumption goods diminish the supply, raise the demand, and produce a new equilibrium? Such questions do not refute Spiethoff's theory or belittle his performance; they do show that there is no room in traditional economics for this special, dynamic theory of the business cycle. A dynamic system of economic theory is required to explain those facts which in Spiethoff's theory are taken as the causes of the economic crisis.

In this country, the counterpart of European Historicism is Institutionalism. It differs from Historicism in its philosophy and political conclusions, but not in its methodological objections to classical economic theory. It is the legitimate offspring of that Pragmatism which is the original and characteristic contribution of America to philosophy. To the historical idea of organic growth, with its conservative implications, Institutionalism accordingly opposes the idea of experimentation and the courage for it. The procedure of the Institutionalist school is piecemeal; its tendency is to be critical of tradition and to favor reform.

Nothing can be more remote from this pragmatic spirit than the idea of a closed structure of thought, a systematic theory. It is true that through Francis A. Walker, F. W. Taussig, Frank H. Knight,[18] and in particular John Bates Clark and Irving Fisher, America has made important contributions to classical and neo-classical theory. But this is tantamount to saying that there is nothing specifically American in the work of these economists. Thorstein Veblen,[19] on the other hand, is most unmistakably American, although there is in his thinking something of that bitter and contemptuous skepticism which is also an element of Fascist thought. As a critic of formidable erudition and keenness of mind, Veblen has rightly been compared with Marx; as a combination of economist, sociologist, historian, and anthropologist, he ranks with the great teachers of Historicism in Europe;

and as a prophet of impending disaster, he is immeasurably superior to them. He did not live to see the realization of his somber prophecy.

Veblen is not the only economist produced by Institutionalism. Its method is conspicuous in John R. Commons'[20] treatment of capitalism in terms of its legal foundations; and on this basis he and his school did for American labor what the Webbs had done for British labor. Spiethoff's counterpart in America is Wesley C. Mitchell,[21] whose standard work on business cycles appeared years before Spiethoff's summary of his findings, although later than his preliminary studies. And Mitchell is in a way more radical than Spiethoff: he does not aim at a final theory but is content to survey the many rival theories and then proceeds to display and sift his enormous mass of material. His book stimulated innumerable factual and statistical studies and provided them with guiding points of view. As a result, every economic theorist is under heavy obligation to the work of the Institutionalists.

VIII. Neo-Classicism

1. THE UNIFICATION OF THE SYSTEM THROUGH UTILITY VALUE

THE growing difficulties that revealed themselves in the system of classical economics naturally suggested a search for a different approach. Cost and labor-value theories had been introduced to deal with the economic paradox stated by Adam Smith; he had thereby departed from the traditional theory of value as utility which had developed with the growth of economic thought. However, this tradition had not been broken. The suggestions of Galiani and the system of Condillac were so elaborate and so obviously correct that they could easily have become serious rivals of the classical system. Say unified the factors of production under the category of utility, which, as we have seen, is the logical alternative to reducing them to labor value, as Ricardo had done. Lauderdale in England, Longfield in Ireland, and Thuenen in Germany developed the productivity theory of the factors of production: their utility is derived from their productivity. The decisive discovery, however, had already been made by Galiani, who anticipated the solution of Smith's economic paradox and so found the key to the new system: the scarcer a good is, the more useful is its acquisition; hence, scarcity coincides with utility. Thus, the alleged conflict between the high utility of bread and its low cost could now be resolved. The utility theory was clearly the alternative to the cost theory. This idea was further developed by Auguste Walras[1] and Senior, but its elaboration was strangely delayed by the authority of the classical theory, and when at last the system of utility value was introduced, it appeared revolutionary.

In the same year, 1871, Carl Menger[2] in Vienna and William

Stanley Jevons[3] in England independently published the new value theory. Jevons based his theory on utilitarian psychology and developed it in terms of a calculus of pleasures and pains. Menger, on the other hand, did not seek a psychological explanation for the individual's valuations but took them as data; this approach recommended itself to him because of its methodological expediency. Three years later, Leon Walras,[4] a Frenchman teaching at Lausanne, propounded practically the same theory—but even more far-reaching in scope—in mathematical terms after having taught it for several years. It soon became apparent that if the credit for the achievement was certainly to be ascribed to all three founders of the theory—and for its further development, to their younger associates and successors: Eugen von Boehm-Bawerk[5] and Friedrich Freiherr von Wieser[6] in Austria; Vilfredo Pareto,[7] an Italian marquess who became Walras's successor at Lausanne; and John Bates Clark[8] at Columbia University—the actual priority belongs to a completely forgotten German theorist who had died in despair over his utter failure to find any response to his fully elaborated system: Hermann Heinrich Gossen.[9] Indeed, the two fundamental laws are now often quoted as the first and second laws of Gossen.

The coincidence that the four doctrines were developed independently was quite properly regarded as the sign of their probable correctness. Meanwhile, a fifth independent source was added: Alfred Marshall,[10] who had gradually developed this theory, from 1867 on, in the course of his incomparably influential teaching career, although his *Principles* first appeared only in 1890. However, he did not represent himself as in any way an innovator; a contemporaneous reviewer (quoted by Keynes) described his book as 'an ingenious attempt to disclaim any credit for discovering it [the truth] on the ground that it was all implicitly contained in the works of earlier writers, especially Ricardo,' and also Thuenen and the Frenchman Cournot. Thus the development of the theory of value as utility appears, if less wondrous, certainly more rational; modern theory, far from revolutionizing classical teachings, rather completes them by adding a neglected element.

The logic of this development can easily be appreciated. To start with Ricardo: market prices deviate from natural prices because goods are not produced in precisely those quantities 'which the wants and desires of people demand.' If these demands were precisely filled by the quantity of goods produced, prices would coincide with values. It appears, then, that value is not something which attaches to any unit of a particular commodity by virtue of the labor time spent in producing it, but only inasmuch as it is a unit of a definite total supply, although Ricardo does not bother to inquire into the factors determining that correct supply. Marshall calls this the 'normal supply.' Marx too recognized utility as a precondition of value. 'Value in exchange,' he said, presupposes 'value in use'; and hence, a quantity of goods will sell at their value only if they are 'proportionate to wants.' And it is this proportionality, which classical theory only postulated as the condition of value, that the modern theory precisely analyzes.

Because of approaching satiation, the satisfaction derived from the consumption of goods increases less in proportion to the quantity consumed; that is, the increment of satisfaction is smaller with each additional unit. This idea is implied in Galiani's concept of scarcity as a ratio. Each additional unit consumed has a diminishing utility; the last has what Wieser called the 'marginal utility,' the smallest in the declining range. (The concept of the margin—though without the name—had already been employed by the productivity theorists Longfield and Thuenen, and even by Ricardo in his discussion of rent, but Gossen was the first to apply this concept to utility and thus became the real founder of the modern theory of value.) Any unit of a given quantity is appraised like the marginal unit and therefore has the same utility; for, if any unit is removed, whatever may have been its original place in the range of diminishing utilities, the result is as if only the marginal unit were removed; that is, only the marginal utility is lost. Accordingly, the value of any individual unit is equal to the marginal utility. This is Gossen's first law. In graphic presentation, if the x-axis represents quantity and the y-axis represents utility, the utility curve will slope down as quantity increases. So does the individual's demand curve for the commodity in question; for the demand curve is derived from the utility curve on the assumption that the individual knows his total income and the prices of all the other goods which he might wish to buy; then he can decide how much of the commodity to buy at any of the different prices at which it may be offered for sale.

However, although the value of each unit of the supply of goods is determined by its marginal utility, the value of the total quantity of a good is not found simply by multiplying the marginal utility by the number of units; for this procedure would fail to take into account the fact that the units diminish in utility as they increase in number. The proper procedure for appraising the value of the total quantity of a good is to sum up the successively decreasing utilities of all the units in the supply from the first down to the marginal unit. In graphic representation, the value of the total supply is not the rectangle formed by marginal value and quantity, but the larger integral formed by the area under the total curve. We can then see that if total value is equal to infinity, this is still compatible with marginal value equaling zero. Any particle of atmospheric air, for example, is completely valueless, is a free good, while the value of the whole is infinite.

A self-sufficient Robinson Crusoe must so apply his strength and time as to make the marginal values of all the goods he produces equal if he is to derive maximum satisfaction from them; the same holds for an individual in a money economy who is to spend his income so that the marginal units of money spent in different goods bring him equal satisfaction. This is Gossen's second law, which defines the proportionality suggested by Marx: it is the maximum satisfaction attainable under given circumstances. Much time and energy was wasted by the Austrians in determining the correct psychological interpretation of this law, but what matters for economic theory is the actions and reactions of men, and these are quite clear. A purified and streamlined version of the psychological theory was given by Philip Wicksteed.[11]

As more money or labor becomes available for allocation among various goods, the amount to be allocated to each must be continually redetermined because of the differences among commodities in the rate at which additional units diminish in utility. The demand curves of the same individual for different goods—given the unit of measurement—begin at different value altitudes (i.e. points on the y-axis of utility) and slope down with different degrees of steepness, depending upon the relative importance attached to any further increment in the quantity of a given commodity. This is Marshall's concept of elasticity of demand. The measure of elasticity is taken as unity when price and quantity vary in inverse proportion, so that total price remains unchanged for different quantities. This condition can be graphically represented by a rectangular hyperbola, the curve of the equation $xy = 1$, where x represents quantity and y represents price. A demand curve which is flatter than this hyperbola is then said to have an elasticity greater than 1, and a steeper demand curve is called relatively inelastic. An elasticity greater or smaller than 1 obtains if, as the supply increases, money is withdrawn from other uses or released for them. The mathematical-statistical investigation of elasticity of demand has become an important field of study under the leadership of Henry Schultz[12] of the University of Chicago.

The grave and insuperable difficulty in value theory is that psychic intensities cannot be objectively measured; one can say that one thing is preferable to another, but not by how much. To a certain extent this difficulty can be evaded by expressing valuations in terms of the prices which men are willing to pay. But this mode of reasoning leads to a vicious circle because it presupposes that individuals already know the prices they have to pay for commodities—prices which are theoretically the indices of their valuations. This difficulty is avoided by the use of in-difference curves (or substitutability curves), which were first devised by Marshall for the purpose of solving a special problem and then further developed by Francis Ysidro Edgeworth[13] and most successfully by Irving Fisher[14] and Pareto. In a system the axes of which represent two commodities, the indifference curve is the locus for all those combinations of different quantities of the two which have equal aggregate utility; thus, it indicates how many units of the second commodity must be substituted for a given number of units of the first commodity in order for the aggregate utility to remain constant. The farther the substitution progresses, the lower will become the rate of substitution (the ratio in which varying quantities of the second are substituted for varying quantities of the first), in accordance with the law of decreasing satisfaction. If we start from another quantitative combination of the two goods, the total utility of which is either higher or lower than that of the first combination, we shall, of course, arrive at a different curve. A system of such curves is then required to provide a complete picture of one person's valuations. In a given situation a similar curve can be drawn to represent the relation between the utility of one commodity and that of all others, which can also be represented by money. This would then be the refined demand curve for that commodity in terms of money, which, however, differs from the usual demand curve. But there seems to be no special harm in using the simpler version for the correct one.

According to classical theory, a product has value to the extent that cost factors are incorporated in it; according to modern theory, cost factors have value, i.e. are useful, to the extent that their product is useful and valuable. Naturally, according to both theories, the value of the product is equal to the sum of the values of the factors producing it. The value of a unit of a cost factor, according to modern theory, is determined by the marginal value of its product; but since the same cost factor can be used in different industries to produce different commodities, the value of the unit of a cost factor will depend on the marginal utility of each of its possible products. In a state of perfect equilibrium, in which all the factors of production are so utilized as to secure maximum satisfaction, these marginal utilities are all equal. The greater the number of industries in which a factor of production is used, the more such marginal units of the factor, all equal in value, there will be. Wieser concluded that the aggregate value of a limited quantity of a cost factor is determined by multiplying the marginal value of each unit by the total number of units. This conclusion is contrary to the accepted proposition that the aggregate value is an integral, and the question was raised whether Wieser's procedure is correct. As usual in such controversies, the issue can be settled by making the proper discriminations and qualifications: what Wieser had in mind was a quantity all units of which are equal, for the reason stated above.

The elaboration of the marginal-utility theory made possible a more precise definition of the cost concept, about which there are two or three different opinions. Since the commodities to the production of which the same cost factors can be allocated do not have equal utilities for the consumers, the cost factors will be allocated to, and used up in, the production of the commodity with the highest utility not yet secured. If all the rest of the commodities to which cost factors could have been allocated are now ranged in the order of diminishing utility, we can define the cost of a commodity in terms of the satisfaction which could have been derived from the consumption of the commodity next in line, that is, the one differing in utility by the smallest margin from the last consumed commodity. In other words, the cost of one form of satisfaction is the next satisfaction which would have to be foregone in the order of diminishing utilities. This is Wieser's theory: marginal value equals marginal cost. The American theorist H. J. Davenport[15] has introduced the term 'opportunity cost' to designate the best opportunity which would have to be foregone below the margin of realization. It has already been noted that many products are related to one another because the same cost factors can be allocated to their production. In the same way, all goods are interrelated through the use of money, which makes them arithmetically commensurable. What any commodity costs us is the satisfaction we could have derived from the one we should have liked to buy next if we had not already spent the available money. Wieser rightly felt that in this way a world composed of nothing but utilities, and unified thereby, is substituted for the purely cost world of classical theory.

However, this theory suffers from a serious deficiency in that it presupposes a given stock of cost factors instead of explaining it. Accordingly, Gossen, the most radical proponent of the pleasure-pain calculus, and Jevons, his successor, using the same method, opposed the idea of disutility to that of utility. Productive work beyond a certain limit becomes increasingly tiresome, even though the pressure of needs may drive a man on to further work. A man will extend his work to the point at which the utility of its product or of its wage is precisely offset by the disutility of further effort. The intersection of the rising disutility curve with the falling utility curve determines the amount of work done, and thus there is added to the theory of marginal utility one dimension that the Austrians neglected. It is not a valid objection to this theory to assert that disutility has an effect on the total supply only at the point where the disutility exceeds the opportunity cost: this situation always prevails at the margin of the supply of the factor. But since disutility is the opposite of utility, the Austrians were right in replacing the concept of the negative utility of work by the concept of the positive utility of leisure, which is the opposite of work, and concluded that, when production is stopped, the utility of leisure must be equal to all other marginal utilities. The same reasoning can be applied to the disutility of the act of saving—refraining from consumption—and to its equivalent, the utility of having savings rather than consumption goods. In this way, the unification of the utility and the disutility systems can be achieved, and for all practical purposes the two coincide.

Against these psychological approaches to the problem of cost, Marshall maintained and reinterpreted the classical theory. 'Real cost' is the amount which must be sacrificed in order to produce the supply of goods or factors of production in the desired quantity. Cost is thus the correlate of demand in the determination of the economic process. In a famous simile, Marshall likened cost and demand to a pair of scissors, whose two blades co-operate in the cutting, although either one alone seems to do all the work when the other remains fixed. The psychological theories of cost must take recourse to technical coefficients of production, e.g. the proportions of labor, ore, coal, etc. that go into a ton of steel, in order to determine how much disutility accompanies the production of any one utility.

Marshall's cost studies have become important. On the one hand, he restored, after a century of discussion, Turgot's unified law of returns, according to which increasing and diminishing returns are but two phases of one development. On the other hand, he gave much attention to the problem of increasing returns. As Cournot had already pointed out, these make competitive equilibrium impossible and seem to lead to monopoly because the larger firm with increasing returns is in a position to increase its advantage over its smaller competitors. Marshall distinguished two categories of reasons for increasing returns, one external and the other internal. The external reasons include improvements in transportation facilities, in the training of workers, etc. and all other benefits which accrue to all firms in the field and hence do not affect their relative competitive positions. Thus, the problem is reduced to one of internal economies. Marshall treated this problem in two ways. In the first place, he introduced the concept of the 'representative firm.' There is a limit, according to Marshall, to the growth of a firm even when conditions are favorable and returns increase. The firm does not simply enlarge automatically. 'The trees cannot grow into the sky,' said Marshall; that is, the vitality of a business firm, which may have asserted itself vigorously in its youth even against adverse conditions, gradually becomes exhausted. In the second place, Marshall introduced the concept of imperfect competition. Products do not compete solely on the basis of price. Each firm tries to take its product out of competition, as it were, by using a brand name and claiming for the product some distinctive feature which makes it unique and incomparable with other products in the same field. Thus, a firm may acquire certain advantages, such as the loyalty of consumers to its brand, which cannot be competed away. Up to a certain point, these advantages may even offset those of increasing returns accruing to a larger competitor. It should be noted that the introduction of the concept of imperfect competition is tantamount to the abandonment of the classical theory of value. Marshall's theory thus takes cognizance of the ever widening area of goods manufactured and distributed with trade marks. Although he himself did not follow up his observations, others did later.

The theory of price follows from the theory of value and cost. Exchange takes place as long as each of the parties engaged in the transaction thinks that what he is getting is more valuable than what he is giving; the exchange stops at the point where one of the parties considers—or both do—the values of the items exchanged to be equal. The market price of a commodity is that price at which the supply of it and the demand for it are equal. If the demand for the commodity falls short of the supply offered for sale at a certain price, the result will be a fall in price in order to equalize demand and supply. If, on the other hand, the demand exceeds the supply, the price will rise until demand falls off and equilibrium is reached. Prices move in accordance with the schedules of demand and cost. Boehm-Bawerk was thus led to formulate price theory in terms of the marginal pairs of buyers and sellers. This can be seen from the accompanying table, which is based on the assumption of discontinuous demand schedules.

Highest price bids of demanders:	300	290	260	245	227	210			
Lowest price demands of suppliers:							220	260	
	100	110	150	170	200	205	200	180	170

Price settles in the interval between the bids of the weakest purchaser whose contribution is needed for equalization of the
market and the strongest demander who is excluded, and between the demands of the least eager seller and the most eager
supplier who cannot sell.

The difficulty in all these formulations of price theory is
that sellers rarely come to the market with a fixed price in mind
below which they will not sell, except when, as in a rural horse
market, they can use the commodity themselves if they do not
succeed in finding a buyer at the price they set. The situation is
different when a disutility or real cost is involved, i.e. when the
commodity has no value to the seller but costs him something
either to purchase or to produce. The device of intersecting curves,
one representing demand and the other cost, with price at the
intersection, was first used, even before Jevons, by Fleeming
Jenkin, a British engineer.[16] This is the classical law of price in
modernized version, in which demand and supply, instead of
being regarded as fixed magnitudes, are conceived as schedules.

The classical distinction between market price and 'normal'
price presupposes a period of time for the adjustment of the
relationship between demand and supply. Marshall elaborated
this element of classical theory. Momentary price prevails when
supply is not given time enough to react to demand; the supply
available is then regarded as 'given,' i.e. as fixed. The concept of
the short-run price presupposes that the existing facilities of production are more or less fully utilized in response to demand.
The long-run price emerges once the size of the industry or
firm concerned has been adjusted—by expansion or contraction
—to the supply-and-demand conditions of the market. This
doctrine has been generally accepted. Cost plays no part in determining momentary price, which is governed exclusively by
demand. However, cost does govern short-run and long-run
prices. Over the short period, the cost schedule is fixed; in the
long run it is changeable. Finally, there are secular price movements in response to changes in knowledge, population, technology, etc.

The fact that demand and supply take the form of schedules makes possible the inclusion of monopoly price in general price theory. Here Marshall leaned on Augustin Cournot, famous French mathematician and one of the most ingenious writers on economics.[17] Three decades before the development of modern value theory, and without any interest in the special problem of economic value, Cournot had taught that an exact approach to economics can be made only by studying the behavior of the individual firm, not by generalizing about the effects of competition. The simplest case, then, is that of the monopolist who is free to sell either more at a lower price or less at a higher price. As he is in quest of maximum profit, his decision will be dictated by the elasticity of demand and cost; he must determine whether the quantity sold will increase more or less rapidly in proportion to the decrease in price and how the increase of output will affect cost and thereby the profit per unit. He will select that combination of price and quantity which yields the greatest profit. Cournot developed the theory by assuming that the monopolist sets the quantity and observes the reaction of the price; Marshall, by assuming that the monopolist sets the price and observes the reaction of the quantity, i.e. the number of units that could be sold at that price. The Italian Maffeo Pantaleoni[18] combined these two approaches. From the simple assumption that the monopolist maximizes his profit, Marshall proceeded to the assumption that the monopolist does not fully exploit his advantage but shares it, to a certain extent, with consumers, like a public gas or power enterprise, or a private railroad which keeps rates down in order to develop traffic and increase profits in the long run by the fuller utilization of its equipment.

2. THEORY OF INCOMES

Cournot had been the first to realize that demand and cost are schedules, that is, that they are not fixed magnitudes, but vary with variations in the quantity of the supply. His discovery was translated into diagrams by the French engineer A.J.E. Dupuit,[19] who was thus the first man to draw demand and supply curves of the type familiar to economists, and whose discovery was repeated, independently, by the German theorist Mangoldt.[20] Dupuit was also the first to conclude that, as prices fall with the slackening of demand, those buyers who were ready to pay more than the price asked enjoy a gain, since they pay less than they would have been willing to pay. The discovery was forgotten and then made again independently by Jenkin. Marshall called this gain 'consumers' surplus' or 'consumers' rent,' measuring in terms of money the benefits to be derived by consumers from any economic arrangement.

The corresponding concept of producers' rent, familiar from Ricardo's theory, was early refined considerably by Hermann and then further elaborated by Marshall. Rent is a surplus, not a cost of production. By taking into consideration the effects of the factor of time upon prices, Hermann was led to the conclusion that much of the entrepreneur's income has the character of rent. If the momentary price is greater than the cost of production, the difference between them appears as rent; but this surplus acts as a signal to producers to expand in the short run, much more in the long run, and in due course is competed away. A gain of the industry as a whole despite the full utilization of its capacity also appears as rent, although it is a signal for expansion in the long run, and is thereby eliminated. These rent-like incomes Marshall called 'quasi-rents.'

The theory of capital also underwent a change as a result of these investigations into the effect of time upon the economic process. Over a short period, prices must be expected to cover current expenses or variable costs, whose magnitude directly depends on the scale of the output. But if prices also cover the overhead, the size of which is independent of the scale of the output, a quasi-rent appears. In the long run even the overhead must be considered variable. This point is important in the theory of the business cycle: the overhead is covered in the boom, but in the depression prices cover only the variable costs.

These are Marshall's observations; the principal authority on the cost structure is John Maurice Clark[21] of Columbia University, the son of John Bates Clark.

Indeed, the most elegant system which neo-classicism has built is that of the elder Clark, the dean of American theorists. He is the direct successor—although himself independent—of Thuenen in making marginal productivity the cornerstone of the structure. Productivity is what makes the cost factors useful and determines their incomes—the incomes of the major classes in society. Since every additional worker on a given piece of land produces less, and since wages must be equal for all, the rent of the land grows; likewise, interest is the rent which accrues to capital as more workers tend the given equipment and hence co-operates with less capital per head. Conversely, the wage can be presented as the rent of a given labor force equipped with growing capital per head; in this process, the marginal product of capital and the rate of its income decreases. Income distribution is thus determined by the marginal products of the factors of production.

Besides being a theory of income distribution, this marginal productivity system is an important contribution to the theory of value, for it solves a problem which had greatly concerned the Austrians from Menger on, namely how separate shares in the product can be imputed to the cost factors when they invariably co-operate in production. Unless this problem is solved, it is impossible to ascertain theoretically the separate values and prices of the cost factors. The Austrians approached the problem by way of a general study of 'complementary goods,' i.e. goods whose value depends on their being used in combination. If either one of a pair of gloves is lost, the other is useless. In this extreme case, in which one of the elements is irreplaceable, its value is regarded as equal to that of the whole combination; we may say that the lost glove assumes the total value of the pair precisely because the remaining one is useless. However, goods differ in the extent to which their loss can be replaced. By the gradual substitution of replaceable for irreplaceable goods, the relative loss can be diminished and—what is more to the purpose —measured; thus, the share of each good in the value of the whole can be appraised. It was along this tortuous path of reasoning that Wieser traveled, finally reaching a point not so far from the position arrived at by Clark. Clark assumed that the loss of any unit is always replaceable, since more units of the factor can always be withdrawn from marginal applications in different industries, where they are equal. This removal, of course, causes a small reduction in the total product—the one imputable to the loss of the unit to be replaced. Clark's method thus was to vary the quantity of one cost factor while leaving the others unchanged; the difference in the product he then attributed to the variation. The limit of production is the point at which a further expansion would involve a loss and short of which a gain would have to be foregone; in other words, it is the marginal productivity of the factors of production. If it be doubted whether there is any practical basis for this theoretical separation of value products in the joint product of different factors, reference need only be made to the fact that a businessman, faced with the problem of deciding whether or not to add—or whether or not to give up—one unit of labor or of capital, ascertains its prospective specific product and compares this with the wage or interest rate. A judgment of this kind is involved in the daily conduct of business—in hiring and firing, in plant expansion and contraction, in the extension of services to customers, and, in fact, in almost every decision that is not merely a part of routine management.

Yet this type of analysis is conspicuously static and unrealistic. If we think of the growth of capital equipment per head in the dynamic process of history, we realize that it is not true that every additional unit of capital is less productive; the law of diminishing productivity is valid only under given technological conditions. As technology improves, productivity rises. Clark was perfectly aware of this fact. What he had in mind were the minor changes in a gradual process rather than the major changes in a revolutionary process. Accordingly, an additional capital investment means not a new structure of technology, as Marx believed, but a slight improvement in a given structure. This mode of reasoning leads to Clark's peculiar concept of capital: capital is a permanent fund of perfect flexibility, as distinguished from capital goods, which are perishable and must be consumed in production in order for capital to remain. It is capital that 'synchronizes' production and consumption: even though production takes time, consumption can go on in the meanwhile because capital keeps the productive process smoothly rolling along; thus Clark denied the role of abstinence. This highly abstract, static theory assumes that, in every case under consideration, capital is so smoothly rearranged in capital goods as always to be fully utilized by the changing numbers of workers and to utilize them fully.

The outstanding single contribution of neo-classicism is Boehm-Bawerk's theory of interest and capital, which had important forerunners in the work of Jevons, and much earlier, of John Rae,[22] a lone thinker outside the traditional schools. This theory was greatly improved by the Frenchman Adolphe Landry[23] and the American Irving Fisher,[24] of Yale University, both of whom refined its psychological presuppositions, and by the Swedish theorist Knut Wicksell,[25] who developed its dynamic implications. The chief merit of Boehm-Bawerk's theory is that it does not, like the productivity theories, juxtapose land, labor, and capital as if they were all on an equal footing, but derives capital from labor and land: capital is labor and land employed for deferred ends. This is what the classical theorists meant when they said that 'previously done labor'—or 'produced means of production'—co-operate with presently available labor. What makes Boehm-Bawerk's theory similar to Senior's doctrine of abstinence is the emphasis on the necessity for bridging the interval of time until the fruits of 'round-about labor' become available for consumption; and what brings Boehm-Bawerk's theory close to the productivity theories, which he criticized with some violence, is the association of higher productivity with this roundabout process of production. Boehm-Bawerk's problem was to show how equilibrium is attained between the value of the sacrifice of time and the value of the increase in productivity thereby achieved.

He found the psychological basis for his theory in the fact that men, because of the uncertainty of their survival, prefer present goods to future goods and are ready to offer interest for a present loan which is to be repaid in the future. Moreover, men are short-sighted and optimistic; they expect to be in better circumstances in the future and underrate their future needs. Yet the correctness of those arguments, which were anticipated by Rae, is somewhat doubtful; Landry and Fisher refined them considerably. According to these theorists, people save even without the stimulus of interest if they believe their present needs to be better met by their present income than they expect their future needs to be met by their future income; if they believe the contrary, they borrow and can pay an interest almost equal to the expected gain—which Boehm-Bawerk called the 'agio' or premium on present goods. The effect is that each man redistributes in time an otherwise unchanged income stream in order to have in prospect equal marginal values of that income per unit of time. Thus we are provided with a description not only of the psychological basis of consumption loans, which are of secondary importance, but also of the motives for saving.

From the point of view of production the problem is one of increasing the size of the income stream through productive investment. Present labor can be converted into capital goods to be used in the future in combination with the labor which will then be available; the result of this combination will be a greater productivity because future labor will be aided by the 'previously done' (stored up) labor incorporated in the present in capital equipment. This is the famous 'third ground' provided by Boehm-Bawerk for the preference given to present over future goods, primarily money capital. On these three grounds, in the credit market, present money for the purchase of present labor is exchanged for future money at a premium. This premium is interest. As Wicksell has pointed out, it is conceivable that stored-up labor is available in such quantities as to bring its marginal productivity down to that of current labor; but as long as the former is relatively scarce, there is a margin of interest.

As more capital is formed, less labor and land remain for current use; consequently, an increase occurs in their marginal productivity and rate of income. At the same time, the marginal products of capital decrease in proportion to the amounts invested, whether for a long or short term, unless there is a special reason to the contrary. However, for arithmetical reasons, this proportionate decrease in the marginal product leaves a relatively larger surplus to the capital invested over a longer period, and thus makes it more attractive than the shorter investment. At an interest rate of 10 per cent, industries with production periods of one year and two years respectively are in equilibrium, that is, the amounts of capital are properly distributed between them, if their products sell for 110 and 231. (See page 99.) A shrinkage of both values by 5 per cent brings them down to 104.5 and 219.945, thus leaving the shorter period with a profit of 4.5 per cent per year, and the longer period with one of about 6½ per cent per year; hence it is the latter industry which primarily attracts the new capitals. Thus the capital structure grows, not only in width but also in height (Wicksell), not only in amounts but also in the time dimension, the extension into the future, under the impact of a larger capital supply and its expression in a lower rate of interest. At the end of the reorganization, the interest will be the same again in industries of differently long periods of production, and lower throughout. More generally, an equilibrium is reached between the length of the period of production and the rate of interest, within the frame of the available labor and land, the magnitude of the fund offered for round-about use, and the different productivities of different periods of production. Although Rae again anticipated, in a somewhat cruder version, Boehm-Bawerk's 'third ground,' the climax of the argument, the synoptic analysis of the determination of the rate of interest by the various factors involved, is Boehm-Bawerk's indisputable achievement.

Durable consumer's goods are also subject to this law if, as the time invested in their production is prolonged, the time needed for them to be consumed is more than proportionately extended. The extension of the period of consumption increases the total utility of the product, makes the use per unit of time cheaper —in other words, increases the productivity of the cost factors employed in the production. In pointing out this fact, John Rae again anticipated Boehm-Bawerk. A third example of deferred consumption is provided by the display of merchandise in large stores for the customers' convenience; although the final use is delayed, the utility of the product is increased because it then fits individual tastes more closely.

Although Boehm-Bawerk was reluctant to admit it, the fact is that he did revive and refine the wage-fund theory. In doing so, he avoided two grave errors of its older version. According to Boehm-Bawerk, the wage fund can be spent over different periods of investment; consequently, the rate of wages is not simply determined by dividing the fund by the number of workers currently employed. Moreover, the wage fund does not consist of goods actually stored up, but it is the money to be currently used for the purchase of the means of subsistence currently in the process of production. Taussig[26] has further elaborated the new wage-fund theory, and Wicksell has drawn attention to the fact that the sellers of land services (landlords), just as much as the sellers of industrial labor, are dependent on getting their incomes advanced out of that fund.

The concept of the period of production is controversial. Frank Knight denies its value altogether,[27] although it should be clear that there is some maximum period to exceed which is not permitted by the available supply of capital. It has been shown, however,[28] that the numerical calculation of the period of production is not so simple as Boehm-Bawerk would indicate. Marxian suggestions make it clear that the production of the fixed capital which precedes the production of final goods has no definite starting point in time; the machine is never, as Boehm-Bawerk would have it, a combination of land and labor only, but invariably the product of preceding machines, which help in the production of ore, coal, and electrical power, and in their combination into the new machine. A circular movement within the sphere of fixed capital complicates the picture of the circulation of factors of production and products as drawn by Quesnay. Yet this consideration, though it invalidates Boehm-Bawerk's solution, in no way mitigates the central importance of his problem.

3. CAPITALISM: PRO AND CON

According to the neo-classical theory, labor and saving have both utility and disutility; they stop at the point at which their utility is equal to their disutility. Thus the total supply of the factors is determined, and the total volume of output and income is determined by these factors, if productivity is given. The various branches of production attract factors in proportion to the anticipated intensity of the demand for their products; more capital flows to those branches of production whose products are expected to be in greater demand. Capital and labor will be so invested as to equalize the marginal products of each factor of production taken separately (the incomes of the units of the factors in their different applications). Thus the maximum satisfaction is achieved on the assumption that the two fundamental factors cannot be substituted for each other. This is a genuine equilibrium.

Of course, the poorer a person is, the greater the marginal value of his money; to a rich person, an additional dollar has less value than to a poor person. Society counts as equal the satisfactions for which equal amounts of money are offered, utility being expressed in terms of money; but the degree of satisfaction derived from the expenditure of the same amount of money will be different for different individuals and groups according to their purchasing power. The equilibrium of society in terms of money coincides with the maximum of each individual in terms of satisfaction; but this is not a social equilibrium because of the difference in satisfaction among different individuals who spend the same amount of money. This is the solution provided by economic theory to the fundamental problem which it was developed to cope with: things are produced in response to the purchasing power which backs the demand for them and in precisely the order demanded—as if this purchasing power expressed the intensity of the need for them—until all marginal satisfactions and all marginal productivities are equal. This is the point of equilibrium, the deviations from which and the tendencies towards which keep the economic process going.

The differences in purchasing power are derived, on the one hand, from differences in the productivity of different persons, and on the other, from differences in the distribution of land and capital properties. In so far as the former differences determine purchasing power, people simply get more as they produce more; society establishes a hierarchy of wants according to the hierarchy of productivities. In so far as purchasing power is determined by the ownership of land or capital, the differences in purchasing power are partly the result of the inheritance of property acquired out of personal remuneration, among which pioneers' profits figure large. However, once the ownership of property is established and passed on to heirs, it becomes an independent source of differences in income. To what extent this random distribution of property acts as an incentive to production or as a drag on it is a moot question, which only a historical-psychological investigation can answer. What economic theory does is to describe how needs are satisfied in the order of a social hierarchy constituted by persons with unequal productivities and unequal amounts of property.

Many theorists, however, observing that exchange continues as long as it seems beneficial to both parties to the transaction, have inferred that a general equilibrium of exchange constitutes the condition of maximum social satisfaction. Gossen, Walras, Jevons, and Pareto seem to approach dangerously near this conclusion, which implies that a capitalist exchange economy is the system best conducive to the common good. But the widespread impression that these thinkers held this view needs correction, in fairness, at least in the cases of Gossen and Walras. Jevons, also, it is true, advocated, 'in the higher interest of society,' public intervention for the preservation of irreplaceable raw materials if free exchange threatens to exhaust the supply; moreover, he was friendly to labor laws. But Gossen and Walras went much farther. They demanded the nationalization of land for reasons considerably more profound than those advanced by Mill and George for the confiscation of ground rent. According to Gossen and Walras, a prerequisite of free exchange and the optimum social satisfaction to be achieved thereby is the freedom of everyone to choose his place of work and his work itself according to his ability. But this is prevented by the private control of land. Hence, the nationalization of land is necessary; and the land would then be farmed out to applicants on the basis of their ability to make good use of it, that is, to pay the community a rent out of their proceeds. It is strange that Oppenheimer should never have realized the support which his geocentric liberalism would have gained if he had referred to two such powerful thinkers. Gossen applied analogous reasoning to the obstacle presented by private property in capital; he completed his system— not without a polemic against Proudhon, whom he far excelled as an economist—by advocating a national credit institution. In this way he proposed that all citizens be placed on an equal footing in regard to capital and land, and made their success in competition dependent on their ability alone. Even Gossen and Walras, however, like Jevons and Pareto, ignored the danger of monopoly as well as the economic crisis: perfect flexibility is always assumed in the doctrine of maximum satisfaction.

Pareto did not criticize this doctrine, but he did not accept it either. After explaining how a relative maximum satisfaction is achieved through free exchange, he listed the advantages of the socialist system and concluded that the decision between capitalism and socialism cannot be made on economic grounds. Thus the systematic criticism of the doctrine of maximum satisfaction was left to Marshall. He approached the problem not as a reformer of society, but as an analyst of free exchange under the given conditions of inequality, regardless whether these are attributable to differences in native ability or in the ownership of property. Marshall's chief objection to the thesis of maximum satisfaction is drawn from the very fact that the incomes of different persons are unequal. A potential increase or decrease in personal income will have different marginal utilities or disutilities for different persons and groups. Thus, if poor men could get a monopoly which would force rich men to buy from them, or if the demand for the products of the rich were to be transferred to those of the poor, the resultant transfer of wealth from the rich to the poor would add a net gain to the total satisfaction of society, because the marginal utility of the additional income for the poor would exceed the marginal disutility of the loss of income for the rich. Furthermore, the total satisfaction of society would be increased if demand shifted from goods produced under conditions of decreasing returns to goods produced under conditions of increasing returns, because the total output will be larger, the cost per unit lower. Hence, a tax on industries operating under conditions of decreasing returns and the use of the tax revenue to subsidize the other industries would increase total output.

Arthur Cecil Pigou,[29] the heir and successor of Marshall at Cambridge, develops these suggestions into a vast edifice of 'welfare economics' by scrutinizing the effects of a whole catalogue of economic, social, and fiscal policies, in a society which has not yet reached the level of planning, upon the total social income and its distribution in the short and the long run, with modifications depending on increasing or decreasing returns. He makes the important discovery that it is incorrect to calculate the costs of production solely in terms of the costs charged to the private producer. There are often other costs of production, like the unemployment or damaged health of the workers, or noise or smoke invading the neighborhood, which are borne by other individuals or by the community. It is likewise incorrect to calculate the gains of production solely in terms of private profit: there may be social gains which do not accrue to the producer who made the original capital outlay. Industries whose private costs are too low thus become too large; industries with too low a private gain, too small. Accordingly, Pigou definitely proves that the success of a business or the outcome of competition is not necessarily to the advantage of society. This really settles the much debated problem of maximum satisfaction. Pigou's results are not affected by the unsolved difficulty of forming a notion of the value to society derived from the incommensurable individual values.

Related to the discussion of maximum satisfaction is that of the problem of socialism. Boehm-Bawerk conceived of the theory of interest as a refutation of socialism, since even in a socialist society interest, which is the expression of man's natural preference for present over future goods, will regulate the periods of production and be chargeable against the capital outlay. Clark, also an opponent of socialism, succinctly stated that, if every function is paid according to its product, so is every person. Both ignored the real issue, namely what persons or classes of persons are assigned by different types of society to the different productive functions and on what basis? Wieser, a non-socialist, accepting Boehm-Bawerk's argument that economic functions are identical in both systems, concluded that socialism is as rational and as feasible as capitalism.[30] According to Wieser, 'natural value' is the value that would exist 'in a perfect or communist society' but is prevented from being realized in present society by the inequality of incomes. Thus, although the laws of value are identical in both types of society, the actual magnitudes of values are different. In this way, Wieser re-established, on a sound basis, the thesis that economic theory discovers the laws governing economic life, but with different systems equally feasible, that is, with proper differentiation in the application of the laws. Smith had believed that the economic system of his day was the only rational one and that the laws governing its operation coincide with the eternal laws of economics. To this view of economic law as eternal, rational, and natural, Marx had then opposed the historical conception of economics: Smith's theory was applicable to only one of several historically possible economic systems and will be followed by another theory applicable to another mode of economic organization. Wieser corrected both conceptions by dissociating economic theory from exclusive reference to any one system of society. A socialist system, if it is to be rational, that is, free from arbitrary and tyrannical distortion, has to apply, in specific form, the general rules of economic theory.[31]

The debate was renewed when Ludwig von Mises,[32] the pupil of Boehm-Bawerk and Wieser, launched what was the keenest and most radical defense of capitalism to be made in recent times. He lumps together as 'destructionism' everything that tends to interfere with the normal formation of exchange values under capitalism, such as social reform, socialism, inflation, Christianity, and war; they all diminish economic welfare. As to socialism, it is most obviously utopian, since the values needed for an exact cost calculation cannot be ascertained by a salaried bureaucrat, but only by private businessmen whose profits depend on the correctness of their calculation. Where there is no free market for cost factors, for instance, the use of capital, prices do not provide an infallible guide for production. The extraordinary vigor of this attack on socialism led to a renewed discussion, which has confirmed once more the fact that the difference be-

tween the two systems is in social arrangements and psychological incentives rather than in purely economic issues.[33]

4. General Equilibrium—Economic Logic

The way from classical to neo-classical economic theory was
far more tortuous than Marshall's loyalty to tradition would
allow him to admit. Smith had taught that under capitalism the
factors of production are continually growing and are invariably
utilized to their full capacity; thus, minor fluctuations and disturbances in this equilibrium of the market are contained in a
harmonious frame, whose current dimensions are determined
solely from within and whose automatic expansion is guaranteed
by the operation of eternal laws. Malthus and Ricardo, although
applying the same methodological procedure as Smith, and no
less firmly convinced than he of the autonomy of the economic
process, were considerably more pessimistic in their conclusions.
Marx, whom Marshall did not count among his teachers, carried
this pessimism to its ultimate end in prophesying the inexorable
doom of the capitalist system as a result of the operation of its
inherent laws. Marshall, on the other hand, was not interested in
the fundamental structure of the economic system and its massive
changes for better or worse, but in the innumerable small variations which lead to innumerable new constellations. Aware of
the fact that the doctrines he had inherited were dated, Marshall
resolved his problem thus: he treated the presuppositions of
classical theory as one set among many others logically possible:
innumerable combinations are equally thinkable. All have a just
claim upon the theorist's attention, but all are treated as purely
hypothetical, and the function of economic theory is to analyze
the implications of each. He formally preserved classicism by
dissolving it in fact; for the result is that no definite structure of
reality emerges. Economics is 'not a body of concrete truth but
an engine for the discovery of concrete truth.'

Others, less skeptical and more ambitious, went farther along this path. They held that the intention of the classical theorists to make economics an exact science failed of realization because too many empirical assumptions were made. The system of economic theory must, then, be purified of all empirical reference by formalizing the functional relations of economic life, i.e. by giving the entire system the character of mathematics or logic. In this way, as in mathematics, all magnitudes—prices, costs, etc.—can be regarded as indefinitely variable, and the relations among them can be studied without reference to historical circumstances. In other words, the entire system can be taken out of history, as it were, and made essentially durationless. Accordingly, there is no reason for distinguishing between the long and the short run, as Marshall had done, on the basis of whether capital equipment remains unchanged or has time to adapt itself to a change in demand; what matters is simply that there is a tendency for capital to adapt itself thus. Nor is there any reason, or justification, for concentrating on a limited section of the total economic system in studying the effects of a change in a particular place. Marshall's geometrical presentation of equilibrium naturally lent itself only to the consideration of a limited sector and thus was subject to severe criticism, since the effects of any cause must be felt throughout an interdependent system. The concept of opportunity cost, for example, clearly permits the range of decreasing opportunities to stretch throughout the system, and the purchasing power released in any individual market through a lowering of price can reappear anywhere else. The only exact approach to economic problems is by way of the concept of 'general equilibrium,' which can be expressed in a system of simultaneous equations.

Given the demand schedules for different goods and the total purchasing power, on the one hand, and the total supply of factors of production and the technically required combination of different units of them in any kind of product, on the other hand: the unknown is the quantities to be produced of the different products and the prices of the factors and consequently of the products. Since all units of a factor in its different applications must have the same price and there are innumerable combinations of the few factors of production in different products, the problem is soluble. And it follows that any change in the supply of a factor or in technology or in the demand schedules must be more or less felt everywhere in the system, which is interdependent throughout and cannot achieve an equilibrium but an all-inclusive one. These effects, naturally, will not be greater than infinitesimal in many places; but an accurate analysis must take account of them.

The founder and head of the school of general equilibrium is Léon Walras, and Irving Fisher has arrived at some of the same results. From Walras to his successor Pareto, the doctrine underwent important technical improvements. He pointed out that the utility of a quantity of a good is not uniquely determined unless we know the quantities of many complementary and rival goods as well. By making use of the indifference curves of Edgeworth and Fisher, Pareto avoided the necessity of assuming that utilities are directly measurable. What is important for economic theory is that they are comparable, i.e. capable of being placed in an ordered scale. Pareto also assumed different types of monopoly and studied their effect on the system of general equilibrium. Schumpeter[34] and Cassel[35] provided simplified versions of the theory, and many other economists made special contributions to it.

According to this theory, any difference of incomes may stimulate further movements towards a more perfect equilibrium. As we have seen, Wicksell argued that the expectation of profit from the use of capital—previously-done labor—suggests the redistribution of labor through time, until the employment of present labor yields as much revenue as previously done labor. If such a state of equilibrium seems highly speculative, others are less remote. There must be an equilibrium among the marginal utilities of all factors of production: their prices must be in proportion to their marginal products, i.e. those factors producing more must cost more to purchase. Otherwise, there would be a tendency for the relatively cheaper factors to be substituted for the dearer ones until equilibrium is restored. Indeed, the prices of the factors of production must be equal to their marginal products, for if a unit of capital or labor yields more or less than its cost in interest or wages, production will be correspondingly expanded or contracted until equilibrium is reached. Furthermore, all the factors of production must be utilized to full capacity; if any unit of capital or labor is idle, its price will fall below that of the other units and there will be a gain from its employment—a reaction which will again restore the equilibrium.

The fundamental motive being given—the search for the maximum satisfaction attainable with the means at hand—there is no doubt that a tendency towards a general equilibrium prevails in the entire system. Yet it is this very motive that—long before equilibrium has been attained—changes the data by stimulating technological improvements and the introduction of new methods of management and production. Consequently, the study of states of partial equilibrium over a short-run period is more realistic because less ambitious. (Of course, the selection of the part of the system to be analyzed is not dictated by logical considerations but is a matter of realistic judgment and turns upon the possibility—whenever there is one—of verifying the data.) Another important inadequacy of the theory of general equilibrium is that it presupposes a fluidity in the factors of production which they do not actually have. In particular, the optimum size of the unit of production—which is the size required for perfect equilibrium—may in fact preclude that perfect competition by which equilibrium is attained and restored: that size may be so large that real competition, the precondition of general equilibrium, is impossible.

The theory is extremely useful, however, if interpreted normatively. Indeed, it is irrefutable if it is understood as a doctrine of what could and should be done to increase total satisfaction. It is for this reason that the general-equilibrium theory finds its most fruitful application to conditions under a socialist dictatorship, that institutional pattern in which alone social norms can be directly realized. Accordingly, Wieser, although not a member of the general-equilibrium school, made use of this method in discussing the socialist system. Pareto himself was well aware of the normative application of his principle, and it is his closest disciple, Enrico Barone,[36] who provided the most comprehensive treatment of the means of maximizing satisfactions in a socialist society.

But from the point of view of theoretical principles, the most interesting contribution is that of the Swedish theorist Gustav Cassel. Price, according to him, is not the result of demand and supply as of random, blind forces. A price 'must' be put on a scarce supply in order to exclude the excess demand which cannot be satisfied out of that supply. This is what he called the 'principle of scarcity' and made the cornerstone of his system. His approach is frankly normative and was intended to replace the older causal and more recent formal-functional methods. The 'invisible hand' is made visible. The application to the socialist economy is explicitly made; but even if no reference were made to socialism, the entire theory, in its normative terminology, reads like the directions to the government of a socialist state, with which Cassel is not at all in sympathy. It is here that the logical consummation of the system of general equilibrium is achieved.

Nothing, on the other hand, can be more remote from the theory of general equilibrium than the theory of the economic crisis, which, whatever may be its causes, must be traceable to some disturbance that is not automatically adjusted by the system. Hence, the one theorist of the general-equilibrium school who engaged in the analysis of the business cycle, namely Cassel —for Wicksell and Schumpeter do not belong to this group— could do so only by ignoring his theoretical system and referring to historical data in a realistic way. His theory of the business cycle, ranking with that of Spiethoff and preceding its final formulation by several years, attributes the crisis to over-accumulation resulting from too low an interest rate, which does not rise promptly enough. How and why such a thing can happen without being taken care of by the forces tending towards equilibrium is not explained. Although Cassel's theory is not necessarily invalidated by this inadequacy, a theoretical explanation is needed in order to make intelligible the periodic occurrence of such disastrous retardations in the self-adjustment of the economic order. Another feature characteristic of his theory, and one that makes it closely akin to Oppenheimer's, is, as Cassel himself pointed out, its distinctly historicist approach to the problem of the cycle: the agricultural surplus population is drained into industrial employment, and it is this influx of labor which makes the expansion possible; but once the source of the labor supply dries up, industrial expansion will come to an end.

5. Imperfect Competition: The Dissolution of the System

The theory of general equilibrium represents one extreme in the reaction against the classical system. The opposite extreme is the complete abandonment of the principal supposition of classical reasoning, namely that of competition. This solution of the problem places emphasis on those rigid factors which obstruct the tendencies towards equilibrium.

The concept of imperfect competition is traceable to the procedure followed by Cournot. It was he who formulated the theory of the individual firm and, after studying the simplest case, that of perfect monopoly, proceeded to introduce a second monopolist acting independently of the first and calculating his output and price on the basis of the output of his rival. Edgeworth[37] concluded that, because the rivalry of the second monopolist changes the conditions on the basis of which the first monopolist made his economic calculations, he will change his policy, and the total situation will be unstable. A wide discussion followed, but it is not particularly instructive because, whatever may be the result in this and similar cases—'duopoly,' 'oligopoly,' etc.—the conditions assumed are highly unstable as long as the rivals do not come to some understanding or merge their businesses. Such a merger or understanding would in the long run best serve their individual interests. The real significance of the discussion lies in the fact that it developed the concept of imperfect competition (monopolistic competition). Cournot had used the term 'perfect competition' to denote an ideal or limiting case in which the total number of competing firms is so great that the sales of any one do not affect the price. This condition prevails in the sale of many staple raw materials but certainly not in the sale of the products of typical modern industrial establishments, which were, however, included in the classical concept of competition. According to Cournot's theory, any situation short of the limit of perfect competition represents a degree of monopolization, since a firm can upset the price structure. This view is the exact opposite of the classical conception of competition as a typical feature of the capitalist system.

The modern theory of monopolistic competition, however, did not immediately follow from these suggestions but from one more observation made by Cournot, namely that perfect competition is incompatible with conditions of increasing returns, which give the larger firms a natural competitive advantage. From this observation Marshall concluded that whatever stability there is in the price structure must be the result of limitations on competition and should be analyzed by comparing the demand curve for the product of the individual firm with the curve of its costs; it is these two curves which between them determine the firm's output and price. The Italian Piero Sraffa,[38] one of Marshall's pupils teaching at Cambridge, was the first to draw the outline of a system in terms of imperfect competition. One further decisive step was taken by another Cambridge economist, Roy Forbes Harrod,[39] who developed the modern tools of monopoly analysis—used independently by others at the same time—, the concepts of marginal cost and marginal revenue.

The terms 'marginal cost' and 'marginal revenue' had formerly denoted the cost of or revenue from the marginal unit in a given quantity: the cost of or revenue from any unit of a given quantity, taken separately, is equal to the marginal cost or revenue. Now, however, the terms 'marginal cost' and 'marginal revenue' are used to denote the net addition to the total cost or revenue produced by the additional unit. This addition in cost or revenue is the difference between the specific cost or revenue from the additional unit and the loss or gain which the addition of a unit brings to each of the preceding units. In other words, the marginal cost and the marginal revenue are the difference between the cost of or revenue from the total quantity and the cost of or revenue from the total quantity minus one unit. The average curve falls when a new unit adds less than the average cost or revenue; it rises if the contrary holds true. Thus, the marginal curve lies below the sloping-down part of the average curve and above its rising part, and cuts it at the turning point. The all-important economic application is that maximum profit is attained when sales have reached the point at which marginal cost equals marginal revenue: one more unit would cost more than it brings; one less unit would cost less than it brings and would leave an unrealized profit. All these propositions are analytic; they follow from the definition of marginal cost and marginal revenue.

The intersection of the curves of marginal cost and marginal revenue is the point at which maximum profit is reached and hence the point at which price settles: this is the modern theory of price. By means of this principle, it has at last become possible to comprehend the two extremes of monopoly price and competitive price under a single law. The special case of perfect competition, as already mentioned, is a situation in which price is not affected by the size of the output of one firm, because this output is too small a fraction of total supply. This case is represented graphically by a horizontal demand (revenue) curve for the products of one firm: in this curve marginal and average revenue coincide. In such a situation the marginal cost curve cuts the marginal and average revenue curves in the same point: price is as low and output as large as possible. In the case of a monopoly, on the other hand, output is expanded only to the intersection of the marginal cost curve with the marginal, not with the average, revenue curve, thus leaving a special profit and making output smaller and price higher than they otherwise would be. The difference between the two cases is in the elasticity of demand, which under conditions of competition is infinite (horizontal) and under conditions of monopoly finite (sloping down); a reduction of output can bring no advantage in the former case but does bring an advantage in the latter case.

Much obviously depends on a knowledge of the structure of costs, which was studied by Marshall's school and by John Maurice Clark, the authority on overhead. It follows from the definition of overhead that it never figures in marginal cost and consequently never influences price.

All this, however, is merely preparatory to the systematic study of the determination of price and output in the many different cases of monopolistic competition. The fact that the logical development of the theory of price can easily be appreciated in retrospect in no way derogates from the merit and originality of those who were the first to elaborate the implications of the theory with the greatest richness of detail, Edward Chamberlin[40] of Harvard and Joan Robinson[41] of Cambridge. Both introduced a new method of determining the general effect of competition on the monopolies. As the profit represented by the distance between average cost and average revenue at the intersection of the marginal curves attracts more competitors, these reduce the demand for the products of the individual firm and thus shift its demand (revenue) curve downward. In other words, a given quantity sells for less; at a given price less is sold; the curve may also become flatter. The profit is thus reduced or obliterated and the output pinned down at an optimum point at which it can neither expand nor contract without actual loss. The shifting down of the demand curve indicates unused capacity, which thus must be traced to the element of monopoly in the situation, represented by the sloping-down demand curve. The effect of the competitive element is the destruction of profit: a given output is produced by more producers at higher cost than necessary, but without profit to them.

According to both authors, and already to Sraffa, a monopoly exists whenever consumers are so attached to the products of any one producer that within certain limits they are willing to pay a higher price than that asked for competing goods. There are limited monopolies of location everywhere in retail trade, and of special brands in the production of consumers' goods; otherwise trade marks would be useless and the money invested in them wasted. These considerations led Chamberlin to an important extension of the field of economic analysis, namely the effect of advertising on the demand schedule, which had long been a stumbling block to a price theory predicated on the assumption that demand is independently given. Chamberlin upheld the objection of the institutionalists to the traditional price theory that the production of additional demand by advertising is an economic, not an extra-economic phenomenon, and includes this phenomenon in his theory by opposing the extra cost to the expected gain in sales, which is represented by the shifting of the demand curve upwards.

The doctrine of imperfect competition, however, cannot be the last word in economic theory. It is indeed alarming that the economists who enthusiastically accept the new doctrine and write textbooks exclusively in terms of it seem blind to the implications of employing it as a substitute for classical and neoclassical teachings. Economics would then cease to be a systematic science and would become a collection of individual case histories representative of the special conditions of particular firms, without any comprehensive organizing principle—a picture of anarchy rather than of spontaneous, although imperfect, order. It is significant that the term 'equilibrium,' which once denoted the coincidence of the maximum satisfaction of the individual with that of society, is now used to denote only the former, although it was reference to the latter that gave the word its weight and normative meaning. And it is equally significant that the one who shares with Chamberlin and Robinson the honor of being the founder of the theory of imperfect competition and who alone has correctly appreciated its implications is a German, Heinrich von Stackelberg.[42] He provides fewer technical details than they do but puts the theory into a frankly Fascist form: if the economic world disintegrates into a wasteful struggle of monopolies without a spontaneously integrating force, then the force of the state must be called upon. 'Order through liberty' was the original program of economics; 'order through force' is the program of the theory of imperfect competition. It is time to recognize that the concept of a system of monopoly is self-contradictory and the very negation of everything economics stands for.

6. Business Cycles

The crucial problem of neo-classicism is the economic crisis: how can a general disturbance arise in a system regulated by price? Say had flatly denied the possibility of such a disturbance. Only the socialists had made the theory of the crisis an integral part of their system of thought, which is dynamic and points beyond capitalism. And before them the two great theorists of the classical school, Ricardo and Malthus, had, in different ways, recognized the possibility of a disturbance. They had come to this conclusion by taking a circular-flow approach to the problem and had found that certain qualitative aggregates have peculiarities which deflect the regular circular flow of economic activities. But their school had repudiated these results. Now it was the neo-classicists who were faced with the problem of the crisis.

In this respect, the neo-classical theorists were under an even greater handicap than were their classical predecessors. The neo-classical objection to classicism is that it did not adhere to the logic of its own argument; for according to classical price theory, the system is self-regulatory by virtue of the price mechanism. The neo-classicists contend that, if the pricing process wipes out qualitative differences everywhere in the economic system, then there is no obstacle to the flow of economic activity. The more neo-classicism progressed in the formal logic of this argument, the further it was removed from economic reality, which is not as smooth as the theory would have it. The theory of the crisis must follow from the general concepts of the system of theory, just as the crisis in reality results from the system of free enterprise; one must reflect the other. The problem is that of deriving a theory of a general disturbance from presuppositions according to which such a disturbance is rendered impossible by the regulatory mechanism of the economic system. This is almost like squaring the circle.

Of the first generation of neo-classical theorists, the founders and their closest disciples, Jevons was the only one to consider the problem; but his approach did not lead him to the crucial issue. For Gossen, Walras, Menger, and Clark the problem does not exist; and Pareto's contribution is of forbidding abstruseness and certainly outside his system of thought. Wieser, who so much surpassed his fellow theorists by his far-sighted critical attitude, explicitly followed Say in denying the possibility of a general disturbance. Boehm-Bawerk, in a passing remark, made it clear that he regarded the theory of the business cycle as the capstone which would complete the structure of economic theory; but he himself never undertook to construct it. And Marshall was so preoccupied with a theoretical analysis of the innumerable small changes in the economic system, in all directions and at every moment, that he treated the massive changes of the cycle, as it were, as a datum and inquired into the reactions of the business world to the business cycle instead of taking the business cycle itself as the problem to be solved.

Various methods of solving it were available. In the first place, the business cycle could be traced to a disturbance coming from outside the system and forcing it to a gradual adaptation to, or absorption of, the disturbing element. No general-equilibrium theory need or can deny the possibility of such an extraneous disturbance; every change is a disturbance in this sense, and the economic system is characterized not by the absence of such outside influences, but by its own resilience, its ability to establish a new equilibrium. Accordingly, Jevons[43] attributed the business cycle to the periodically recurrent disturbances caused by sun spots, which produce fluctuations in agricultural crops; an increase in these, in turn, stimulates the demand for industrial goods and hence increases employment. The same theory had already been suggested by Juglar,[44] whose name must head every list of business-cycle analysts, and a variant was later employed by the mathematical economist Henry Ludwell Moore[45] of Columbia University. Even if the assumption is abandoned that there is a periodicity in the fluctuation of agricultural crops, it is still possible that a chance expansion of agricultural production may result in an expansion of business. This more restricted theory has been elaborated by Pigou,[46] who has most fully investigated the impact of rising crops on business and credit. But whatever the merits of Pigou's theory, it can never be, and was not intended as, more than a partial explanation of the business cycle; the theory presupposes that productive resources are not fully utilized, since otherwise production could not be expanded in response to improved agricultural conditions.

A second way out of the impasse must be credited to Pigou, who had the wisdom to realize that there is no logical reason why the recurrent disturbances of the economic system should have but one cause; no logic can preclude the possibility that different causes take turns in the history of the phenomenon or combine in the same cycle. Pigou has stressed a possibility that had already been recognized by his predecessors, namely that booms and depressions are caused by miscalculations on the part of businessmen with regard to future market conditions. It is a fact that 'business confidence' or lack of it feeds on itself, since the holding back of sales in the expectation of higher prices or the rushing of sales in the expectation of lower prices cannot fail to bring about at least a short-lived boom or depression. However, it is questionable whether this explanation really gets to the bottom of the matter; such fluctuations in business sentiment may be only one phase in a cycle and may be traceable to more fundamental causes in the economic system. Although the logic in the argument which attributes the periodic breakdown of the self-regulatory mechanism of the economic system to cumulative errors on the part of those in charge of the system is unassailable, the argument itself is certainly not impressive.

The contribution of Irving Fisher[47] can perhaps be characterized as parallel to Pigou's. Fisher describes an important phase of the cycle, which reinforces it, once it begins for other reasons. As prices rise, money depreciates in value, and the real value of the nominal rate of interest diminishes. From the nominal rate one has to deduct the expected rate of depreciation of money, that is, of the loan when it will become due. In other words, for the real rate to remain unchanged, the nominal rate would have to increase by the depreciation rate of money. This argument presupposes the price rise of the boom; the contrary holds as prices fall in the depression. Fisher's theory thus explains a strong incentive to further expansion on the basis of credits in the boom and to contraction in the depression.

The third way out of the impasse is to ignore the general structure of the system of economic theory and to concentrate on the analysis of the cycle as an isolated problem. This way suggested itself to those who were opposed to economic theory on principle. It was only natural that the serious analysis of the business cycle should be inaugurated by economists who rejected the theoretical system according to which a crisis is impossible. The lone and long-ignored pioneer in this analysis is Juglar, who, as early as 1860, took the decisive step from the idea of the crisis as a periodic breakdown of an otherwise smoothly working system to a statistical investigation of the business cycle. According to Juglar, 'the sole reason for the crisis is the boom'; the capitalist system develops, not along a straight line broken by periodic depressions, but with wide fluctuations of employment, income, and output, in which every phase follows from the preceding one, and there is no equilibrium. In this way, the problem was for the first time fully understood: what is the reason, not of the crisis, but of boom and crisis, that is, of the cycle? It is on this basis that the great achievements of Spiethoff and Mitchell stand. These we have already discussed. For all their merits, however, their explanations of the business cycle proved incomplete because unrelated to a general system of economic theory which could explain the movements that were supposed to lead to the fluctuations. Cassel's theory is open to the same criticism; although, unlike Spiethoff and Mitchell, he is a neo-classical economist, he in no way relates his theory of the business cycle to his general-equilibrium theory and does not explain the contradiction between them. This point too has already been discussed.

Thus, Mises[48] and Schumpeter must be credited with having made really significant progress because, instead of being content with highly original theories of the business cycle, they integrated their own original theories into the general system of economic thought. The question then is: to what extent was the problem solved?

Mises reversed the socialist argument. The socialists had pointed to the crisis as the sign that capitalism is unstable and decaying. Mises, who more than any other economist regards laissez-faire as the system of equilibrium, blames the crisis on arbitrary tampering with that delicate mechanism. Whereas Cassel's theory of the crisis cannot be fitted into a system of thought built around the price theory, Mises's theory, and that of his disciple Hayek, is an integral part of the system because it describes an illegitimate but regularly recurrent interference with the natural flow of economic activities. This disturbing element is the inflationary proclivities of both governments and banks, which lead to over-expansion of credit. It would be quite possible to keep these tendencies towards inflation under control, just as, according to Smith, it is possible to control the tendency towards monopoly; but in reality the harmful forces assert themselves.

Businessmen always cry for 'cheap money'; governments, in their eagerness for popularity, are prone to yield to this pressure; and banks gladly lower the rate of interest by creating additional loans and thus increasing their business. Accordingly, everything conspires to deflect the rate of interest from its proper position as analyzed by Boehm-Bawerk and thereby to make so long a period of production—so large an output of producers' goods —appear profitable that the available subsistence fund is not sufficient to sustain producers for so long a period. When this situation becomes apparent, consumption goods rise in price and producers' goods fall, bringing losses to their producers. Thus the structure of production is disrupted. The difference between the prices of producers' goods and those of consumers' goods is the profit which accrues from the use of the former for the production of the latter; Boehm-Bawerk and his pupils contend that under conditions of equilibrium the interest rate is equal to this profit. Hence, Mises argues that the rise in the price of consumers' goods in relation to the price of producers' goods restores the correct rate of interest by disrupting the distorted structure of production resulting from the distorted rate of interest.

This theory has been further elaborated by the Austrian-born London theorist Friedrich A. von Hayek[49] and has become one of the major business-cycle theories of our day. According to Hayek, the rise of prices resulting from the creation of new, illegitimate bank credit forces the recipients of fixed incomes, or of incomes which do not rise in proportion to the rise in prices, to forego the services of factors of production which they formerly used. The same thing happens when people voluntarily save their money. But the 'forced saving' imposed by credit expansion on those who cannot afford to buy at the higher price is not likely to be continued when the credit inflation stops; the former level of consumption will be immediately restored, whereas voluntary savings are likely to be continued. The restoration of the former level of demand then draws factors of production into the consumers' goods industries and may leave the far-reaching projects of expansion unfinished and the capital invested in them lost. Lionel Robbins[50] of the London School of Economics has undertaken to verify this thesis by using the statistical material provided by the great depression of 1929. The main objection to Hayek's theory, raised by Neisser,[51] is that the restoration of the consumption level does not have harmful effects if the expansion stimulated by credit inflation has already resulted in enlarged output; the total level is then higher than it was. Apart from its political implications, however, the Mises-Hayek thesis certainly gives an accurate picture of what happens in the last phase of the boom, when labor is fully employed and a continuous stream of credit raises wages and destroys profit.

The explanatory value of theories like those of Mises and Hayek is, of course, limited because of the fact that the disturbing element to which they trace the cycle is regarded as illegitimate, i.e. outside the activities necessary for the carrying on of the economic process. Hence, the importance of these theories in the development of economic thinking is considerably surpassed by Joseph A. Schumpeter's[52] achievement in at last providing a theoretical understanding of the cycle as a phenomenon quite legitimate and even indispensable in capitalism. Each cycle leaves a net gain in income, output, and employment, as evidenced by the hundred years of progress between the Napoleonic Wars and the First World War. This led Sombart, the historian, and Schumpeter, an Austrian-born Harvard theorist, to interpret the business cycle optimistically as the special form in which capitalist industry grows, an encouragement to all sorts of experiments in the boom and a severe test of soundness in the depression.

Schumpeter solves the problem of the business cycle by introducing into the system of static equilibrium a dynamic factor which upsets the equilibrium, namely the entrepreneur, in the new and specific sense of the person who does not simply produce things desired by the consumers in the traditional way, but conceives of new products, new methods of production, and new industries. In the system of static equilibrium, all the factors of production and all purchasing power are needed for normal circulation; thus, in order to be able to bend factors to his own purposes, the entrepreneur must be given command over them. It is the banker who provides him with newly created purchasing power, after considering the many projects submitted for financing; the banker limits the total volume of his loans, in order to remain liquid, by charging an interest that is intended to exclude the weaker applicants or those who are less reliable. The entrepreneur then uses the credit to purchase factors of production; he can offer higher wages, and thus divert the factors of production from the channels of the static economy, because he expects higher profits to result from the application of his new ideas. In this way, additional purchasing power circulates, wages and prices rise, and the boom begins. Once the new production has come to an end, the output becomes larger and cheaper, the credits are repaid from the proceeds of the new sales, and the volume of purchasing power shrinks. For these reasons the return to static equilibrium comes as an unpleasant surprise but also indicates that the whole process is self-regulating.

What Schumpeter describes is essentially the rise from one state of equilibrium through a disequilibrium to a new state of equilibrium on a higher plane. In other words, the crisis is not inevitable; what happens is only that static equilibrium is restored after the rush to a higher plane, and the crisis could be avoided if people were not thrown into panic by the interruption of the boom. Graphically represented, the cycle would appear not as a wave fluctuating around a rising average but only as the upper half of such a wave. Thus it can be seen that Adam Smith's idea of harmonious growth guided by price still exercises an important influence upon the theory of this most advanced neo-classical economist and places a limitation even on his epoch-making achievement. In Schumpeter's most recent presentation of his doctrine the crisis is again absent from the primary development of his principle and introduced only in a second step.

Schumpeter's achievement is not confined merely to the development of a new theory of the business cycle; he opened up an entirely new vista. What he provides is a theory of economic dynamics, different from the equilibrium which is the subject matter of the static theory. According to Schumpeter, the crisis is not produced by extraneous disturbances, miscalculations, or illegitimate influences on credit policy; what happens is that there is movement and growth, which in due time has to give way to the readjustment of the economic system by the tendency towards equilibrium. The only predecessor of Schumpeter to hold such a dynamic conception, although he approached it from a different standpoint, is Marx; Schumpeter, however, makes full use of the refined neo-classical instruments of thought, the beginnings of which Marx had spurned.

Credit, profit, and interest, according to Schumpeter, are phenomena only of the expanding phase of the business cycle and vanish with it. Prosperity is, in fact, always accompanied by increasing credits and profits, and it has become an accepted doctrine that in a state of equilibrium, in which aggregate price covers aggregate cost, including interest, there is no room for profit beyond this. Thus, the classical theory, which identified profit with interest, is justified anew: it always is a theory of equilibrium, which in Schumpeter's system is reduced to the second phase of the cycle. However, the moot point in Schumpeter's theory is the exclusion of interest itself from the static equilibrium. According to Schumpeter, once equilibrium is reached, round-about production becomes synchronized with consumption; that is, both processes are simultaneous and continuous, consumption need not wait for production to be completed, and no limitation need be placed on the period of production. This argument had been employed by J. B. Clark against Boehm-Bawerk; Schumpeter uses it to deny the possibility and necessity of interest in a state of static equilibrium. Moreover, he cannot, from his starting point, provide an analysis of the peculiarities of the structure of fixed capital.

IX. The Emergence of the System of Economic Fluctuations

THE economic and social turmoil after the First World War, first in Germany and then in the other occidental countries, naturally stimulated the quest for a new principle of economic theory—different from the principle of equilibrium—which would logically lead to a theory of fluctuations as the normal condition of capitalist industry. In other words, the shackles of classical and neo-classical price theory had to be broken by the unqualified acceptance of the circular-flow principle in order that the theory of the business cycle, and more generally the theory of economic fluctuations, could be adequately formulated.

The discussion was opened by a group of German theorists who later came to the United States. Adolph Lowe[1] acted as the herald of the new doctrine in the struggles of the 'twenties, demanding the reconstruction of economic theory in terms of the circular-flow principle. He sees in technical progress, as did Marx and Schumpeter, the dominant dynamic force of this age, and sketched a system of thought which would renew, with modern means and in the light of modern developments, Marx's attempt to describe periodic fluctuations around a general course of economic transformation. Emil Lederer,[2] like Schumpeter, laid greater emphasis on the credit phenomena accompanying technical progress. He made an exhaustive study of the many different cases in which technical progress may or may not lead to unemployment, depending on whether or not the immediate dismissal of workers is offset by the effects of general expansion. A new industry, financed by new credits and producing new goods, enlarges both the total supply and the total demand; it is in this way that capitalism has continually grown. But, according to Lederer, Lowe, and Neisser,[3] the mechanization of existing industries may lead to a shrinkage in the economic system. This argument is disputed by the 'compensation theory' of the classical school, according to which the dismissal of workers resulting from the introduction of labor-saving devices is compensated by the setting free of their wages for reinvestment, which cannot fail to reabsorb the workers. However, the re-employment of the workers requires additional capital for the equipment of new jobs as well as the old wage fund—where is this capital to come from, unless it is provided by chance? Moreover, those who receive the money saved by the dismissal of the workers—consumers if the product sells at a lower price, producers if the price remains the same—must use this money to buy the things produced for the dismissed workers; otherwise these products would remain unsold and the crisis would begin. But then that money cannot be used for reinvestment, and the dismissed workers remain excluded from employment and consumption. This reasoning, based on the principle of the circular flow of goods, is sound. But, though it demonstrates the possibility of permanent technological unemployment, the theory does not provide an explanation of the business cycle, which, whatever its ultimate source, is directly caused by a fluctuation in purchasing power.

This point is taken into consideration in Lederer's theory of the business cycle, which, though taking its start from Schumpeter's theory, is free from the classical prejudice of economic harmony. The additional credit which is granted to entrepreneurs introducing new projects necessarily results in a profit margin over aggregate cost, since the covering of costs would have required only unchanged purchasing power. Profits are preponderantly invested in further expansion, while the lagging-behind of wages undermines the demand for the new larger output and brings about the crisis; in the downward movement again, profits fall first and wages lag behind, thus bolstering up demand and eventually stopping the downward movement. Hans

Neisser, starting from Say's law of markets, has provided what is up to the present day the most comprehensive catalogue of such changes in both production and consumption as may lead to a withdrawal of purchasing power from the market and thus to a crisis. Following a suggestion of Schumpeter, Neisser also shows how the international division of labor makes the study of the cycle in only one country inadequate, since the successive phases of the same cycle may occur in different countries.

The main approach to the rebuilding of the system of economics was, logically, from the side of purchasing power, i.e. of monetary theory. Wicksell, Schumpeter, and Hahn were the pioneers, who also influenced the economists of Lederer's group. Keynes is the undisputed head of this school.

Wicksell[4] was the first, after 150 years, to establish a connection between the theory of money and that of interest. No one since David Hume had done so; everybody was awed by the insistence of the classical economists that a policy of 'easy money,' which businessmen invariably demand and the confused mercantilists recommended, could not lead to anything but inflation. Starting from the classical conception of capital and credit, Wicksell called 'normal' or 'natural' that rate of interest at which the available supply of capital was absorbed by those seeking funds for profitable investment; in other words, the rate of interest at which saving is equal to investment. This rate is thus equal to marginal profit. Now if the chances of making a profit are improved by technical progress or other causes, the unchanged interest rate of the banks proves to be too low to meet the increased demand for credit. The demand must be satisfied by creating new money, which, in this age of bank accounts and checks, is not technically distinguishable from the already existing money. Entrepreneurs use the loans to pay higher incomes to workers and landowners, and the demand for goods increases. Hence the price level rises as long as interest, although rising, has not caught up with profits; the price level falls as long as interest is too high, even though it too is falling. In other words, the boom and the depression result from the lagging of interest rates behind profits. What is implied in this theory, although not explicitly formulated at that early date (1898), is Keynes's thesis that there is an upward movement if investment exceeds savings and a downward movement if investment falls short of savings.

Schumpeter's much more radical theory of credit and interest is an integral part of his dynamic theory, which we have discussed above. Though original, it was anticipated in one important respect by the Scottish banker Henry Dunning McLeod,[5] whose voluminous writings in the second half of the last century had been contemptuously rejected by his contemporaries. According to McLeod, credit is not a transfer of purchasing power from a saver through a bank to a debtor-investor, but purchasing power is created by the bank—in the form of bank accounts—for the express use of the debtor. McLeod had then traced the business cycle to fluctuations in the volume of bank credit, which varies incomparably more than the volume of money saved. Schumpeter likewise takes bank credit as capital—the means of building up new enterprises—but he deviates from McLeod in limiting the possibility of bank credit to a dynamic development, that is, such applications for credit as are designed to transform production. Only such credit as serves to direct resources into new productive channels and thus anticipates future additional goods is capital and can earn an interest, since interest must be paid out of entrepreneurial profits. Accordingly, in a state of static equilibrium, there is no credit and no interest. The bank must charge an interest on its credits because the circulation of its credits diminishes its liquidity; the interest so charged places a limit on the number of applications for credit and on the ensuing loss of liquidity. Thus, Schumpeter is the founder of the new theory of interest, which was called the theory of liquidity preference, first by Hahn and then by Keynes. According to Schumpeter and Hahn, interest does not make saving equal to investment, as the classical theory holds; interest makes investment equal to bank credit. Savings, says Schumpeter, are too insignificant to support the dynamic development of production, and the interest that they receive is only reflected from the interest on the investable funds created by the banks. This point had already been made by Hermann, as early as 1832.

McLeod's theory was made respectable and refined considerably by R. G. Hawtrey[6] of the British Treasury, according to whom the business cycle is a 'purely monetary phenomenon' governed by variations in the interest rate. These variations, although too small to influence industrial investments directly, are of decisive importance for the carrying of merchants' stocks and consequently for the orders from merchants to manufacturers. Hawtrey holds that the gold standard is responsible for the downward trend, which is the result of the rise in interest rates needed to protect the gold reserve, and he recommends to the authorities a policy of credit control in order to stabilize the flow of purchasing power, which consists almost exclusively of bank money. The specific role assigned to interest and the association of the business cycle with the gold standard makes this a somewhat frail theory.

The contribution of Albert Hahn,[7] a former German banker, is remarkable despite the fact that it was ignored by the English-speaking theorists. In his credit theory he follows McLeod rather than Schumpeter; his emphasis is on the technical mechanism of credit and its operation. His theory of interest is that of Schumpeter. But Hahn suggests new approaches to the problem of the relation between saving and investment. He revived the thesis of Malthus, later much emphasized by Keynes, that saving, far from automatically bringing investment with it, is in itself a reduction of effective demand. Moreover, Hahn added what Keynes later called the doctrine of the rising propensity to save or falling propensity to consume, in the normal progress to greater wealth. Hahn infers from this doctrine and from the theory of Malthus that, if a crisis is to be avoided, rising investment must offset rising saving. This thesis is also at the center of Keynes's system. Whereas Wicksell, who held a similar theory, had presupposed full employment, Hahn associates the fluctuations of investment with those of employment and output.

All these motives were richly elaborated by John Maynard Keynes,[8] now Lord Keynes, a Cambridge man, and used as material in the building of a new structure of thought. Keynes goes far beyond Wicksell and Hahn in developing the theory of saving and investment, proving that saving and investment, for all their dynamic relationship, are always equal for the economy as a whole. Total income is equal to total output and spending is equal to consumption; hence, income that is not spent but saved, and production that is not consumed but invested are equal. But the intentions of savers on the one hand and investors on the other are not connected and may diverge. There may be more intended investment than saving, the momentary result being that stocks of consumption goods fall short of demand and are depleted. In other words, this rush for goods brings about an unintended disinvestment, which reduces aggregate investment to an amount equal to savings. In the longer run the depletion of consumers' goods leads to more orders, more investment, higher incomes, and a rising saving quota, until saving equals intended investment. If saving exceeds investment, the demand for goods falls short of the supply, and the expected disinvestment does not take place; this unintended investment raises total investment to an amount equal to saving in the short run, and reduces orders, investment, and income in the longer run, until the saving quota out of a lower income is only equal to intended investment. This is the mechanism which, within the fundamental condition of equality between saving and investment, makes for fluctuations of income and employment.

Like Hahn, Keynes holds that the rising propensity to save is the gravest and ever-present danger to the stability of the system. This theory must be classified with the underconsumption theories, like that of Malthus, because they all trace the downward movement of the economic process to the inability of the community to consume its growing income. And this tendency is not easily reversible. Alvin H. Hansen[9] of Harvard, the leading representative of the theory in the United States, has demonstrated how vast is the amount of more or less irrevocable, institutionalized saving, e.g. in private and social insurance. The use of boom profits for hastily writing off new plants, while considered sound financial practice from the point of view of an isolated enterprise, does much to break the boom. Investment, on the other hand, fluctuates with the prospects of net profit, which is the difference between expected gross profit and interest. Gross profit depends on the application of new ideas, which raise the 'marginal efficiency of capital.' Interest, however, is regarded as independent of such considerations and determined solely by the liquidity preference of the public.

This theory of interest assumes a new dimension in comparison with those of Schumpeter and Hahn, which connect interest only with the liquidity preference of the credit-issuing banks. Keynes's extension of the theory of interest is an application of Marshall's theory of money, which has been handed down by an almost purely oral tradition, and of the coincident, independently conceived, theory of Mises. Marshall and Mises replace, in the quantity theory of money, the inconvenient and unsystematic concept of the circulation velocity by its reciprocal, the demand for money, in the sense of people's desire to hold it in order to be liquid. This desire will normally be for the equivalent of a certain quantity of goods in order to cover the period between expected income payments or expected business proceeds, and to meet possible emergencies. The demand for money in this sense will thus rise as prices rise and fall with falling prices, but will be lower in the expectation of rising prices (since people try to purchase goods before their prices rise and thus add to the inflation by adding to the demand) and will be higher when a fall in prices is expected, with the opposite effect. The desire to hold money in the expectation of falling prices is the third motive for liquidity added by Keynes; the speculative motive for holding money. When prices—e.g. bond prices, which rise as the general rate of interest falls—have sufficiently risen to make some owners apprehensive of the future price, these owners liquidate their assets and hold cash. Only if prices fall and interest rises again will they part with their money, and the rate at which they do so is the measure of their liquidity preference. Hence, interest is determined by forces independent of investment and may be, and actually is for long periods of time, too high for that volume of investment which would provide full employment.

The relation between interest and saving is here the opposite of that posited by classical theory, according to which a rise in the rate of interest not only checks investment but stimulates saving, and a fall in the rate of interest has the opposite effect; in this way, a unique equilibrium is reached between saving and investment, which are not naturally equal. According to Hahn's and Keynes's doctrine, the volume of saving is not only dependent on the rate of interest but on the size of the income out of which the saving is to be done: the saving rises with the income and more than the income. Hence, a rise in the rate of interest, by checking investment, diminishes income and both the absolute and the relative amounts of saving out of that income; conversely, a lower rate of interest stimulates investment—if there is a given expectation of profit—and increases income and the absolute and relative amounts of saving. What interest equates is neither saving and intended investment nor bank credit and intended investment, but the supply of money issued by the banking system and the amount which the public wants to hold; this amount is determined by the schedule of liquidity preference and by the size of the income, which in turn is determined by the volume of investment at the given rate of interest.

Two special theories fit into this system of thought and help to explain the modes and sizes of the fluctuations in the economic process. The first is the 'multiplier' theory: any increment to the circulating purchasing power, such as is invariably connected with the rising phase of the business cycle, causes an addition to total income larger than the amount of the increment. The reason is that the first recipient, into whose income the additional money enters, buys additional goods and, in payment therefor, passes the money on to his supplier, for whom in turn it is again additional income. Thus, the original increment is 'multiplied' in any one income period, according to the circulation velocity of incomes, until theoretically one circuit is completed and the money arrives at its starting point again. This idea was closely analyzed by Pigou,[10] who gave the credit for it to Walter Bagehot,[11] famous British financial expert and writer of the last century. Later, in the great depression, R. F. Kahn[12] of Cambridge investigated the effects of relief payments on total income and added to the theory the important observation that even if payments continued indefinitely, the effect would not be multiplied to infinity, because leakages diminish the amount passed on at every step in the circulation, as debts are repaid to grocers and bakers and by these to wholesalers and banks; furthermore, the amounts paid for imported materials leave the circulation of the country. Kahn shows that, given a stable percentage of leakage at every step, the effect of the original payment is multiplied over an indefinite period of time by the reciprocal of the leakage, e.g. three times if the leakage is one third. Further discussion, climaxed by the work of John Maurice Clark,[13] showed the impossibility of assuming that the percentage of leakage is constant, since debt repayments reach their end, new savings may or may not follow, etc. The main result of the discussion was the realization that the tangible effects of an increase in income are limited to a relatively short period of time. Keynes generalized the multiplier theory: any addition to purchasing power, whether inaugurated by public policy or private investment, produces a multiplied effect, and the downward spiral must be explained conversely.

The other special theory is of incomparably greater importance. It is called variously the 'theory of the accelerator' or the 'principle of derived demand' or the 'principle of the relation,' and was first developed by the French theorist Albert Aftalion;[14] Spiethoff too suggested it. The chief authority on this subject too is Clark,[15] and Harrod[16] has integrated the theory into the Keynesian system of thought. According to this theory, the fluctuations in the demand for durable goods—both producers' and consumers'—are far more violent than the fluctuations in the demand for transient goods, because, once durable goods have been produced, the demand for them has been satisfied for several years to come, and normal production is reduced to the annual replacement quota. Suppose the latter is 10 per cent, and the demand increases by 10 per cent of its former volume, the output for one year must then be raised to twice the former amount (which was only the replacement quota) and then reduced to whatever the new replacement quota may be. Conversely, a decrease of the demand by 10 per cent would temporarily halt production, since one of the ten replacement quotas would no longer have to be filled. Any change in the mere rate of increase or decrease of the demand thus produces a cyclical movement in production because of the key position of the replacement quota in the durable-goods market. The Norwegian Ragnar Frisch and Clark[17] have greatly refined this theory and have again shown that crude arithmetical reasoning must be avoided. But the unsettling consequences of the operation of this principle can be appreciated when it is realized that demand shifts more and more to highly durable goods. And the even more significant conclusion follows that, with heavy industry geared to the demand of a rapidly expanding and mechanizing industrial world, any diminution in the rate of expansion is likely to bring disaster. In an appraisal of the future of an unregulated system, the decreasing population rate, which diminishes the demand for houses, and the cessation of capital export as young countries provide for their own industrialization, must be accounted unfavorable tendencies, while the spread of further technological improvements makes for a more favorable prospect; the deciding factor may be the post-war reconstruction demand and assistance to backward countries in raising their productivity.

Keynes's system of economic theory is far from complete. It is a dynamic theory of employment and makes reference to the factors which bring about the business cycle, but it is not yet a real theory of the cycle. The way out of our difficulties through the creation of additional demand, either by public investment or public consumption, is not controversial in principle, although its political implications are. But some implications of the theory are dubious. As popularly understood, Keynes's theory traces the discouragement of investment to an interest rate that is too high. But this interpretation is not quite consistent with the doctrine that the cycle is traceable to violent fluctuations in the expectation of profit while liquidity preference is much more stable. The rate of interest cannot be lower than zero, yet even a zero rate would be 'too high' for a period in which losses are expected from investment.

More generally, Keynes's system, first conceived in the great depression, may seem to later historians as a reflection of special troubles rather than as a balanced presentation of the economic world as a whole. His theory may be said to over-emphasize Quesnay and Marx as against Adam Smith. For the equilibrating forces of the price mechanism, although too weak to prevent the depression, were still too strong to permit the system to be completely disrupted; a minimum of spontaneous order survived even in the crisis. And the problems of equilibrium, overshadowed by the depression, would be raised again if specific conditions of stability in the financial and in selected industrial sections of the economic system were realized. More specifically, modern theory has swept aside rather than refuted or considered older theories. In a reorganized and stabilized world the length of the period of production as studied by Boehm-Bawerk would be of paramount importance again, and neither profit expectations nor liquidity preferences would fluctuate as violently as in the past once freedom from fear removes the main reasons for such fluctuations.

Keynes's system is predicated on a very definite assumption with regard to wages, namely that the present institutional organization of society makes it impossible for workers to increase employment by lowering their real wages, even if they wanted to do so, because a cut in money wages may bring down prices and thereby raise real wages. This doctrine is tantamount to the assumption that wages are more or less stable—an assumption which inevitably leads to a number of consequences at variance with orthodox reasoning. Here then is the point on which the attack on Keynes's system seems to concentrate: the system is supposed to be valid only if wages are kept from fluctuating with prices, a condition which in itself, whether or not it can be altered, is contrary to the classical theory of a price-regulated economy. Pigou,[18] the main target of Keynes's criticism, has rejoined by pointing out this implication. If this criticism is well founded, the 'general theory' of Keynes would be revealed as a special theory distinguished by realism and closeness to the facts of history, but not necessarily in conflict with the more abstract classical doctrine. Much bewilderment and confusion, which inevitably attends the advance into new territory, would thus be relieved.

NOTES

CHAPTER I

1. Adherents of the economic interpretation of history should find nothing objectionable here. Their doctrine is on a different plane. According to it, the political authority is formed by those who own the means of production. Once the authority is established, however, it is in political control, and this is what we are discussing. For in the authoritarian system, the political power, even if established by the owners of the means of production, organizes economic activities directly; in a system of laissez-faire, the government, again derived from the owners, has only the function of a custodian, but economic activities are self-regulating, being so geared as to reproduce the supremacy of property. In the first case, the power of property, assuming that it is the 'ultimate determining power,' asserts itself through the orders of its government to producers, in the second case through 'the free play of forces.' What we are discussing is the difference between two techniques of economic control, and this discussion is compatible with any philosophy of history.

2. This last point will be illustrated below, page 208. The terminology here employed is, of course, arbitrary. The *Gestalt* of any future economic society will require a theory to describe it and make it transparent; such a theory, more general, would be parallel to what is correctly called 'theory' in the other social sciences. The uniqueness of traditional economic theory, however, well justifies the reservation of a special name for it. Of the uniqueness of its method every social scientist who attends a discussion between economic theorists becomes immediately aware. The reason for this uniqueness is the problem of economic theory: how does proportionality between independent economic units come to be established?

3. A brilliant example is the book by Charles Gide and Charles Rist, *A History of Economic Doctrines*, 1915 (translated from the French edition of 1913).

4. The outstanding example is the contribution of Joseph Schumpeter, 'Epochen der Dogmen- und Methodengeschichte,' in *Grundriss der Sozialoekonomik*, vol. I, 2nd edition, 1925.

5. Karl Marx, *Theorien ueber den Mehrwert*, 3 vols., edited by Kautsky, 1905-10 (no translation), is the classic model. A recent example is Erich Roll, *A History of Economic Thought*, 1939. Gunnar Myrdal's essay, *Das Politische Element in der Nationaloekonomischen Doktrin-*

bildung, 1932, represents a much more mature development of this approach.

6. This is the doctrine, presented with a most extraordinary amount of learning, of Karl Mannheim, *Man and Society in an Age of Reconstruction*, 1940.

CHAPTER II

1. His economic discussions are in his *Politics*, Book 1, and in the *Nicomachean Ethics*, Book v.

2. For a very good survey of ancient and medieval thinking on economic matters, see Edgar Salin, *Geschichte der Volkswirtschaftslehre*, 2nd edition, 1929, Part 1.

3. On mercantilism, see Gustav Schmoller, *The Mercantile System and Its Historical Significance*, 1895 (translation of a chapter from his *Studien ueber die wirtschaftliche Politik Friedrichs des Grossen*, 1884); William Cunningham, *The Growth of English Industry and Commerce*, vol. 1, 4th edition, 1905; and Eli Heckscher, *Mercantilism*, 2 vols., 1935 (from the Swedish), whose point of view appears less acceptable to this author.

4. 1530-96.

5. 1571-1641.

6. 1623-87.

7. 1626-92. *Der teutsche Fuerstenstaat*, 1656.

8. 1635-82. *Politischer Discurs von den eigentlichen Ursachen des Auff- und Abnehmens der Staedt, Laender und Republicken*, 1668.

9. 1634-1712. *Oesterreich ueber alles, wann es nur will*, 1684.

10. For the cameralists, see Louise Sommer, *Die Oesterreichischen Kameralisten in Dogmengeschichtlicher Darstellung*, 2 vols., 1920 and 1925, and Kurt Zielenziger, *Die Alten Deutschen Kameralisten*, 1914.

11. The dynamic character of mercantilism has been particularly emphasized by Werner Sombart, *Der Moderne Kapitalismus*, 2nd edition, chapter 56.

12. *Réponse . . . aux paradoxes de monsieur de Malestroict touchant l'enchérissement de toutes les choses*, 1568. An abstract in translation is found in A. E. Monroe, *Early Economic Thought*, 1924.

13. Gerald Malynes, *Consuetudo, vel Lex mercatoria*, 1622.

14. Sir Josiah Child, 1630-99. *A New Discourse of Trade*, 1693.

15. *Some Considerations of the Consequences of the Lowering of Interest and Raising the Value of Money*, 1691.

16. *England's Treasure by forraign trade*, 1664; new edition edited by W. J. Ashley, 1895.

17. *Six livres de la République*, 1576, Book vi.

18. *Verbum sapienti, or an account of the wealth and expences of England . . .* 1665, published as an appendix to *The Political Anatomy of Ireland*, 1691.

19. *The Fable of the Bees: Or, Private Vices, Publick Benefits*, 1714.

20. *A treatise of taxes and contributions*, 1662. It is amusing to see that Karl Marx's preoccupation with his exploitation theory, as well as his generosity towards supposed predecessors, made him re-interpret this proposition in such a way as to suggest that Petty is really the orig-

inator of the Marxian doctrine: *Theorien ueber den Mehrwert*, vol. I, p. 3.
21. *Political Arithmetick*, 1682.
22. Good historical analyses are Arthur Eli Monroe, *Monetary Theory Before Adam Smith*, 1923, and E. A. J. Johnson, *Predecessors of Adam Smith*, 1937.
23. 1623-87. His most important writings in economic theory, except *Quantulumcumque concerning money*, 1682, have been mentioned in footnotes 18, 20, and 21. His collected economic-statistical writings were republished in two volumes in 1899.
24. 1641-91. *Discourses upon Trade*, 1691.
25. 1622-1704. *Some Considerations of the Consequences of the Lowering of Interest and Raising the Value of Money*, 1691; *Two Treatises concerning Government*, 1690.
26. 1680-1734. *Essai sur la nature du Commerce en général, traduit de l' Anglois*, 1755.
27. No book has ever had a stranger history. The—imperfect—French translation is supposed to have been done by the author himself, who had a home in Paris. Why he should have chosen publication in French at a time when he lived in London is among the mysteries of the story. The extraordinary delay, by twenty-one years, in the posthumous publication is another mystery. The book was quoted by Adam Smith in his chapter on wages but then forgotten. It was rediscovered by W. S. Jevons in 1881 and republished by Henry Higgs in both the French and English versions in 1931, with richly documented biographical essays by both Jevons and Higgs. A German translation also appeared in 1931, with an equally valuable introduction by F. A. Hayek.
28. Ludwig von Mises, *The Theory of Money and Credit*, 1934, translated from the German edition of 1912.
29. 1711-76. *Political Discourses*, 1752. This collection includes a number of papers on economic matters, among them papers on interest, on money, and on the balance of trade.

CHAPTER III

1. Two older works deserve to be consulted: James Bonar, *Philosophy and Political Economy in Some of Their Historical Relations*, 1893, and Wilhelm Hasbach, *Die Philosophischen Grundlagen der von François Quesnay and Adam Smith begruendeten Politischen Oekonomie*, 1890. Also Heinrich Dietzel, 'Individualismus,' in *Handwoerterbuch der Staatswissenschaften*, 3rd edition, 1912. For a monographic study of Leibniz and Locke as laying the philosophical basis of classical economics see the first essay of W. Stark, *The Ideal Foundations of Economic Thought, Three Essays*, 1943.
2. See above p. 19 and later p. 142.
3. 1694-1774. None of his publications appeared under his name, and there are a number of unpublished manuscripts. Most publications were in the form of articles in periodicals and in the *Grande Encyclopédie*. The sole exception is the *Tableau Economique* itself, which was privately printed in 1758, but the stock was soon exhausted; it was re-

printed in the supplementary volume to the book of Victor Riquetti Marquis de Mirabeau, *L'Ami des Hommes*, 1760. The first printing was reproduced in facsimile after its rediscovery in 1894. Somewhat abridged translations are to be found in the collection, *Early Economic Thought*, edited by A. E. Monroe, 1924, and in Othmar Spann, *History of Economics*, 1930 (London edition, *Types of Economic Theory*; from the German *Haupttheorien der Volkswirtschaftslehre*, a book whose sound scholarship is overshadowed by vicious propagandistic distortions; it should immediately be added, however, that the author did not yield to the Nazis and died in a concentration camp.) This is the so-called *Grand Tableau*, as distinguished from the *Petit Tableau* in the article *Analyse du Tableau Economique*, first published in 1766. The *Grand Tableau* has never yet found a satisfactory explanation; we follow the *Petit Tableau* and Quesnay's analysis of it. For all the anonymity of his writings, Quesnay exerted an enormous influence through his personal position and the circle of his devoted friends and pupils, who were organized as a scientific club. The list of Quesnay's writings was compiled by August Oncken, and he also edited the first (almost) complete edition of Quesnay works—in 1888! The *Analyse du Tableau Economique*, along with another important article, the *Maximes générales du gouvernement économique d'un royaume agricole*, has also appeared in a German translation, 1921; no English translation. For a survey of, and excerpts from, the manuscripts see G. Weulersse, *Les Manuscrits économiques de François Quesnay et du Marquis de Mirabeau*, 1910. On the physiocrats, see August Oncken, *Geschichte der Nationaloekonomie*, vol. 1: *Die Zeit vor Adam Smith*, 1902; Henry Higgs, *The Physiocrats*, 1897; G. Weulersse, *Le mouvement Physiocratique en France de 1756 à 1770*, 1910.

4. 1727-81. *Reflexions on the Formation and distribution of Riches* (French original 1766; many editions and translations). It should be mentioned that the influence of Turgot's economic writings was at least equaled by that of his outline of a philosophy of history, which anticipated Comte's doctrine of the three stages in the history of human thinking by distinguishing the animistic, speculative, and scientific stages: *Discours sur les progrès successifs de l' Esprit Humain*, 1750.

5. 1720-93. *L'ordre naturel et essential des Sociétés politiques*, 1767. This book was recognized by the physiocrats as the best summary of their system.

6. 1728-87. *Della moneta libri quinque*, 1750; *Dialogues sur le Commerce des bleds*, 1770. On Galiani's theory of value (in his book on money) see later pp. 107-8.

7. 1723-93. *Theory of Moral Sentiments*, 1760; *An Inquiry into the Nature and Causes of the Wealth of Nations*, 1776. Numerous editions and translations. Edwin Cannan in 1896 published *Lectures on Justice, Police, Revenue, and Arms, delivered in Glasgow by Adam Smith, from Notes taken by a Student in 1763*. Thus it can be seen that Smith's life-work comprised social ethics, political science, and economics. Like Locke and Hume, Quesnay and Turgot, and like Mill, Marx, and Oppenheimer after him, Smith was not an economist in the modern specialized sense of this word; he, precisely like Marx, was a philosopher

who developed his economic theory as a special chapter of his philosophical picture of the world. All these men believed in a relatively autonomous sphere of economics. But it would not have occurred to any one of them to disregard the joints which connect economic life with general social life; such narrowness of mind, however, has become the professional disease of too many specialized economists of the highly technical modern training, who rationalize their deficiency by insisting on the methodological wisdom of discussing economics in a vacuum outside the world. On Smith, see John Rae, *Life of Adam Smith*, 1895. (The author of this book is not the theorist of the same name whose ideas will be discussed in a later context.) That Smith was the founding father not only of economics, but of sociology as well is shown, with rich documentation, by Albert Salomon, 'Adam Smith as Sociologist,' *Social Research*, 1945.

8. 1670-1733. *The Fable of the Bees: Or, Private Vices, Publick Benefits*, 1714. The first edition 1705 appeared under the title, *The Grumbling Hive, or Knaves Turn'd Honest*.

9. See later p. 107-8.

10. Adolph Lowe, *Economics and Sociology*, 1935.

11. *Traité d'Economie Politique*, 1803. On Say, see p. 107 ff.

CHAPTER IV

1. For an excellent history, see Edwin Cannan, *A History of the Theories of Production and Distribution in English Political Economy from 1776 to 1848*, 3rd edition, 1917. A spirited defense, copiously documented, of the Classical School against its misrepresentation by its historicist (and institutionalist) critics can be found in Richard Schueller, *Die Klassische Nationaloekonomie und ihre Gegner*, 1895.

2. 1766-1834. *An Essay on the Principle of Population as it affects the Future Improvement of Society, with remarks on the speculations of Mr. Godwin, M. Condorcet, and other writers*, 1798 (anonymous; five more editions of increasing volume, under slightly changing titles, with the author's name, during his lifetime; numerous further editions and translations): *An Inquiry into the Nature and Progress of Rent*, 1815; *Principles of Political Economy, considered with a view to their pracical application*, 1820. Most important are Malthus's letters to Ricardo. On Malthus see James Bonar, *Malthus and his work*, 1885, and the charming essay of John Maynard Keynes in his *Essays in Biography*, 1933.

3. See the article by Ludwig Elster, 'Bevoelkerungslehre und Bevoelkerungspolitik,' in *Handwoerterbuch der Staatswissenschaften*, 4th edition.

4. 1543-1617. *Delle cause della grandezza e magnificenza delle città*, 1589.

5. 1712-69. *Lezioni di economia civile*, 1769.

6. 1713-1790. *Riflessioni sulla populazione delle nazioni par rapporto all' economia nazionale*, 1790.

7. In the article 'Hommes,' written for the *Encyclopédie* but not published, rediscovered only in 1890, and published in volume 1 of the *Revue d'Histoire des doctrines économiques et sociales*, 1890.

8. 1706-90. *Observations Concerning the Increase of Mankind* etc., 1755.
9. 1756-1836. *An Inquiry Concerning Political Justice* etc., 1793.
10. 1743-94. *Esquisse d'un tableau historique des progrès de l'esprit humain*, 1794. The famous philosopher—the title of his book shows his dependence on Turgot—was co-author of the Declaration of the Rights of Man issued by the French Revolution and shortly afterwards became a victim of the Revolution.
11. It is strange that so erudite an author as Cannan should have denied Malthus's knowledge of the law of diminishing returns, in view of the arithmetical series, which is plainly illustrative of the law.
12. 1772-1823. *The high price of bullion, a proof of the Depreciation of Bank-Notes*, 1809; *An Essay on the Influence of a low Price of corn on the profits of stock*, 1815; *Proposals for an Economical and Secure Currency*, 1816; *The Principles of Political Economy and Taxation*, 1817; 3rd edition, with a new chapter 'On Machinery,' 1821. Ricardo's letters to Malthus and other friends are important. It is worth mentioning that, as a member of parliament during the last years of his life, Ricardo proved far from a doctrinaire adherent of laissez-faire in its application to either international trade or social problems. Cf. on Ricardo's doctrines in a wide context of preceding and contemporaneous writings Karl Diehl, *Sozialwissenschaftliche Erlaeuterungen zu David Ricardo's Grundgesetzen der Volkswirtschaft und Besteuerung*, 2 vols., 3rd edition, 1922.
13. 1783-1828. *An Essay on the Application of Capital to Land*, 1815.
14. 1739-1808. *An Inquiry into the Nature of the corn laws*, 1777.
15. *An Inquiry into the Nature and Progress of Rent*, 1815.
16. *Observations sur la mémoire de M. de Saint-Péravy*, 1768.
17. *A Tract on Monetary Reform*, 1923.
18. *The Purchasing Power of Money*, 1903.
19. *Staatswissenschaftliche Untersuchungen*, 1832.
20. Bastable, *Theory of International Trade*, 1897. Taussig, 1859-1940. 'Wages and Prices in Relation to International Trade,' *Quarterly Journal of Economics*, 1906; *Tariff History of the United States*, 1888 (7 later editions); *Wages and Capital*, 1896; *Principles of Economics*, 1911 (numerous editions and translations).
21. 1760-1850. *An Inquiry into the Nature and Effects of the Paper Credit of Great Britain*, 1802.
22. *The Theory of Social Economy*, 1932 (German edition 1918).
23. Born 1890. 'International Trade under Depreciated Paper. The United States 1862-1879,' *Quarterly Journal of Economics*, 1922; *The Abolition of Unemployment*, 1932; *Social Goals and Economic Institutions*, 1942.
24. Born 1892. *Canada's Balance of International Indebtedness*, 1924.
25. 'International Trade under Depreciated Paper,' *Quarterly Journal of Economics*, 1917.
26. 1767-1832. *Traité d'Economie Politique*, 1803; many editions.
27. *Della moneta libri quinque*, 1750. Selected sections from this book are rendered in English by A. E. Monroe, *Early Economic Thought*, 1924. On Galiani see also above p. 62.
28. 1714-80. *Le Commerce et le Gouvernement relativement l'un à l'autre*, 1776.

29. 1783-1850. *Der Isolierte Staat in Beziehung auf Landwirtschaft und Nationaloekonomie*, part I, 1826; part II, 1850-63. The term 'isolated state' denotes not anything political, but the Ricardian method of abstraction from connections unessential to the problem.

30. Born 1868. *Ueber den Standort der Industrien, Teil I: Reine Theorie des Standortes*, 1909; *Kulturgeschichte als Kultursoziologie*, 1935.

31. On Clark see below p. 197 ff.

32. Later von Hermann, often quoted thus, 1795-1868. *Staatswissenschaftliche Untersuchungen*, 1832, several editions. This book, remarkable for perspicacity and careful presentation, was regarded as a classic and regularly quoted by Marshall. In political history Hermann was also distinguished as one of the leaders of the then strongly liberal German universities; the abortive liberal revolution of 1848 made him a leading member of its parliament.

33. 1802-84. *Lectures on Political Economy*, 1834.

34. 1759-1839. *An Inquiry into the Nature and Origin of Public Wealth*, 1804.

35. 1790-1864. *An Outline of the Science of Political Economy*, 1836. On Senior, see M. Bowley, *Nassau Senior and Classical Economics*, 1937.

36. 1806-73. *System of Logic*, 1843; *Essay on some unsettled questions of political economy*, 1844; *Principles of Political Economy, with some of their applications to social philosophy*, 2 vols., 1848 (numerous editions and translations); *On Liberty*, 1859; *Considerations on Representative Government*, 1861; *Dissertations and Disquisitions*, 4 vols.

37. 1844-1931. On Brentano see below p. 178.

38. 1840-97. *The Wages Question*, 1876; *Political Economy*, 1883.

39. 1813-80. *On Labor*, 1869.

40. On both see below p. 202.

41. 1773-1836. *Elements of Political Economy*, 1821.

42. 1801-50. *Harmonies of Political Economy* (French original, 1850).

43. 1793-1879. *The Past, the Present, and the Future*, 1848; *Principles of Social Science*, 3 vols., 1858-9.

44. The most recent presentation, F. J. Normano, *The Spirit of American Economics*, 1943, again completely misunderstands Carey.

45. On both see below p. 167.

CHAPTER V

1. 1773-1842. *Nouveaux Principes d'Economie Politique*, 1819.

2. 1789-1846. *The National System of Political Economy* (German original 1841; several editions and translations); *Le Système Naturel d'Economie Politique*, written 1837, published for the first time, with a German translation and scholarly introduction, by Edgar Salin and Arthur Sommer, 1927. On List cf. Arthur Sommer, *Friedrich List's System der Politischen Oekonomie*, 1927.

3. Cf. Alfred Meusel, *List und Marx*, 1928.

4. In his *Report on Manufactures, communicated to the House of Representatives*, 1791.

5. *Statement of Some New Principles on the Subject of Political Economy*, 1834. On Rae see p. 199 ff.

6. Born 1872. *Schutzzoll und Freihandel*, 1905; *Die Klassische Nationaloekonomie und ihre Gegner*, 1895.

7. 1824-68. *Grundriss der Volkswirtschaftslehre*, 1863. Mangoldt was, like his teacher Hermann, a theorist of considerable merit, whose contribution well deserves a fuller exploration than it has found.

8. 1783-1833. *An Inquiry into the Principles of the Distribution of Wealth most conducive to Human Happiness*, 1824; *Labour Rewarded*, 1827. For a detailed study see W. Stark, *The Ideal Foundations of Economic Thought*, 1943, second essay.

9. 1799-1850. *A Lecture of Human Happiness*, 1825.

10. 1809-95. *Labour's Wrongs and Labour's Remedies, or The Age of Might and the Age of Right*, 1839.

11. 1787-1869. *Labour Defended against the Claims of Capital, or The Unproductiveness of Capital*, 1825. For a detailed study see W. Stark, *The Ideal Foundations of Economic Thought*, 1943, second essay.

12. Gunnar Myrdal, *Das Politische Element in der Nationaloekonomischen Doktrinbildung*, 1931.

13. 1760-1825.

14. 1770-1857.

15. 1805-75. *Zur Erkenntnis unserer Sozialwissenschaftlichen Zustaende*, 1842; *Soziale Briefe an v. Kirchmann*, 1850-51; *Das Kapital*, published from an unfinished manuscript in 1884. Rodbertus took an active part in the liberal movement in Germany and served as a member of parliament and even, for a short time, as a Minister of Education in the liberal revolution of 1848. Cf. Heinrich Dietzel, *Karl Rodbertus, Darstellung seines Lebens und seiner Lehre*, 2 vols., 1886-8.

16. 'Handelskrisen und Hypothenkennot,' *Gesammelte Schriften*, vol. IV.

17. *Poverty of Philosophy, A Reply to M. Proudhon's Philosophy of Poverty*, French original, 1847.

18. 1809-65. *Système des contradictions economiques, ou philosophie de la misère*, 2 vols., 1846; *Qu'est-ce que la propriété?* 1840; *Organization du crédit et de la circulation*, 1848. Proudhon, a self-taught man, fertile in ideas but without intellectual discipline, was an extremely prolific writer and very active in public life, particularly in the revolution of 1848. On his profound insights, see the chapters devoted to him in Georges Gurvitch, *L'Idée du droit social*, 1932.

19. 1812-78. *Die Nationaloekonomie der Gegenwart und Zukunft*, 1848. On Hildebrand, see below p. 178.

CHAPTER VI

1. 1818-83. Best biography and appraisal of his intellectual development: Robert Wilbrandt, *Karl Marx*, 1918 (vol. 261 of the series, *Aus Natur und Geisteswelt*). See also A. D. Lindsay, *Karl Marx' Capital*, 1925.

2. Sources of Marx's philosophy: *Communist Manifesto* (with Friedrich Engels), 1847; Preface to *Contribution to a Critique of Political Economy*, written 1859, published by Karl Kautsky, 1902. For more profound studies: Karl Marx, *Der Historische Materialismus*, edited by S. Landshut, and J. P. Meyer, 2 vols., Leipzig 1932, containing Marx's philosophical manuscripts 1840-46, of which several were here pub-

lished for the first time, with an able introduction by S. Landshut; shortly afterwards they were also published in the collected works edited by the Marx-Engels-Lenin Institute in Moscow (D. Rjazanoff). No translation. For a popular summary of the philosophy: F. Engels, *Socialism, Utopian and Scientific* (first edition in French, 1880).

3. For a fuller discussion see E. Heimann, 'Marxism and Christianity,' in *Christianity and Society*, Spring 1942.

4. For a fuller discussion see E. Heimann, *Communism, Fascism, or Democracy?* 1938, Chapter III.

5. *Das Kapital*, vol. I, 1867; vols. II and III edited from unfinished manuscripts by F. Engels and published 1885 and 1895 resp. Several English editions. As a supplement: *Theorien ueber den Mehrwert*, 3 vols., ed. by K. Kautsky from partly unfinished manuscripts, 1905-10; no translation. Best systematic survey of Marx's and Marxian economics: Paul M. Sweezy, *The Theory of Capitalist Development. Principles of Marxian Political Economy*, 1942.

6. *Der Kapitalprofit*, 1920.

7. *Das Grundgesetz der Marxschen Gesellschaftslehre*, 1903.

8. 1820-97.

9. *Karl Marx and the Close of his System*, 1898 (published in German as an article, 1896; integrated into the later German editions of his *Geschichte und Kritik der Kapitalzinstheorien*).

10. *An Essay in Marxian Economics*, 1942.

11. *Capitalism, Socialism, and Democracy*, 1942.

12. 'Zur Berichtigung der grundlegenden Theoretischen Construction von Marx im Dritten Bande des "Kapital,"' *Jahrbuecher fuer Nationaloekonomie und Statistik*, 1907, summarized by Sweezy, *op. cit.*

13. 1871-1919. *Studien ueber die Bewegungsgesetze der Gesellschaftlichen Entwickelung*, 1922.

14. 1877-1941. *Das Finanzkapital*, 1910.

15. 1870-1919. *Die Akkumulation des Kapitals. Ein Beitrag zur oekonomischen Erklaerung des Imperialimus*, 1912, and *Die Akkumulation des Kapitals, oder Was die Epigonen aus der Marxschen Theorie gemacht haben. Eine Antikritik*, 1917.

16. 1858-1914. *Imperialism*, 1902.

17. 1864-1943. *System der Soziologie*, in four double volumes, of which the third contains the system of economic theory, a readaptation of the *System der Reinen und Politischen Oekonomie*, 1910; a somewhat abridged but still voluminous version was published in Holland in 1937 under the title, *Das Kapital—Kritik der Politischen Oekonomie*. For specific questions, earlier writings must still be consulted, in the first place *Wert und Kapitalprofit*, 1916; monographs on Malthus, Marx, and Ricardo in 1901, 1903, and 1909 respectively. The other volumes of the *System der Soziologie* include the general sociology and social psychology (I), the political theory (II), and the economic and social history (IV). Of all these writings only a preliminary version of the political doctrine has been published in English (and many other languages): *The State*, 1914, 4th edition 1926. For a brief survey, see E. Heimann, 'Franz Oppenheimer's Economic Ideas,' *Social Research*, 1944.

18. 1833-1921. *Kritische Geschichte der Nationaloekonomie und des Sozialismus*, 1871; *Kursus der National- und Sozialoekonomie*, 1873.
19. 1839-97. *Progress and Poverty*, 1879.

CHAPTER VII

1. 1817-94. *Grundriss zu Vorlesungen ueber die Staatswirtschaft nach Geschichtlicher Methode*, 1843; *System der Volkswirtschaft*, 5 vols., 1854-95.
2. 1812-78. *Die Nationaloekonomie der Gegenwart und Zukunft*, 1848.
3. 1821-98. *Die Politische Oekonomie vom Standpunkt der Geschichtlichen Methode*, 1853; *Geld und Kredit*, 3 vols., 1873-9.
4. 1838-1917. *The Mercantile System and Its Historical Significance*, 1895 (translated from a chapter of *Studien ueber die Wirtschaftliche Politik Friedrichs des Grossen*, 1884); *Grundriss der Allgemeinen Volkswirtschaftslehre*, 2 vols., 1900-1904; 'Volkswirtschaftslehre,' in *Handwoerterbuch der Staatswissenschaften*, 3rd edition.
5. 1844-1931. *Die Arbeitergilden der Gegenwart*, 2 vols., 1871-2; *Der Wirtschaftende Mensch in der Geschichte*, 1923; *Geschichte der Wirtschaftlichen Entwickelung Englands*, 3 vols., 1927-9.
6. 1842-1926. *Die Bauernbefreiung und der Ursprung der Landarbeiter in den aelteren Teilen Preussens*, 2 vols., 1887; *State Theory of Money* (German original in 1905).
7. 1847-1930. *Die Entstehung der Volkswirtschaft*, 1893 (later editions much enlarged); *Arbeit und Rhythmus*, 1896.
8. 1864-1920. *The Protestant Ethic and the Spirit of Capitalism* (German original as an article 1904-05); 'Agrarverhaeltnisse im Altertum,' in *Handwoerterbuch der Staatswissenschaften*, 3rd edition, 1909, now in *Gesammelte Aufsaetze zur Sozial- und Wirtschaftsgeschichte*, 1925; *Wirtschaftsethik der Weltreligionen*, from 1915 on; *General Economic History* (German edition, 1921); *Wirtschaft und Gesellschaft*, 1921; etc.
9. 1863-1941. *The Quintessence of Capitalism*, 1915; *Der Moderne Kapitalismus*, 6 vols., 1919-27; *Der Proletarische Sozialismus*, 2 vols., 1924; etc.
10. 1849-1919. *The Growth of English Industry and Commerce*, 3 vols.; *Western Civilization in its Economic Aspects*, 2 vols., 1898-1900.
11. 1860-1927. *An Introduction to English Economic History and Theory*, 2 vols.
12. *Untersuchungen ueber die Methode der Sozialwissenschaften und der Politischen Oekonomie insbesondere*, 1883; *Die Irrtuemer des Historismus*, 1884. Schmoller's reply in his *Jahrbuch fuer Gesetzgebung*, 1883.
13. 1828-1911. *Histoire des classes ouvrières en France*, 1867.
14. Sidney Webb, born 1859; Beatrice Potter Webb, 1858-1943. *History of Trade Unionism*, 1894; *Industrial Democracy*, 1897; etc.
15. Cf. Melchior Palyi, *Der Streit um die Staatliche Theorie des Geldes*, 1922.
16. Born 1873. Articles in *Jahrbuch fuer Gesetzgebung und Verwaltung*, 1902, 1903, 1909, 1920; 'Krisen' in *Handwoerterbuch der Staatswissenschaften*, 4th edition, 1925.

17. 1819-1905. *Des Crises commerciales et de leur retour périodique en France, en Angleterre, et aux Etats-Unis*, 1860.
18. Born 1885. *Risk, Uncertainty, and Profit*, 1921; *The Ethics of Competition and Other Papers*, 1934. The former book gives a critical and balanced survey of the entire field of classical and neo-classical theory, far beyond what the title announces; its function today is comparable to that of Hermann's *Staatswissenschaftliche Untersuchungen* in an earlier phase of the development.
19. 1857-1929. *Theory of Business Enterprise*, 1904; *The Instinct of Workmanship*, 1914; *The Engineers and the Price System*, 1921; *Absentee Ownership and Business Enterprise*, 1923; etc. Cf. Joseph Dorfman, *Thorstein Veblen and his America*, 1934.
20. Born 1862. *Legal Foundations of Capitalism*, 1924; *Institutional Economics*, 1934; *History of Labor in the United States* (with eight others), 4 vols., 1918-35.
21. Born 1874. *Business Cycles. Vol. I: The Problem and Its Setting*, 1913. (No second volume).

CHAPTER VIII

1. *De la Nature de la Richesse et de l' Origine de la Valeur*, 1831.
2. 1840-1921. *Grundsaetze der Volkswirtschaftslehre*, 1871. See also p. 178 above.
3. 1835-82. *Theory of Political Economy*, 1871; *Investigations in Currency and Finance*, 1875. Also *The Coal Question*, 1865.
4. 1834-1910. *Eléments d'economie politique pure*, 2 vols, 1874-7; *Etudes d'economie sociale*. 1896; *Etudes d'economie politique appliquée*, 1898.
5. 1851-1914. *Capital and Interest*, 1890 (translated from the first edition of *Geschichte und Kritik der Kapitalzinstheorien*, 1884); *Positive Theory of Capital* (German edition, 1889); 'Macht and Oekonomisches Gesetz,' in *Gesammelte Schriften*, 1924.
6. 1851-1926. *Ueber den Ursprung und die Hauptgesetze des Wirtschaftlichen Wertes*, 1884; *Natural Value* (German edition, 1889); *Social Economics* (German edition, 1914).
7. 1848-1923. *Cours d'économie politique*, 1895; *Manuale di Economia Politica*, 1906 (French translation 1909); *Traîte de sociologie générale*, 2 vols., 1917-19 (English translation as *The Mind and Society*).
8. 1847-1938. *The Distribution of Wealth*, 1899; *Essentials of Economic Theory*, 1907.
9. 1810-58. *Entwickelung der Gesetze des Menschlichen Verkehrs und der daraus entspringenden Regeln des Menschlichen Handelns*, 1854. The tragic figure of Gossen even today is far from being duly appreciated. Four years after the publication of his book he withdrew it, despondent over its utter failure, and died soon afterwards of consumption. In 1874 an English scholar came across his name and spent four years in search of a copy of the book in the catalogues of old-book shops of Germany—it was in no library. When he finally succeeded, he called it to the attention of Jevons, who, generous as later in the case of Cantillon, hastened to state emphatically Gossen's priority over himself in the preface to the second edition of his *Theory*, 1879.

Finally, in 1885, Gossen was extolled as both a scholar and a reformer by the related genius of Walras, whose paper was reprinted in his *Etudes d'economie sociale*, 1896. Gossen's book has been republished in Germany, but no translation is available; its clumsiness and pretension are in its way. Gossen is now generally recognized as the author of the value doctrine, but the radical liberalism of his program of reform, which is the logical climax of his system, is generally ignored—despite Walras, whose reputation is similarly incomplete. For a detailed study, see the third essay in W. Stark, *The Ideal Foundations of Economic Thought*, 1943.

10. 1842-1924. *Principles of Economics*, 8 editions from 1890 on; *The Economics of Industry*, 1879; *Memorials of Alfred Marshall*, ed. by A. C. Pigou, 1925, with a beautiful biography by J. M. Keynes.

11. 1844-1927. *The Commonsense of Political Economy*, 1910.

12. 1893-1938. *The Theory and Measurement of Demand*, 1939.

13. 1845-1926. *Mathematical Psychics*, 1881; *Papers Relating to Political Economy*, 1925.

14. Born 1867. *Mathematical Investigations into the Theory of Value and Price*, 1892; *The Purchasing Power of Money*, 1903; *Theory of Interest*, 1907; *The Rate of Interest as Determined by Impatience to Spend and Opportunity to Invest*, 1930.

15. 1861-1931. *The Economics of Enterprise*, 1913.

16. 1833-85. *Graphic Representation of the Laws of Supply and Demand*, 1870.

17. 1801-77. *Researches into the Mathematical Principles of the Theory of Wealth* (French edition, 1838), translated by Irving Fisher, 1892. Cournot did not live long enough to see his work praised and continued by Jevons, 1879, Marshall, 1890, and Fisher.

18. 1857-1924. *Pure Economics* (Italian edition, 1889).

19. 1804-66. *La mesure de l'utilité des travaux publics*, 1844; *L'utilité des voies de communication*, 1849; both memoranda were republished under the title, *De l'Utilité et de sa Mesure*. 1933.

20. See above page 134.

21. Born 1884. *Studies in the Economics of Overhead Costs*, 1923; *Strategic Factors in Business Cycles*, 1934; *The Economics of Planning Public Works*, 1934; *Preface to Social Economics*, 1936.

22. 1796-1872. *Statement of Some New Principles on the Subject of Political Economy*, 1834. The book was quoted by Mill, but only for its advocacy of an educational tariff, not for its theory of capital and interest. It shared the fate of several books of similar ingenuity in being completely ignored and soon forgotten. Only after the publication of Boehm-Bawerk's theory, in 1895, did C. W. Mixter rediscover this book, and in 1905 he published it in a new, rearranged form, with his own introduction, under the title, *The Sociological Theory of Capital*. Since that time, Rae has been given his proper place in the distinguished and melancholy company of Cantillon, Longfield, Cournot, and Gossen.

23. Born 1874. *L'Intérêt du capital*, 1904.

24. *Theory of Interest*, 1907; *The Rate of Interest as Determined by Impatience to Spend and Opportunity to Invest*, 1930.

25. 1851-1926. *Ueber Wert, Kapital, und Rente*, 1893; *Interest and Prices*

(German edition, 1898); *Lectures on Political Economy*, 2 vols., (Swedish edition, 1901 and 1906).

26. *Capital and Wages*, 1896.

27. In several articles in the *Journal of Political Economy*.

28. Fritz Burchardt, 'Die Schemata des Stationaeren Kreislaufs bei Boehm-Bawerk und Marx,' *Weltwirtschaftliches Archiv*, January 1932.

29. Born 1877. *Wealth and Welfare*, 1912; *The Economics of Welfare*, 1920; *The Political Economy of War*, 1921; *Industrial Fluctuations*, 1927; *Socialism versus Capitalism*, 1937.

30. *Natural Value.*

31. See our discussion of this point above, page 10.

32. Born 1881. *Socialism* (translated from the second edition of *Die Gemeinwirtschaft*, 1932); *Liberalismus*, 1927; *Theory of Money and Credit*, 1934 (German edition, 1912).

33. For a detailed history of the theory of a socialist economic system, see E. Heimann, in *Social Research*, 1939.

34. *Wesen und Hauptinhalt der Theoretischen Nationaloekonomie*, 1907.

35. 1868-1945. *Theory of Social Economy* (German edition, 1918); *The Nature and Necessity of Interest*, 1907; *The World's Monetary Problem*, 1921; *The Downfall of the Gold Standard*, 1936.

36. 18 -1924. 'The Ministry of Production in the Collectivist State,' in *Collectivist Economic Planning*, ed. by F. A. Hayek, 1935 (Barone's article had appeared in Italian in 1908); *Principii di Economia Politica*, 1908 (available also in German translation).

37. 'Pure Theory of Monopoly' (Italian version, 1897), in *Papers Relating to Political Economy*.

38. 'The Laws of Returns under Competitive Conditions,' *Economic Journal*, 1926.

39. Born 1900. 'Notes on Supply,' *Economic Journal*, 1930; 'The Law of Decreasing Cost,' *ibid.* 1931; *The Trade Cycle*, 1936.

40. Born 1899. *Theory of Monopolistic Competition*, 1933.

41. Born 1903. *The Economics of Imperfect Competition*, 1934.

42. *Marktform und Gleichgewicht*, 1934.

43. *Investigations in Currency and Finance.*

44. *Des Crises Commerciales et de leur retour périodique*, 1860.

45. Born 1869. *Economic Cycles, their Law and Cause*, 1914; *Generating Economic Cycles*, 1923.

46. *Industrial Fluctuations.*

47. *Booms and Depressions*, 1933.

48. *Theory of Money and Credit.*

49. Born 1899. *Monetary Theory and the Trade Cycle* (German edition, 1929); *Vom Widersinn des Sparens*, 1930; *Prices and Production*, 1931; *The Road to Serfdom*, 1944; editor of *Collectivist Economic Planning*, 1935.

50. Born 1898. *An Essay on the Nature and Significance of Economic Science*, 1932; *The Great Depression*, 1937.

51. 'Monetary Expansion and the Structure of Production,' *Social Research*, 1934.

52. Born 1883. *Wesen und Hauptinhalt der Theoretischen Nationaloekonomie*, 1907; 'Epochen der Dogmen- und Methodengeschichte,' in

Grundriss der Sozialoekonomik, vol. 1; *Theory of Economic Development* (German edition, 1912); *Business Cycles*, 2 vols., 1939; *Capitalism, Socialism, and Democracy*, 1942; important articles in *Archiv fuer Sozialwissenschaft und Sozialpolitik* etc.

CHAPTER IX

1. Born 1893. 'Wie ist Konjunkturtheorie ueberhaupt moeglich?' *Weltwirtschaftliches Archiv*, 1926; *Economics and Sociology*, 1935.
2. 1883-1939. *Aufriss der Theoretischen Oekonomie*, 1931; 'Konjunktur und Krisen,' in *Grundriss der Sozialoekonomik*, vol. IV, 1925; *Technical Progress and Unemployment*, 1938; *The State of the Masses*, 1939.
3. Born 1895. *Der Tauschwert des Geldes*, 1928; 'Lohnhoehe und Beschaeftigungsgrad im Marktgleichgewicht,' in *Weltwirtschaftliches Archiv*, 1932; 'General Overproduction,' in *Journal of Political Economy*, 1934; *Some International Aspects of Business Cycles*, 1936.
4. *Interest and Prices; Lectures on Political Economy*, vol. II.
5. 1821-1902. *Elements of Political Economy*, 1858; etc.
6. Born 1879. *Good and Bad Trade*, 1913; *Currency and Credit*, 1919; *Monetary Reconstruction*, 1923.
7. Born 1889. *Volkswirtschaftliche Theorie des Bankcredits*, 1924; 'Kredit,' in *Handwoerterbuch der Staatswissenschaften*, 4th edition, 1925. The *Theorie* was heatedly discussed in Germany and appeared in three editions in a few years. From the third edition on the author has drastically revised his doctrine and reverted into the fold of neo-classicism.
8. Born 1883. *The Economic Consequences of the Peace*, 1919; *A Tract on Monetary Reform*, 1923; *Treatise on Money*, 1930; *General Theory of Employment, Interest, and Money*, 1936; *How to Pay for the War*, 1940.
9. Born 1887. *Full Recovery or Stagnation?* 1938; *Fiscal Policy and the Business Cycle*, 1941.
10. *Industrial Fluctuations*, Chapter v.
11. *Economic Studies*, 1880; *Lombard Street*, 1873.
12. 'The Relation of Home Investment to Unemployment,' in *Economic Journal*, 1931.
13. *The Economics of Planning Public Works*, 1935.
14. Born 1874. *Les Crises périodiques de surproduction*, 2 vols., 1913.
15. *Strategic Factors in Business Cycles*, 1934.
16. *The Trade Cycle*, 1936.
17. Discussion in *Journal of Political Economy*, 1931.
18. 'The Classical Stationary State,' *Economic Journal*, 1943.

Selected Bibliography*

J. A. Schumpeter, *History of Economic Analysis*, 1954. Unfinished and un-edited posthumous work by one of the great economists; of unrivaled erudition, the standard work for a long time to come, but very uneven and somewhat arbitrary; 1200 pages in close print.

J. A. Schumpeter, *Ten Great Economists*, 1951. Brilliant sketches of Marx, Walras, Marshall, Keynes, etc.

Charles Gide and Charles Rist, *A History of Economic Doctrines*, 1948. Translated from the seventh French edition (1st edition, 1909). Written in the eclectic manner described on page 13 above, rich and scholarly, but somewhat uneven and leading only up to the beginning of the century, with two chapters on International Trade and Conflicting Theories of Crises recently added. The history of economic thought has long been cultivated in France, more than in other countries. Among recent works are

René Gonnard, *Histoire des doctrines économiques*, 1941, and

Emile James, *Histoire des doctrines économiques*, 1950.

Erich Roll, *A History of Economic Thought*, 1939. Represents the approach in terms of the economic interests for which the theories stand, as de-scribed on page 14 above. Particularly good on labor theory of value; business cycle theory is almost entirely omitted.

Gunnar Myrdal, *The Political Element in the Development of Economic Theory*, 1954. Swedish original, 1932. Related to Roll's book, but superior in method; a running comment rather than an account of the develop-ment of economic theory.

Highly commendable are the following three books:

Alexander Gray, *The Development of Economic Doctrine*, 1931. Learned and colorful.

L. H. Haney, *History of Economic Thought*, 4th edition, 1949. Includes the post-Keynesian development; scholarly, rather detailed, and not too difficult.

Edgar Salin, *Geschichte der Volkswirtschaftslehre*, 4th edition, 1951. A brief but learned book, with the emphasis on the history of the ideas within which economic thought develops; presupposes some knowledge. One of

*This Selected Bibliography was thoroughly revised in 1962 for the paper-back edition of this book. In a few cases, there may be discrepancies between earlier editions of books quoted in notes and later editions quoted here.

255

its most brilliant chapters corrects the prevailing opinion on medieval economics, as does Schumpeter's big book; the best authority in English on technical details in this field is Raymond de Roover. See his articles in *The Quarterly Journal of Economics,* November 1951 and May 1955, and in *Kyklos,* 1957, No. 2.

Very valuable books of more limited scope and much rigorous technical detail are:

T. W. Hutchison, *A Review of Economic Doctrines, 1870-1929,* 1953.

G. J. Stigler, *Production and Distribution Theories: The Formative Period,* 1941.

R. L. Heilbroner, *The Worldly Philosophers,* 1953. A more popular and highly readable but still quite scholarly book on the main figures in the history of economic thought, fairer to the heretics than to the great academic achievements.

Two fine books on the history of socialism are:

Eugen Duehring, *Kritische Geschichte der Nationaloekonomie und des Sozialismus,* 1871, 4th edition, 1900. Distinguished by vigor and originality and still worth studying.

Alexander Gray, *The Socialist Tradition,* 1946. Charming, learned, and highly personal.

Commendable books on special periods or of a special point of view are:

Eli Heckscher, *Mercantilism,* 1935, 2 vols. Original in Swedish.

Arthur E. Monroe, *Monetary Theory before Adam Smith,* 1923.

E. A. J. Johnson, *Predecessors of Adam Smith: The Growth of British Economic Thought,* 1939.

August Oncken, *Geschichte der Nationaloekonomie,* Band I: *Die Zeit vor Adam Smith,* 1902. No second volume appeared. A scholarly book that does not become obsolete.

Werner Stark, *Ideal Foundations of Economic Thought: Three Essays on the Philosophy of Economics,* 1943.

Werner Stark, *The History of Economics in Its Relation to Social Development,* 1944. Brief, learned, instructive.

Some books of a limited scope are particularly important although, or because, they each argue their special case. They are:

Karl Marx, *Theories on Surplus Value,* 1951. Unfinished posthumous edition of draft for a fourth volume of *Das Kapital.* A monument to Marx's erudition. Edited by K. Kautsky, translated by G. A. Bonner and Emile Burns.

Edwin Cannan, *A History of the Theories of Production and Distribution in English Political Economy from 1776-1848,* 3rd edition, 1917.

Eugen von Boehm-Bawerk, *History and Critique of Interest Theories,* Vol. I of *Capital and Interest* (1st German edition, 1884), 1959.

Joseph Dorfman, *The Economic Mind in American Civilization, 1606-1865,* 1946, 2 vols.

Adolph Lowe, *Economics and Sociology,* 1936. A slim but brilliant volume.

Index